Origins of Arthurian Romances

Origins of Arthurian Romances

*Early Sources for the Legends
of Tristan, the Grail
and the Abduction of the Queen*

FLINT F. JOHNSON

McFarland & Company, Inc., Publishers
Jefferson, North Carolina, and London

Drawings provided by author.

LIBRARY OF CONGRESS CATALOGUING-IN-PUBLICATION DATA

Johnson, Flint.
 Origins of Arthurian romances : early sources for the legends of Tristan, The Grail and The abduction of the queen / Flint F. Johnson.
   p.   cm.
 Includes bibliographical references and index.

 ISBN 978-0-7864-6858-4 ∞
 softcover : acid free paper

 1. Arthurian romances—Sources. I. Title.
PN685 .J64 2012
809'.93351—dc23   2012030664

BRITISH LIBRARY CATALOGUING DATA ARE AVAILABLE

© 2012 Flint F. Johnson. All rights reserved

No part of this book may be reproduced or transmitted in any form or by any means, electronic or mechanical, including photocopying or recording, or by any information storage and retrieval system, without permission in writing from the publisher.

Front cover images © 2012 Shutterstock

Manufactured in the United States of America

McFarland & Company, Inc., Publishers
 Box 611, Jefferson, North Carolina 28640
 www.mcfarlandpub.com

Table of Contents

Preface — 1
Source Abbreviations — 3
Introduction — 5

PART ONE: THE ABDUCTION OF THE QUEEN

1. Introduction to the Material — 9
2. Chrétien's Known Sources and Influences — 14
3. The Characters and Their Roles — 31
4. Literary Tools for Supplementary Material — 38
5. Motifs and Details: Clues of Celtic Origins — 46
6. The Sixth Century in Chrétien — 64
7. Conclusion — 71

PART TWO: THE HOLY OBJECT

8. Introduction to *Le Conte du Graal* — 75
9. Philip of Flanders, Life and Influences — 79
10. Grail Theories — 83
11. The Characters and Their Roles — 100
12. Literary Tools for Supplementary Material — 107
13. Religion in Fifth and Sixth Century Britain — 118

14. Motifs and Details: Clues of Celtic Origins	122
15. The Sixth Century in Chrétien	129
16. Conclusion	131

PART THREE: TRISTAN

17. Introduction to the Tristan Legend	137
18. The Characters and Their Roles	146
19. Thomas of Britain	155
20. The Literary Source Material	158
21. Motifs and Details: Clues of Celtic Origins	167
22. The Sixth Century in Tristan	172
23. Conclusion	176
Appendix: Additional Thoughts	179
Chapter Notes	185
Bibliography	211
Index	225

Preface

This book began as an exploration of the more interesting elements of a single Arthurian story, the abduction of Arthur's queen, and slowly developed into an examination of its Celtic source materials. Certain details to be found there suggested a connection to the grail, and so the study was expanded as a result. Theories of both stories' development and ideas about the nature of the grail and grail culture came naturally after that. The result was the formation of a broad methodology for examining materials from a period without strictly historical documents. The Tristan legend was the next logical step because it provided a counterpoint to all of the positive finds encountered in the first two stories; Tristan belongs securely in the realm of myth.

The result of writing in this manner is that this book is, essentially, an expanded comparative study of three Arthurian romances. Each story is treated in isolation, with all of its medieval versions discussed in terms of the development of characters and plot as well as the progression of its themes and motifs. A brief look at the bias of each author serves to demonstrate much of the variation between renderings.

With all three of the stories, there is a primary continental writer from which all later authors derived their materials. This author's biography, skills, patrons, and personal knowledge are explored more fully. Each story is then cross-referenced against the Celtic myths and legends, medieval and ancient tales, and even the culture of the period and places in which the romances were written.

The expansion beyond a traditional comparative study is due to the fact that the author is not limited by a literary approach; the methodology is cross-disciplinary in nature. Parallels for certain episodes and motifs in all the Arthurian tales have been found through the years in the history, laws, and archaeology of the Britons and Irish. These and the additional data the author was able to research add greatly to our understanding of the subject.

Making use of the historical information will prove greatly beneficial, because of where it will lead. Many of those aspects normally associated with the Arthurian romances seem to fit equally well to both the time in which they are known to have been written on the continent and to post–Roman Britain in the fifth and sixth centuries. Many more details and scenes belong exclusively to that era of British history. Comparative history, extant law texts, and recovered archaeological finds of the era provide clues and insights to the three romances not found in any other approach.

Combined, the employment of additional perspectives brings the Arthurian stories, so regularly and for so long seen purely as creations of the High Middle Ages derived from Celtic folklore, into a fuller light. They show that recoverable pieces of post–Roman history are lodged within them.

The following pages are an examination of three pillars of Arthurian literature using a heretofore untried methodology of applying the knowledge from several disciplines. In each of the three cases, critical studies will be utilized in determining how that story will be applied to the overall approach. With flexibility to the individual subjects, very different and more plausible theories emerge regarding the genesis and development of the Arthurian stories than have been considered previously.

Reconstructing the romance tales of the Arthurian era or any other period is not the extent of the method's applications, however. As the author hopes to demonstrate in future publications, this method is applicable to all aspects of history, which seems to defy traditional historical studies. The myths of the Æsir, Conchobar, Perseus, Achilles, Gilgamesh, and Maui would benefit from the same approach. Their historicity might be demonstrated by it, and the periods they lived in might be broadly mapped by applying the same tactics. In the immediate future, the author intends to show the versatility of the methodology in a study of Arthur as a historical figure and in another where the absolute and relative dates of personalities from his period are roughly laid out.

A great deal of time has passed since the manuscript was a Ph.D. thesis, and apart from the conclusions very little of what was there remains. And so, though I would again like to record my thanks to Charles Warren, Dave Schleh, Kari Fuller, Marina Moschovidou, Professor Graham Caie, Professor Rachel Bromwich, Atia Chowdhury, Dr. Richard Wilson, Professor Rex Whitehead, Professor William Gillies, and Dr. Alison Rawles; they are the people who helped me to finish the manuscript. It is to Michelle Klein that I owe the debt of helping me find the will to see my work through to publication.

Source Abbreviations

A	Antiquity
ASE	Anglo-Saxon England
B	Bulletin of the Board of Celtic Studies
CMCS	Cambrian (Cambridge) Medieval Celtic Studies
CR	The Chaucer Review
DVJ	Deutsche Vierteljahrsschrift für Literaturwissenschaft und Geistes geschichte
EC	Étude Celtique
EHR	English Historical Review
LlC	Llên Cymru
MA	Medium Ævum
MLN	Modern Language Notes
MLR	Modern Language Review
MP	Modern Philology
NMS	Nottingham Medieval Studies
PMLA	Publications of the Modern Language Association of America
PBA	Proceedings of the British Academy
PSAS	Proceedings of the Society of Antiquaries of Scotland
R	Romania
RP	Romance Philology
S	Speculum
TCWAAS	Transactions of the Cumberland and Westmoreland Antiquarian and Archaeological Society
TDGNAHS	Transactions of the Dumfriesshire and Galloway Natural History and Antiquarian Society
THSC	Transactions of the Honourable Society of the Cymmrodorion
TYP	Trioedd Ynys Prydein: The Welsh Triads, Rachel Bromwich (ed. and trans.)
VL	Die deutsche Literatur des Mittelalters
WHR	Welsh History Review
ZCP	Zeitschrift für Celtische Philologie
ZDP	Zeitschrift für Deutsche Philologie
ZDA	Zeitschrift für Deutsche Altertum

Introduction

In about 1136, a Welshman named Geoffrey of Monmouth wrote an ambitious composite of British literature and pseudohistory known as *Historia Regum Britanniae*. It featured a famed British figure named Arthur, who had been hitherto obscure to the continent.

Arthur was an immediate hero in medieval Western Europe, and as a result Geoffrey's book would take a back seat only to the Bible in terms of copies made in the Middle Ages. His main character would even go so far as to be named one of the three Christian Worthies by antiquarians within a few centuries.

Arthur's fame was fortuitously supported by the political landscape of the time as well. Henry II was the dominant force in the Celtic lands at this time. He controlled a large portion of the Welsh population, Scotland, England, and half of France. His political control allowed for the unimpeded spread of the Arthurian legend to France. From there it spread to all of the literary and musical minds of the French musicians/poets known as the *trouvères* and *troubadours*. Because of their efforts, the legend would spread to all of Europe.

It was not long before other British heroes were associated with Arthur.[1] The trouvères and troubadours formulated courtly personalities for them based loosely on their legends. In the twelfth century, several romance poets would pull stories out of this fast-growing body of information and write on them. The greatest of these was Chrétien de Troyes, who did much to create a new genre of literature with his Arthurian romances. He successfully blended a British plot with the concept of courtly love and a broad knowledge of ancient and contemporary literature. The subject matter introduced by Geoffrey of Monmouth and the manner of presentation brought to fruition by Chrétien de Troyes influenced and at times served as an inspiration for thousands of medieval and modern writers. Their authority continues to do so to the present.

However, the British sources of information for Geoffrey, Chrétien, and many of the early romance writers remain in doubt. Geoffrey undoubtedly drew on Welsh genealogical tracts and Bede,[2] but beyond a few specific examples, much of the source material he used remains uncertain. With Chrétien and many early romance writers, nothing but a British plot and characters' names have been distinguished.

The trends in Celtic scholarship would also favor caution about pinpointing a specific source or sources for the romances. Every major British written source for this period has come under scrutiny in the past forty years. Gildas' historical prelude to his denunciation of several contemporary British kings in *De Excidio Britanniae* (c. AD 535) is often vague. He is often demonstrably historically incorrect when he does manage to be specific. In several major articles Professor Dumville has demonstrated that *Historia Brittonum* is a composite, pseudohistorical book with only limited uses as an historical source.[3] Kathleen Hughes's study of *Annales Cambriae* has demonstrated that the original document was compiled in St. David's beginning in AD 795.[4] She has also shown that from the years AD 613 to 795 it drew on Irish chronicles and the *Northern British Chronicle*.[5]

Professor Jackson, Dr. Jarman, and Professor Dumville have advocated a more tentative stance to the poem *Y Gododdin* concerning its historicity and reliability as a literary source of the sixth century.[6] In addition, Professor Sims-Williams has stressed that few of the literary materials may be dated more specifically than pre–1150. Thus, much of the native Welsh material cannot be proven to be free of Geoffrey's influence, especially when it comes to Arthur.[7]

The present work is in part a response to their labors. The above-mentioned scholars have cumulatively demonstrated the seeming futility of reconstructing fifth-century British history with the limited resources available and therefore have inferred the desire for more material with which to work. This is the service I am attempting to render here. The conclusions I have come to may well be shown incorrect in the future, but a better understanding of the period must be the result of such labors. I believe it more useful to propose a new and possibly incorrect thesis than never to make the attempt.

It is my contention that other, ancient literary sources of information did exist in Britain at one point. These oral and literary records dealt mainly with fifth- and sixth-century figures and were the rudimentary beginnings of the King Arthur of the medieval literary world. Later these records were transferred to the continent as tales or, less probably, as sagas.[8]

Further, I believe that four of the five extant Arthurian poems written by Chrétien were based on one or several of these sources of information from Britain. His poems in their turn became the inspiration for variations of his plots in particular and the Arthurian corpus in general. For this reason, it seems necessary to start with him.

This book will explore only two of Chrétien's four romances: the abduction of Guinièvre and the grail. They were chosen because they have not been given the one-dimensional sovereignty label of *Yvain* and *Erec*. Because their nature has never been widely agreed upon, the author needs only to focus on the evidence and where it leads instead of breaking down accepted theories point by point. It is good fortune that these two are also the most deeply enriched in the Celtic tradition and have the most and earliest versions. Because of these facts, they will yield the strongest findings.

The contentions I begin with are twofold and may seem radical at first. However, the pages below will bear them both out. First, it is possible to reconstruct the British prototypes of the abduction and grail stories with the use of several parallel versions also dependent on British sources. Second, one might date these prototypes safely to the ninth century and tentatively as early as the sixth century. The idea that the Arthurian romance writers of the late twelfth and early thirteenth centuries were historians in any sense is not suggested. Certainly no sixth-century warrior crawled across a sword, as Lancelot does in *La Charrette*. I would, however, suggest that the persons who wrote on these stories of the abduction and the grail accessed a body of sources deriving from the sixth century.[9]

Central to the tales under study here will be Chrétien, the first and most imitated court poet of the continent during the Middle Ages. It is through an understanding of him that a clear picture of the original version of these tales is achieved. The transition between heroic tale and romance is also most clearly seen through him. Every scene and detail that is out of place or unnecessary in his poems will be scrutinized for such anomalies.

Having determined them, the question of where such oddities might have been derived will be posed; here the work of previous scholars has suffered because there is only a paltry amount of knowledge about early Britain. Very little was written and even less preserved from the Arthurian period. So, the theory of Hakam's Razor will be employed to postulate a most likely cultural scenario for the timeframe in question. Knowledge of the pre–Roman British culture will be derived from Roman, Greek, and the occasional native sources. The law texts and the observations of eleventh- and twelfth-century writers regarding contemporary Welshmen will give a strong picture of medieval society. The most reasonable transitional culture between the societies of Roman Britain and historical Wales will be assumed, guided by what little contemporary evidence exists for the period in question.[10]

Chrétien's influences will also be discussed at length, most notably his two patrons. Their hand will also be looked for in both poems, and reasons for their influence on certain aspects of the poems will be examined. In these scenes and details Chrétien has in some cases apparently been asked to edit or disguise an established line of the plot because it ran counter to the patron's wishes. In these cases, Chrétien inevitably replaced the offending scene or detail with something especially palatable to his patron. Knowing the motivations of both Marie de Champagne and Philip (of Flanders), it is possible to identify and retrace these instances. I will then compare the segments where these instances occur to what can be discovered of sixth-century Britain using the meager sources at hand. Among these elements a significant number will be uniquely tied to British culture before AD 900. A larger number of these elements can be placed there more easily than in the twelfth century.

However, Chrétien will not be the only author studied here. With both stories, all versions showing some independence from him and contain traditional British information are discussed to determine the earliest possible date at which their common original must have existed.

Parallel to developing a more accurate period of origin for the source materials for both stories is an evolution of our understanding of the characters and their predictable roles in a reconstructable original. The analysis of all analogous material is employed to fine tune this method.

The process outlined here is designed to reveal the most historically accurate elements in literature that was entirely created as fiction. This approach will no doubt raise eyebrows among specialists in British historical and archaeological circles. But the study is not purely one of historical or archaeological research. It is, by the very nature of the evidence at hand, a multidimensional one: the techniques of each field must be applied. It must be kept in mind that the various approaches are just as valid within their own fields as the historical and archaeological approaches are within theirs.[11]

PART ONE:
THE ABDUCTION OF THE QUEEN

1
Introduction to the Material

Over a century ago and in his work on *Le Chevalier de la Charrette* (1883), Gaston Paris began the painstaking process of proving that Irish mythology had provided a great many of the motifs and plots for the French romances. During their respective careers, Sir John Rhys[1] and Professor Roger Sherman Loomis[2] both expanded this tenet to include the *medieval* Arthurian romances from all the countries of Europe. Using the Welsh versions of the continental tales, Loomis and Rhys documented their transmissions from an unRomanized Ireland to France through Britain.[3] Modifying this theory, Professor O'Rahilly, and later Dr. Proinsias Mac Cana and Dr. Bromwich, developed a trend toward thinking of the common Irish, British, and Arthurian themes as pan–Celtic motifs. This thinking has certainly gained ground in the past few years.[4] However, a latent tendency to see the Celtic themes in the continental romances as the result of a purely Breton/Welsh connection still exists.

Since the middle part of the century, Rachel Bromwich and others have initiated a more thorough research method using onomastic features within the Arthurian romances and Welsh stories as their guide. She has shown that the legend of Arthur was transmitted to Europe both orally and through written means by analyzing how the names of established characters have altered in the comparable Insular and continental tales. She has also demonstrated that this material came with a setting comparable to that in Welsh tales and retaining the names and personalities of many of the characters.[5] Her position that the Welsh literary traditions supplied the original stock to the continental Arthurian romances now stands uncontested by all who study the Celtic side of the Arthurian phenomenon. The details about the method of transference to the continent and the name transformations of individual Arthurian characters, on the other hand, remain open to much debate.[6]

Celtic scholars have for the most part stood clear of Arthur, except as a literary figure.[7] However, some of their studies during the past thirty-five years will have some bearing on the proposed topic as well. The work of Dr.

Rachel Bromwich, Professor Patrick Sims-Williams, Dr. Brynley Roberts, and a host of others have improved the level of understanding of Middle Welsh literature concerning Arthur. The scholarly efforts of Dr. Kathleen Hughes, Dr. Peter Bartrum, Dr. Molly Miller, and Professor David Dumville have given Welsh scholarship a clearer perspective on the historical sources for the period.[8] Work on the heroic-age milieu by Professor Hector and Dr. Nora Chadwick has yet to be equaled.[9] The pertinent Middle Welsh literature has been thoroughly edited and discussed by Sir Ifor Williams, Professor Kenneth Jackson, Dr. Rachel Bromwich, and Dr. Marged Haycock.[10] An idea of post–Roman Britain's customs was given a solid framework upon which to build by Dr. Nora Chadwick. This framework was initiated through her work on the *Mabinogion* collection and the Irish stories, mainly the tales of the Ulster cycle.[11] The work of Dr. David Binchy and Professor Fergus Kelly on Old Irish law texts have also made vast contributions to our knowledge of Dark Age society.[12]

In material pertaining uniquely to the study of the grail, Dr. Bromwich, Dr. Nora Chadwick, and Professor Charles Thomas have examined certain aspects of the extent of Christianity in Dark Age Britain.[13] The work chiefly of Dr. Graham Webster, Dr. Margaret Murray, and Dr. Clare Stanfliffe has opened up a new understanding of the nature of the British beliefs as they were practiced in sub–Roman Britain.[14] Dr. Glenys Goetinck has done the most comprehensive study of the romance *Peredur*.[15] From the turn of the nineteenth century renowned French scholars such as Viscount Villemarqué, Professor Gaston Paris, Professor Alfred Nutt, Sir John Rhys, Dr. Jessie Weston, Dr. Roy Owen, Dr. Arthur Brown, Professor William Roach, Dr. William Nitze, Professor Roger Loomis, Dr. Eugene Weinraub, and Professor Norma Lorre Goodrich have added their understanding of the grail question to the growing body of literature.[16]

With regards to the Tristan legend, a number of scholars have made their important contributions. Professor Joseph Bédier made important advances in the development of the legend on the continent.[17] Gertrude Schoepperle, Professor Joseph Loth, Dr. Helaine Newstead, and Dr. Bromwich made great strides in our understanding of the source materials.[18] Professors Kuno Meyer and Heinrich Zimmer worked on key translations to the parallel materials.[19] Work on individual Tristan romances by W. T. H. Jackson, Eugène Vinaver, Professor Tony Hunt, Professor Geoffrey Bromiley, Professor Owen, and Professor Douglas Kelly has allowed for a better understanding of their interrelationships.[20] Loth and Dr. Oliver Padel delved into the Cornish aspects of the legend.[21]

The intervening thirty-nine years since *Arthur's Britain* have produced a great deal of scholarship in archaeology, too. An increased number of digs and a more complete view of early medieval political geography and culture have greatly improved our understanding of the people of Celtic heritage and their settlement choices. Archaeologists such as Dr. Kenneth Dark have also become interested in the political boundaries of the Celtic kingdoms following the Roman occupation.[22] The broad knowledge and interests of the archaeologists Professor O. G. S. Crawford, Professor Stuart Piggott, Dr. P. K. Johnstone, Dr. Lloyd Laing, Professor Charles Thomas, Professor Leslie Alcock, and many others have been integral in this process. The increased comprehension of Pictish as a language and cultural group separate from the British, but similar, has helped fill in many voids as well. The accumulation of knowledge regarding warfare, social organization, and architecture since 1971 is based almost entirely upon the subsequent digs that have been conducted in the intervening period.

A great deal of knowledge has been acquired pertaining to sub–Roman Britain and the literary connections between themes and motifs of the Arthurian romances and those of the British people. Yet there remains the tantalizing statement by Dr. Bromwich of something more substantial: "But there is little reason to believe that the authors of the [French] poems had any specific knowledge of the places in Arthurian Britain."[23] How, then, did they come to have access to the precise details regarding Arthur, the names of his men, and the peculiar traits of these heroes? Certainly a bard could describe the terrain of a particular scene, but continental romances demonstrate a knowledge of the toponomy of many areas in Scotland, northwestern England, Cornwall, and Wales. This implies a supply of knowledge much more precise than an oral source. Certainly the antiquity of several elements in both poems under study here will imply a source older than the work of the twelfth-century *latimari*,[24] as will be seen. Unquestionably, much of the Arthurian puzzle has yet to be solved. A tentative solution will be forthcoming; the romances' primary British material derives from sources whose history stretched back centuries before Chrétien de Troyes began writing.

The following pages are an attempt to show that this hypothesis is not only defensible, but is the most likely possibility. To demonstrate the verifiability of such a claim, the author will begin by examining the sources and influences of the most influential Arthurian poet, Chrétien de Troyes. His hand can be seen in all the later material, so that he was crucial to those who followed him. The study will begin by focusing on understanding the influences upon Chrétien in his writings. This will include Celtic and continental literary materials and the influence of Marie de Champagne and Philip of Flanders. The chapter will provide some idea of his and his patrons' *sens*. Chrétien was a master of integrating hundreds of concepts, scenes, and other elements into a flowing text. However, it will be seen that this ability made for his own limited role in creating any of the scenes or motifs in his poems.

With a solid foundation, the study of the two stories will be divided. In each case, one chapter will be devoted to identifying the original roles of the major characters. A discussion and brief analysis of all early literature regarding these stories will also be conducted. The purpose of this exercise will be threefold: First, it will serve to point out that the romances similar to the two Chrétien poems had derived from a common original by 1100. Second, those items unique to each redaction will point out a degree of independence from Chrétien. Finally, they will show a dependence on a common Celtic source. The author will use the term *Glas* for the source material for *Le Chevalier de la Charrette* and *Dysgyl* for *Le Conte du Graal*. As it seems reasonable that similar material on the same group of characters would derive, to some degree, from the same source, the author will call their common knowledge bank *Cadegr*.

Going beyond this, the author will follow Sir John Rhys[25] and Sir Ifor Williams[26] in proposing that the romances are loosely based on stories told during the British heroic period. The present author is hardly the first to conceive of such a notion.

> It follows that if one wished to make a comprehensive collection of the sagas about Arthur, one would have to take the romances into account, since things even of mythological interest have been lost in Welsh, and are now only to be found in the Anglo-Norman versions and those based on them.[27]

This account will be followed by a discussion focusing on a search for Celtic patterns of the British Heroic Age.[28] This in turn will preface a look for potentially historical Celtic material that is not based on a specific motif. These studies will be concluded with close examinations of the motifal and historical elements of the poem. These elements will serve to demonstrate most simply the antiquity of both stories by the twelfth century.

Concerning *Le Conte du Graal*, however, something more will be required. First, a chapter will be assigned to carefully defining the main grail theories. The purpose here will be to demonstrate the inability of any one of the theories to fully explain the grail. It will also show the mutual dependence of three grail theories to satisfactorily explain the grail and the ceremony surrounding it in the romances. It is a Celtic ceremony with a Christian and possibly Jewish mask layered on it.

Second, I will examine the state of religion in Britain during the fifth and sixth centuries. This examination will bring out the prominence of Celtic cults through the year AD 500 and the prominence, particularly in *the North*, of the fertility god Belatacudros, or Beli. In turn, these findings will begin to explain the presence of Pelles in the romances. He is no more than a euhemeristic version of a well-known British deity, and many of Belatacudros' qualities are shared by the grail itself.

However, to begin one must first summarize the poems as a reference point. *Le Chevalier de la Charrette* will be first:

Chrétien de Troyes's poem begins in Arthur's court. The evil prince Meleagant rides into Camelot's hall alone and demands the king's wife as a boon. Arthur shows some apprehension, so Meleagant appeases him by giving Guinièvre a chance for freedom. He will fight a champion for possession of her. Arthur accepts this arrangement, though the court is flabbergasted by the audacity of Meleagant's request. This is followed by a scene in which Sir Keu manipulates the king and queen into allowing him to be Guinièvre's champion; he promptly loses the battle and Guinièvre.

However, Keu has been followed by Gauvain and Lancelot, who now pursue Meleagant. Lancelot kills two horses in pursuit of him and eventually submits to riding in a criminal's cart in order to hear news of Guinièvre, who has been taken to the island of Gorre. In time Lancelot and Gauvain are escorted to a nearby castle, the Cart Castle. That night they sleep in its hall. The two knights take different paths to Gorre the next day. Gauvain decides to cross to Gorre by a mysterious water bridge, and Lancelot will take a perilous sword bridge route. Before attempting it, Lancelot defeats a knight at a ford, has an odd rendezvous with the lady of another castle,[29] lifts a perilous tomb, crosses a perilous stony passage, defeats another knight,[30] participates in a liberation battle, and finally crosses the Sword Bridge and arrives in Gorre.[31] Here he is welcomed by Bademagus father of Meleagant,[32] and finds Guinièvre.

Lancelot defeats the antagonist in two duels soon thereafter, but Guinièvre saves Meleagant and Bademagus' request on condition that there be a decisive battle in a year's time. Lancelot accepts these terms and departs, but he is soon captured by Meleagant's men and imprisoned in one of Meleagant's castles. Meanwhile Guinièvre and the now-returned Gauvain get word that Lancelot has returned to Camelot, and they leave Gorre to join him. There Guinièvre learns he is not with Arthur. She organizes a tournament to draw him out. Through a gentleman's promise, Lancelot is allowed to go to the tournament incognito and return. He does so, but when he comes back Meleagant moves him to an isolated tower. At this point, Chrétien breaks off and Godefroi de Leigni completes the narrative. The story's scope necessarily diminishes somewhat. Lancelot is eventually released from prison by the sister of Meleagant who nurses him back to health just in time for Lancelot to defeat and behead Meleagant, thus ending the story.[3]

2

Chrétien's Known Sources and Influences

In the 1170s a Frenchman with extraordinary literary abilities wrote a romance for his patroness, Marie de Champagne. It was not Chrétien de Troyes's first offering in that milieu, but it is the most celebrated; they were all groundbreaking. The tales he told, beginning with *Erec et Enide* and followed by *Yvain* and *Le Conte du Graal*, soon became the basic model of all Arthurian tales. His progressive development of Gauvain and Keu was molded in his poems to the stereotypical figures that are recognized today. The timelessness, the grail adventure, even the modest, often weak-minded Arthur of the romances has his origins in Chrétien's works. Creating the Arthurian setting as modern society understands it, however, was only one of the ways in which he was an inventor. His poems were the first of courtly love ever introduced into the literature of the North of France. This innovation alone places him in a unique position in medieval literature.

Because of his central importance in the literature of continental Europe from his era on, Chrétien's known sources and influences are of great importance to any study of the origins of the Arthurian legend. Chrétien himself insists on using the terms *sens* (meaning) and *matière* (material) when discussing the origins in his prologues. Because of this, his intended meanings for these two words would appear to be crucial to an understanding of his sources and influences. So, too, would a good understanding of the medieval prologue in which he first mentioned them.

The prologue had a universal purpose in literary circles of the Middle Ages, one derived from the monastic traditions of Western Europe. Throughout the period after the fall of Rome, it was these institutions alone that were willing and able to preserve the writings of the ancient periods, in particular the works of Greek and Roman writers. It was because of their role, and the necessity of handwriting each copy of the manuscripts, that the monks developed a genuine respect for the classical writers. This respect ran so deeply that it was believed nothing they had written was contrary to the *Bible* or to the Christian faith. In fact, the wisdom of the Greek and Roman writers could not be surpassed, only put in language more easily understood by a contemporary audience. For medieval ecclesiastic writers, this was the sole purpose of writing a book. For lay writers, it meant that everything that was worth writing about had already been written.[1]

With this in mind, the material of a work, the *matière*, was unimprovable.[2] The meaning, or *sens*, was the only aspect that could be altered to enable a more accurate and subtle understanding of the thoughts of the superior minds that had preceded them. The presence of the concepts of *sens* and *matière* in a prologue, and an understanding of those concepts, allowed for a great deal of poetic license. As long as one used an old tale (*matière*), one was free to give to the material any presentation (*sens*) that the author chose.[3] At the same time, by following monastic convention and claiming to be making use of an old theme a poet could mold a prologue into a tool to give a sense of humility to his work. It gave him a place to introduce an imaginary source where necessary or, more often, to praise one's patron for providing it. This segue would introduce the individual funding the work and provided for an excellent opportunity to praise the largesse of one's benefactor in hopes of additional financial reward.[4] Chrétien's use of the terms *sens* and *matière*, then, indicates nothing as to the true nature and history of his sources; he may well not have known them. His use of the terms only shows his proper education in the medieval form of writing.

What Chrétien otherwise tells us about his personal contributions to the poems and the nature of his source material may leave the reader wanting. However, his writings have produced modern criticism from many different perspectives and especially from Celtic and French scholars. These two fields have combined to give a good indication of Chrétien's material and lend true significance of matière and sens to his works. The focus of these studies has been chiefly literary by nature. However, there have been other, broader scopes and topics. The main interest in this chapter will be divided between the Celtic and French schools of thought on Chrétien's sources and his use of them. It will be seen that the two schools are mutually compatible.

The Celticists, led by Rachel Bromwich, have developed the idea that the hero Arthur and a discernibly British cast of characters were transferred from British–speaking Britain to the continent in conjunction with him. To quote her: "This body of names constitutes the most important and incontrovertible evidence for the Celtic contribution to Arthurian romance."[5]

The focus of their studies has mainly been in the geographic and chronological origins of the material. The form and manner by which it was transmitted has been of greatest interest. To this the current author will add the theory that the *Northern Memoranda* or some allied material could have been the ultimate source for these tales. As has been said of the more historically based information on Arthur: It is surely legitimate to conclude that the Nennian *Arthuriana* section came from a source closely related to the *Northern Chronicle* that underlies *Annales Cambriae*, even if this source was not the same.[6] Surely it is probable that a similar source might have proved to be rich in lore on Arthur. The evidence gathered in chapters 4, 5, 13, and 14 will support this theory.

Deriving the point of origin for the British–based literature, however, has proven nearly impossible. If the tales evolved from heroic-age poetry, then one might reasonably believe that the corpus had begun developing near where Arthur and other prominent chiefs lived.[7] One can imagine a petty king generously rewarding the fortunate poet who had most recently extolled him. However, this simple solution holds several complications.

First, around AD 550 the British language shifted so significantly that the vocabulary that antedated this watershed would have become archaic and, very quickly, incomprehensible to contemporary speakers. Any bardic verse composed around AD 450 would not have been understood by around AD 600. Because of this, any literature written in AD 450 or before would not have been understood well enough to be recopied as soon as AD 600.[8] The history remaining in that state would have been lost. In fact, it is possible that literature written only a generation before about AD 600 would have met with similar fate. It is, after all, with the poetry of the late sixth-century bards Taliesin and Aneirin that British rhyme first emerges.

Additionally, it may very well be that certain living poetry would not have survived beyond this point, either. It must be remembered that secular history often was stored in tightly rhymed verses and that the rhyme scheme allowed the basis of historical knowledge to be kept intact.[9] Without it, such knowledge was quite fragile. Dozens of examples of prominent chieftains are mentioned in *TYP* or by later poets who would seem to have had extensive sagas associated with them at some point. Yet these sagas have not survived. This void can easily be explained by the extinction of the Cumbric language, and with it much of the oral history of the northern British regions disappeared.[10] It may well also be that changes to the language over the centuries rendered those rhymes that managed to survive the watershed of AD 600 incomprehensible anyway.

What remained of the poetry and sagas apparently became the basis for the oral tradition that has endured the centuries.[11] And, as the Arthurian corpus was a part of that oral tradition, it may be implied that any territory in British hands up to around AD 550 could have been the point of origin for the Arthurian tales. Yet the origins of these materials are an important aspect of the equation and cannot be left in such a broad state if they are to prove useful.

The argument that Wales is the earliest location for the Arthurian material is the easiest to defend on literary grounds, so the review will start there. The linguistic evidence shows that *Preiddeu Annwn*, *Culhwch ac Olwen*, and probably similar works had been developed in what would become Modern Wales prior to the emergence of Chrétien de Troyes.[12] Loomis pointed out that a Welsh point of origin was suggested by the less commonly found names in the poet's writings, whose sources he believed came directly from Wales without alteration. Loomis also listed well-known names such as Gauvain and Modred, which he saw as adaptations made when translating the stories from Welsh into French.[13] Such conclusions still seem undeniable.

The evidence for Cornwall and Somerset as a source for Arthurian information is most apparent in Geoffrey's account of Arthur's conception at Tintagel. However, some place-name evidence there corresponds to other key events in his life.[14] At least part of the Tristan element of the Arthurian legend clearly derived from Cornwall as well. Several of the place-names embedded in the romances about him are undoubtedly from that region.[15]

The Bretons may also have developed the legend of Arthur. Loomis saw the Breton names Ivanus (Yvain), Moraldus (Morhaut), and Winlogee (Guinloie) as intermediaries between their Insular and French counterparts,[16] suggesting they may well have been the facilitators of the legend onto the continent. The author will expound on that thought below, during the discussion of the means of transmission for the Arthurian materials.

Besides the Welsh, Cornish, and Breton claims to being the founders or continuators of the Arthurian legacy, certainly what had been Roman Scotland cannot be excluded from the search for source material. Parts of the area fell under the domination of the Anglo-Saxons some decades after Arthur's traditional obit (516 × 542), indicating military activity during his proposed floruit and implying the very heroic poetry from which the Arthurian corpus might have developed.[17] The Arthurian characters Rion, Yvain, Tristan, and Perceval, and the place names Galvoie, Loenis, and Cardoel are of northern origin in the forms of Urien, Owain, Drust, Peredur, Galloway, Lothian, and Carlisle. It has also been noted that all the earliest known poets were predominantly northern figures.[18] This suggests that whatever powers were at work over the centuries allowed more poetic information about the North to survive than that from other areas that were long conquered by the twelfth century.

In addition, the possibility exists of a known written, historical source from this region. Thurneysen was the first to argue the existence of a body

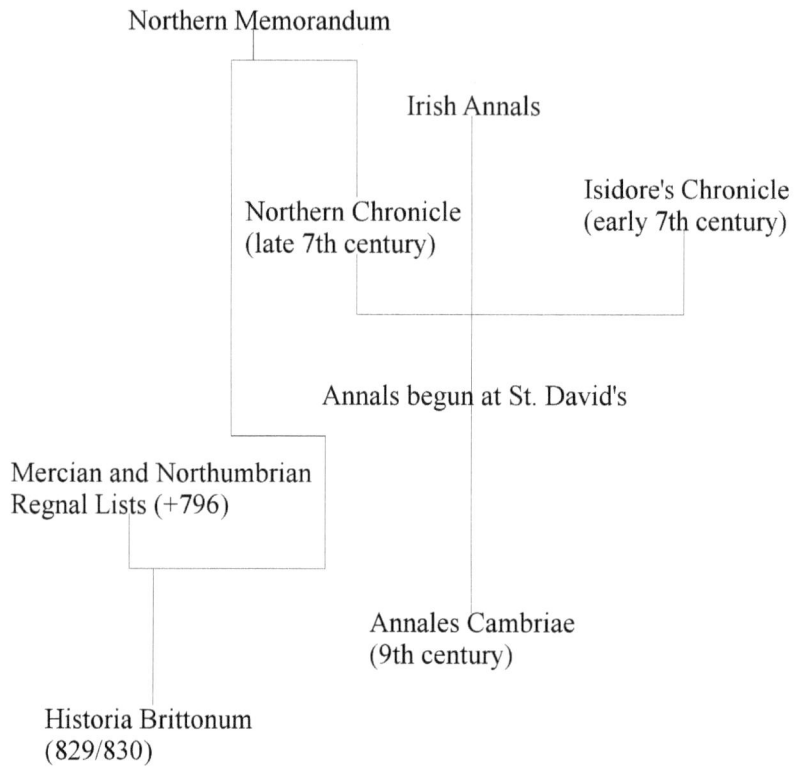

A hypothetical development of the *Northern Memoranda* based on the work of Rudolph Thurneysen, Robert Bruce, Nora Chadwick, David Dumville, Kathleen Hughes, and John Koch.

of pseudohistory, which he termed the *Northern Memoranda*. This body of materials may well have been a source for the *Historia Brittonum*, *Annales Cambriae*, the two extant lives of St. Kentigern, and possibly other literary works, both extant and lost. Thurneysen's hypothetical source has been accepted by several prominent scholars.[19] Professor Dumville and Dr. Hughes, among others, have helped refine how the works influenced this source as it developed. What these scholars have come up with will prove helpful to the author's current project.

The general locale of the above works favors a "northern Britishness."[20] The kingdoms of Mercia and Northumbria were located in what is now northern England, and the names of places and battles given in the sources are not of Germanic origin. In fact, they are occasionally quite ancient. Also, the northern British section of *Historia Brittonum* is devoted entirely to British leaders of *Y Hen Ogled* (The Old North) and the details about five British bards associated with Outigern would have been pertinent only to a British audience. Even the inclusion of the Gwynedd kings in that section pertains to the North. The northern hero Coel is given credit for being the ancestor of the dynasty. The *Vita Kentigerni*, too, is a northern-based work.

The mention of British bards argues for the existence and use of a source of some age by Ninnius. No independent record of the poets named exists. It may be assumed that all but Taliesin and Aneirin would have been forgotten relatively quickly after their floruits, as they were not political leaders and have apparently left no extant poetry. Therefore, the person who recorded the names of the other three bards surely lived well before the late eighth century; it seems probable his lifetime crossed theirs. Judging by the relative chronology of the surrounding chapters, all five lived in the mid-sixth century, which means he was likely active no later than AD 600.

So, too, the place names. Several of the locations mentioned were inside Germanic kingdoms by AD 600, and the British versions of their names must have been out of use within a few generations of that. Yet they appear in *Historia Brittonum* in their British forms. The evidence points to a British source no later than the seventh century for the *Northern Memorandum*.

The *Vita Kentigerni* provides further evidence for such an early dating. Jackson dated the stock materials for both saints' lives to the eleventh or possibly the tenth centuries based on the language of the *vitae*.[21] However, MacQueen, Carney, and more recently Koch have used other methods and postulated a date in the seventh or eighth century for the first version of the legend.[22]

Nora Chadwick came to the same conclusion by different means: "There can, I think, be little doubt that many of the picturesque details of the narrative and the static epithets are of this [sixth or seventh century] origin."[23] She goes on by noting that *Historia Brittonum* ends with Penda, who died at or before AD 655, and its last battle is that of Nechtanesmere in AD 685.[24] Therefore, according to her the source ends with the last years of the seventh century and was most likely last edited shortly after Nechtanesmere.

Professor Koch used a third method. He has also attempted to date the *Northern Memorandum* to 685–700 on the basis that this was the period when the northern British kingdoms would have most benefited from the lapse in Northumbrian aggression. The English genealogies and chronological tie-ins between English and British events could thus be explained by the conquest of Cumbria in the seventh century and the subsequently increasing number of English religious men in the Cumbrian monasteries.[25]

The general location of origin for the *Northern Memorandum* is easy enough to determine. A clue comes in the same sentence that tells us the date of the original *Historia Brittonum* manuscript. Ninnius, one reads, wrote in

King Merfyn's fourth year of rule.[26] Merfyn and his heir Rhodri are known to have taken a considerable interest in North British history in order to build a national consciousness. To this end, they gathered and published much of the records from the North. Since the only surviving British state in ninth-century Scotland was Strathclyde, it seems most probable the *Northern Memorandum* was kept somewhere within its borders. As has been seen, the *Vita Kentigerni* was created from it, and such a work would only have been appropriate coming from the saint's region of activity. The *Northern Memorandum* must have been stored there for several decades at least. And while its specific location of storage is unknown, it is unnecessary information for the purposes of this paper.[27]

As to the nature of the *Northern Memorandum*, the annalistic format of *Historia Brittonum* and *Annales Cambriae* suggest it was written.[28] Further, the specific uses the extant sources put to it hint that the original source was considerably larger than one finds in *Historia Brittonum*. The evidence from *Historia Brittonum* and *Annales Cambriae* indicates that it contained historical, pseudohistorical, and literary materials. Thurneysen, Bruce, and Bromwich have added the *Arthuriana* section of the *Historia Brittonum* to the northern history chapters. If this theory continues to hold up, then much of our Arthurian information may have come from the *Northern Memorandum* as well.[29] If that is true, it may well be that *Cadegr* was a part of the *Northern Memorandum*.

As uncertain as the geographic origin of the legend of Arthur and its subsequent heroes are, the precise form in which this corpus made its way to France is fairly certain; it was primarily oral. Loomis was for many years the biggest proponent of this belief. He devoted the majority of his first chapter in *Arthurian Tradition and Chrétien* to listing the widespread evidence for oral transference before, during, and after Chrétien's period.[30] This is the best assembly of evidence to the current author's knowledge.

Dr. Bromwich has asserted the debt to oral transference by noting that the French/Welsh equations were unknown to Geoffrey and his adapters, yet can be found in both Welsh and French stories. Some of these equations are Girflet fis Do/Gilfaethwy fab Don, Maheloas/Melwas, Mabonagrain/Mabon, and Caradues Briebras/Caradawc Freichfras. Dr. Bromwich then proposes that oral tradition was probably the reason the names used by Chrétien and his successors were unrecognizable. She puts this succinctly in *The Legend of Arthur in the Middle Ages*.

> Although a proportion of names in Chrétien correspond with names in existing Welsh poems and triads and native tales, the large number of names in the French romances which cannot be explained, and which have obviously been borrowed in forms which are corrupt, favours the belief that oral transmission

2. Chrétien's Known Sources and Influences

was by far the most frequent and widespread means of transference of Celtic names and stories into French; though we must allow always for several significant instances of written borrowings.[31]

This is indeed what one would expect to find if the material was transported orally.[32]

Finally, the question of who passed the British information on to poets such as Chrétien has been the subject of ongoing debates. Three major theories have been created to account for the phenomenon. They all involve different intermediaries in primarily the same role. The proponents of each have been roughly equal in number. In these proposals, the protagonists are the Bretons, Welsh, and the unskilled tradesmen and military personnel of the Angevin kingdom. A brief overview will outline the main points of each school of thought.

In 1055 a Gwynedd king named Gruffydd ap Llywelyw united the kingdoms of Gwynedd, Powys, Deheubarth, and Morgannwg under him. During that period, those kingdoms constituted most of what remained of Wales and the British legacy. The political unity allowed by Gruffydd's activities allowed individuals of the bardic class interstate travel on a scale that had previously been unthinkable, and they made good use of the new freedom. The exchange was such a lucrative one that it created a renaissance of British culture. Wales became a receptacle of northern British, Cornish, and Irish historical, pseudo-historical, and literary materials.[33] As a result, the mid-eleventh century generated a large body of material about Arthur as well. And so, by the end of the century, the vehicle for easy transference to the continent was in place.

In 1066, William the Conqueror of Normandy assumed the English throne. By the time he died in 1087, William had control of a large part of Britain as well as his hereditary estates in Normandy. By 1100, this Angevin Empire stretched over much of France and the South of Wales, not to mention Scotland and England. With it, a constant stream of information and individuals flowed back and forth from every corner of the kingdom. As much as Wales was a receptacle of Arthurian knowledge by 1100, the Angevin Empire was prepared to be a vehicle of transference. The literature needed only an anima in the form of Geoffrey of Monmouth to create an interest and send *Arthuriana* pouring forth onto the continent. The Arthurian material could then have found its way to the continent by several means; soldiers, monks, crusaders, or noblemen each could have brought Arthur to France, and undoubtedly many representatives of these groups did.

However, the Welsh were the keepers of British history and legend as the only remaining receptacle of British culture in Britain, and others have believed that this is the only important point. It is known that there were bilingual communities in the South of Wales who spoke both their native language and French fluently.³⁴ Professional storytellers from these communities, known as *latimari*, would have been able to translate any Arthurian material from Welsh to French as the situation required. And it is very likely they were put in situations like that often. The latimari were renowned for their linguistic prowess and often served as translators throughout Britain. These men may have served in France as well and carried with them their traditional stories as entertainment.

It is also possible the Bretons may have learned the materials and translated them on their way back to their homeland. It is known that the Bretons were among the more numerous of William the Conqueror's allies. After his assumption of the throne, they were allotted territory in Wales as well as England and France. This act made them one of the more powerful groups in the Angevin realm. Their language was also intelligible to the Welsh, helping the two groups form a bond in English- and Norman–dominated Britain. These factors could have contributed to help form a bridge of unimpeded transmission of material from Wales to the continent as well.

The *troubadours*, professional storytellers of southern France, are also part of the Arthurian equation. Undoubtedly, they were bearers of early versions of Arthurian stories. *Troubadour* poetry is known to have predated Chrétien and all extant Arthurian romances. For instance Tristan was known to them before 1145, and Perceval is referred to in a poem prior to 1160, anticipating Chrétien by some twenty-five years.³⁵ In fact, an overwhelming number of references to Arthurian characters are to be found in the *troubadours'* literature,³⁶ indicating a strong and early foundation in southern France.

It was also probably the *troubadours* who modified and softened the Welsh literature involving Arthur. It was they who created what can be considered the framework for the romance pattern that is now associated with Arthur and made him fully palatable to the French courts. It was in their tales that Tristan became the best lover, Yvain the first model of fashion, and Arthur the courtly standard for kingliness.

That is not to say, however, that the troubadours in any way created the plots in which we later find these characters. However, the vast majority of what is integral to the romance literature of the period found its impetus in the Celtic tales. As Alfred Nutt put it over a hundred years ago: "The spirit of the age, akin to the Celtic, recognized in Celtic tales the food it was hungering for."³⁷ Regarding the poets of northern France (*trouvères*), this statement has gone generally unchallenged, and in the South the work of Dr. Joseph Anglade and Dr. Rita Lejeune have greatly substantiated this claim.³⁸

One can be certain that some of Chrétien's data for *Le Chevalier de la Charrette* originated in Scotland, Wales, Cornwall, or Brittany (or any combination of these places). It was transmitted by professionals through Breton and/or Welsh bard/translators, in oral and, possibly, written form. Informally, Breton soldiers, settlers, or any class of people who traveled throughout the empire of Henry II (the great-grandson of William) transmitted the data, specifically the names and attributes of the heroes. This information was likely stripped of its rough edges and made courtlier by the troubadours and trouvères of Chrétien's native kingdom. This is the extent of Celtic research on the transmission of Arthurian material.

The French perspective on the question of transmission is based mainly on the relationship between *matière* and *sens* of which Chrétien speaks in his prologues, what little is known of his personal life and his literary influences, and his patrons.

Professor Gaston Paris admitted to Celtic influences of some sort and of some degree (both undefined).[39] Still, he saw most of Chrétien's work as being the product of his reading of classical writers, which is one reason why he is often labeled a clerk, priest, or other holy person.[40] The following pages of this chapter will demonstrate the degree to which Chrétien's learning has molded his poetry by showing how he successfully integrated his knowledge of Latin, Greek, and contemporary scholars with the Celtic plots, motifs, and names he is known to have used.

Ovid was most clearly one of Chrétien's guiding forces in technique and manner of presentation. In addition, Ovid was the expert on the topic of love for the twelfth-century reader.[41] His belief that the institutions of love and marriage were innately opposed to each other permeated much of the thinking of the time. Chrétien himself claimed to have written a version of several Ovidian poems: "The Art of Love," "The Shoulder Bite," "The Metamorphosis of the Hoopoe," "Swallow," and "Nightingale."[42] In two of his Arthurian poems, *Cligès* and *Le Chevalier de la Charrette*, he seems to follow Ovid's principles of love. Lancelot and Guinièvre as well as Cligès and Fenice all have relations out of wedlock. Further, Ovid's method in *Heroide* of capturing the emotional thoughts of the characters and then commenting on them is well matched in "Cligès" where Soredamors allows us a glimpse of her thoughts.[43] It is also found in *La Charrette*, when Guinièvre ponders suicide on hearing Lancelot is dead.[44] Noble further sees the couples Lancelot and Guinièvre as well as Yvain and Laudine as Ovidian lovers. This is because the male is obedient to the whims of his idol, the female, who is most willing to test those feelings.

However, Ovid was clearly not a welcome influence. In *Cligès*,[45] Chrétien reveals his conscience through a regular denunciation of the heroine of the *Tristan* cycle, Isolde, whose romance with Tristan was outside of marriage as well. In *Le Chevalier de la Charrette*, he disclaims responsibility for matière and sens altogether. Curiously, he did not finish this poem. As has been mentioned, he gave it to Godefroi de Leigni to finish. Ovid's love philosophy was something Chrétien apparently could not personally accept.[46]

On the other hand, four of Chrétien's Arthurian poems—*Erec et Enide, Yvain, Le Conte du Graal,* and part of *Cligès*—extol marriage. This betrays his strong moral sense.

There are, then, strong indications that Chrétien had a strongly negative view of Ovidian love philosophy. Dr. Guyer's thesis, *The Influence of Ovid on Chréstien de Troyes*, only reinforces this appraisal. He lists two compelling examples of this theory in *Le Chevalier de la Charrette*. First is Lancelot's attempt to jump from the top of a tower to rescue Guinièvre. She is at that moment safely and slowly riding by the castle in which he is staying. Second is Lancelot's mental absorption with Guinièvre during his first duel with Meleagant. Upon seeing her, he becomes so enraptured with her that he allows his opponent to work his way around him to face Guinièvre, forcing Lancelot into the error of turning his back to his foe.[47] In caricaturing Lancelot, the personification of the perfect lover, Chrétien is belittling courtly love. Peter Noble's book *Love and Marriage in Chrétien de Troyes* lists many additional examples of excessive behavior from Lancelot that demonstrate Chrétien's personal disgust with Ovidian love and respect for marriage.

Following Ovid's lead, and formalizing and adapting it to the twelfth century, Andreas Capellanus systematized the ideology now known as courtly love. A few of its guidelines will be sufficient to clarify its main theme.

I. Causa coniugii ab amore non est excusatio rects.
XI. Non decet amare, quaram pudor est nuptias afectare.
XII. Verus amans alterius nisi sui coamantis ex affectu non cupit amplexus.
XIV. Facilis perceptio contemptibilem reddit amorem, dificilis eum carum facit haberi.
XXVI. Amore nil posset amore denegare.[48]
1. Marriage is no excuse for no loving.
11. One should not love another whom one should be ashamed to court.
12. A true love desires only his beloved.
14. The more difficult love is the more it is prized.
24. Every act must end in the thought of the lover.
26. Love can deny nothing to love.[49]

Within this fashionable concept, Chrétien began to create the poems for which he is praised today. The evidence of this courtly code is clearly delineated, especially in *Le Chevalier de la Charrette*. The entire love element in the story would not be possible without Capellanus's first rule. And though no one can love two people, he does say that two people may love the same person.⁵⁰ This precept is not in Ovid's works but is central to Capellanus's writings.

Chrétien did not write with only Ovid and Andreas Capellanus in mind, however, as has been demonstrated by a wide variety of scholars. Geoffrey of Monmouth, great progenitor of the legend of Arthur to the reading world, gave Chrétien his setting. Wace, his French translator, was also an influence. In *Erec* Chrétien first mentions the Round Table which was first introduced by him.⁵¹ Dr. Owen and Margaret Pelan have additionally noted dozens of other examples.⁵²

La Chanson de Roland, an epic French poem and a precursor to the romances, gave Chrétien inspiration in *Cligès*. The retreat of the traitor Angres, descriptions of resplendent tents, and jousting among the enemy are all reminiscent of similar themes in the classic.⁵³ So is the segment when Alexander combats the enemy. Alexander names each of his comrades in turn, beginning with a close friend, as in *La Chanson*.⁵⁴ Both lists include an epic pair.⁵⁵ In both cases the enemy attempts a night raid that is defeated by a premature rising of the sun.⁵⁶ None of the above is from Geoffrey or Wace.

Other details of Chrétien's romances that relate directly to *La Chanson de Roland* include two heroes named by Chrétien: Fernagut and Forre. Both were killed by Roland.⁵⁷ A comparison Chrétien makes between Yvain and Roland is overt in its influence, making clear he was familiar with the general form of *La Chanson de Roland* (*Yvain*, ll. 3235–7). The similarity of the Roland-Oliver-Aude relationships to that of Gauvain-Alexander-Soredamors in *Cligès* and the reference to Ganelon are also plainly derived from the French epic.⁵⁸ Finally, the translator Owen made note of a strong likeness between Arthur's statements about the betrayer Angres and Charlemagne's comments about his own traitor in the respective poems. The evidence for the influence is overwhelming in *Cligès*, though possibly this has some connection to the relative independence of *Cligès* from Celtic influence.

He also uses the theme of the beloved being recognized by her golden hair in this poem, a concept he borrowed from either Vergil's *Aeneid* or the *Roman d'Eneas*. Chrétien refers specifically to the Old French version of this poem,⁵⁹ and uses the name Lavinia of Laurentium — Aeneas's wife.⁶⁰ The actions of the two maidens in preparing Enide's hair are strongly reminiscent of a similar scene in *Aeneid* involving Dido and her maidens.⁶¹ Even the monologue Soredamors develops in *Cligès* seems to be based on the Dido monologue in Aeneid.⁶²

The great poet owed a heavy debt to other classical writers as well. Dr. Laurie saw evidence of Propertius's stream of erotic poetry in *Elegiae*.⁶³ In Alexander's lament for Soredamors she saw a resemblance to Lucretius's *De Rerum Natura*.⁶⁴ A link to Caesar's *De Bello Civili* can be seen in the rise of

Erec and his subsequent problems,[65] and Enide's self-examination resembles the Cornelia character of Lucan.[66] Chrétien mentions Macrobius, author of *Saturnalia*, by name.[67] Chrétien has also been seen to mimic Quintilian in his treatment of the queen in *Cligès*. Her manner of detecting the signs of love between Soredamors and Alexander are also similar to Quintilian.[68] The wedding scene of *Erec et Enide* is blatantly stolen from Statius's *Venus*.[69] Chrétien even touches on mythology with his introduction of Medea.

Christian writers influenced Chrétien as well. Dr. Laurie detected the Augustinian concept, "The will finds rest in knowledge itself."[70] She also discovered that St. Augustine's *Confessions* was Chrétien's source for the motif of deliverance from evil.[71] The concept that a "touch of resignation is real enough" given to Lancelot about Guinièvre[72] and the belief that the soul is informed of the world through the body is also taken from St. Augustine's *Confessions*.[73] The sequence of the plot in *Cligès* is similar to a hymn attributed to the pure of heart.[74] The axiom is follow by a biblical sequence.

In addition, the trees in *Yvain* covered by sweetly singing birds seem to be taken directly from those of *Navigatio Sanctii Brendani* and its Anglo-Norman version.[75] Dr. Owen found one comparison between *The Gospel of Nicodemus* and *Le Chevalier de la Charrette*: Lancelot's trip to Gorre imitated the gospel's version of Christ's crucifixion and his Harrowing of Hell.[76]

Chrétien also drew from the Tristan legend. He claims to have written a version of it in *Erec* and inserts in that same poem a comparison of Enide with Iseut's blonde hair.[77]

Some of these comparisons are without a doubt subjective, but together they do form a consistent pattern. One may see that Chrétien made use of the works of Ovid and Andreas Capellanus, as well as those of Wace, the early Tristan romances, and scores of classical and ancient Christian authors. One may also see that he is able to take these ideas and manners of presentation and sew them seamlessly into an already structured plot.

One must now turn to Chrétien's major and most watchful influence — his feminist patron, the countess Marie de Champagne. What little is known of her character tells us a great deal about her. Her mother, Eleanor of Aquitaine, had been one of the most formidable women in all of Europe during her heyday. Her most noteworthy action was her decision to marry King Henry II of England after being divorced by King Louis VII of France. This was not only a personal affront to Louis VII, but it effectively gave one quarter of France to England and his rival. Her actions had great personal and political repercussions for all of Western Europe.

Her later divorce from Henry again altered the political scene, as she intended. Seeking to establish her independence once more, she created her own court at Poitiers. There she went on to fund the maturation of the

2. Chrétien's Known Sources and Influences

The Angevin Kingdom, c. 1100. With Henry of Anjou's inheritance of Britain, his kingdom was a perfect vehicle for the transfer of government and soldiers, culture, ideas, and Arthuriana to and from the continent.

romance movement. She began by making her daughter the head of her own court. She devoted this court to romance, and her daughter's strong personality and her regular commissions of romantic tales soon made it the center of romantic thought in Western Europe. In time it would make rulings on romantic issues. It was in this setting that Marie, through Eleanor, was able to create the ambiance that would become a mainstay of Arthurian literature.[78]

Because of her contributions and her finances, Marie was also a figure of note throughout Europe. In addition, she was a widow of the Count of Champagne, which meant she had land and money in her own right. These three facts demanded that she be treated with respect, if not endearment, among her male peers. She made the most of the attention that garnered. In her lifetime, letters were written not only to, but about her. One correspondence was addressed to the bishops of Sens, Reims, and Meaux as Marie lay on her deathbed and spoke of her contributions to society.[79] Two contemporary historians described her as acting *viriliter*, that is, "in manly fashion."[80] In a world where women were by definition considered inferior, that was high praise. She deserved it; she actively and repeatedly took charge of situations, as when a small group of nobles decided to gather on her property so that they could figure out how best to control the young king Philip Augustus. After her relationship with the king had settled, she had the audacity to approach him and request that he intervene when a treaty that had assigned her son and daughter a wife and husband was in danger of being ignored. The matter was conducted to her satisfaction.

It was this decisive woman for whom a succession of poets worked, and it is apparent that she took an active role in the creation of many of their works. Her commission of a translation of Genesis points this out most of all. Three versions of this work have survived in manuscript. They have been named "A," "B," and "C."

Scholarship by Dr. Henderson has concluded that manuscripts "B" and "C" are later versions of "A"[81] because the intense feminist attitudes in "B" and "C" are not found in "A." Henderson believes this feminism was due to Marie's direct supervision.[82] Considering this assumption Dr. McCash believes the third book of *De Amore* tells us something more of the environment Marie created. Andreas Capellanus finished writing it around 1186, and it recants some of the more Ovidian principles on love. Coincidentally, he is not to be found in any of Champagne's legal charters from about this time, implying he no longer was a part of Marie's circle. Whether he was allowed to finish the book in her court or was expelled before he wrote it, the third book of *De Amore* was not condoned on Marie de Champagne's property. It seems the author of such writings was not allowed, either.[83]

With the completion of *La Charrette*, Marie must have reached the height of her power in the cultural world. Her brothers Richard the Lionheart and John Lackland would fight their father and later, each other for the kingdom. She could not do this. She was condemned to marry a count and be a wife and later a widow. She was forced into the role of a woman in a man's world, and she must have hated it. In the literature her court produced, though, and particularly in *La Charrette*, she got some measure of revenge. In it Lancelot is the perfect knight in all respects, bowing to every whim of his lover as though she was his master. This was the sens that Marie wanted to integrate into the British tales, and the sens for which Chrétien wanted no credit. This influence also helped create the otherworldliness of the Arthurian world that has so tightly linked it to fairy tales and mythology, and therefore the one that must be accounted for if one is to gain an accurate view of the original British tales.

As I wrote at the beginning of this chapter, the Celtic and French approaches are not mutually exclusive, in fact they occasionally complement each other. No French scholar claims that the impetus for much of the early Arthurian romances derived from anywhere but Britain. The French scholars do not argue the tales could have been transferred to the continent by any oral or written means, either. Scholars see many Celtic themes and names in the early romances, but the references to classical writers make it clear that Chrétien was also aware of them and made use of his wide readings. Therefore, it is clear that Chrétien used British sources for the plots and many of the individual scenes. It is also clear that he integrated other sources, both classical and contemporary, when it suited his personal tastes or the desires of his patrons.

The accumulated facts allow the critical analyst to gain some perspective on Chrétien's creativity concerning the material that influenced him. Much of where Chrétien found many of his themes and perspectives are known. He was unmistakably well read in the Greek, Roman, and medieval authors and especially so with the *chansons de geste* (songs of heroic deeds), *Historia Regum Britanniae*, and Wace. It appears that Chrétien remolded the Celtic stories in his poems and elaborated on his source with the techniques of literary scenes and with figures of the classical and medieval worlds. As Dr. Owen, translator of the poet, has remarked: "At times his memory of some narrative appears to condition his presentation of important sections of a romance as he takes elements from it, adapts them to his needs and insinuates them into his text."[84]

However, there are minutiae that are not from the literary masterpieces of the ancient and medieval worlds. As has been noted, the names, several motifs, and themes are Celtic; much more remains unconnected to the classical or contemporary worlds. Much of this material, and the energy of the romances, derives from British sources. This is because the primary source of the poems is always British. The other influences on the verse are generally transitory and appear to have been superimposed on the plot.[85] A first step toward proving this thesis has been taken by demonstrating Chrétien's dependence on a large number of classical writers. A second step was taken in establishing the existence of an early body of historical and literary material from which the Arthurian abduction and grail romances may have derived. Finally, a survey of possible manners of transference to the continent has provided the means by which Chrétien may have accessed them.

In the following chapters the author will show evidence, both motifal and historical, why several early forms of the abduction scenario were not totally dependent on Chrétien. In addition, the author will bring forth evidence to show that at times these alternative forms drew directly on a British source, or at least one of their antecedents did in a line independent of Chrétien. Thus, several different romance writers drew directly on British sources. This in turn means that each writer may be employed to define the prototype for the abduction.[86] The author hopes to show that there was originally a single post–Roman British tale on both topics from which the various authors drew. Likely it was oral in nature, likely it varied greatly with each redaction, but it was essentially the same tale.

3

The Characters and Their Roles[1]

The previous chapter showed evidence that a significant percentage of the material in the Arthurian stories came from Britain. In this essay, the focus will be on the main characters in the traditional abduction story. No one denies that the names of the chief players—Meleagant, Guinièvre, Keu, Gauvain, Arthur, and Lancelot—and their occurrence in the literary material present incontrovertible evidence for the ultimately British origins of the story.[2] However, three topics must be discussed in order to fully understand their true nature: the strange imposition of Urien/Valerin as the alternate abductor, the exact role of each of the main characters in the presumed original tale, and the birthplace of the name Lancelot.

Lanzelet and *Diu Crône* employ an alternative Valerin/Urien as the antagonist.[3] As all the other characters are consistently present and retain their functions in the different versions, it seems reasonable to assume that either Melwas or Urien is a later intrusion on the story, instead of deciding there might have been two. Common sense suggests that Urien is the later addition.[4] The fact that Urien of Rheged was both memorable and active during the same heroic age as the Arthurian figures is the telling piece of information here. As a rule, such individuals tend to be drawn into the orbit of more popular leaders as their stories gain wider circulation, and this scenario may well be what happened here.[5] The fact that no evidence of his presence exists in the tale may well mean nothing. However, etymology offers an alternative solution.

The earliest and overwhelming majority of the sources use *mel* for the first syllable of the antagonist. The second syllable tends to vary, but in its earliest form is *was*. Professor Sims-Williams translates *melwas* as "honey-youth."[6] The other theory, proposed by Dr. Bromwich, is that of Melwas<*mael* "prince" + *gwas* "lad," "servant."[7]

The translations "prince-lad" and "honey-youth" both sound like titles or nicknames. In the context of *Ymddiddan Gwenhwyfar ac Arthur* or *The*

Dialogue between Gwenhwyfar and Arthur, such an appellation would be applicable as the moniker for a well-known character, such as Urien. On the other hand, it could simply be a poetic invention for a nameless hero as has been believed. Apart from this story and that found in the second *vita* of Gildas, Melwas is unknown in Britain.

While a Melwas/Urien theory may not have strong supporting evidence, it is viable and explains the later transposition on the continent. As will be seen below, the authors of both *Lanzelet* and *Diu Crône* had direct access to Insular source materials. It could be that their source named Valerin/Urien directly. However, no matter what route the antagonist took — as a nameless individual who was later supplanted by Urien or as Urien who during the golden age of the Arthurian literature was known by his nickname — the character in the poems was a consistent one.

Guinièvre seems like a very obvious and necessary element of the tale as well. She is present in all versions as both Arthur's queen and the victim of a kidnapping. However, there is some negative evidence that this character was not an old one. Both Guinièvre and her progenitor Gwenhwyfar are unknown in any tale whose orthography dates before the twelfth century. She is not to be found in the oldest group of triadic material, either. Using any literature's composition, one cannot with certainty date the introduction of Guinièvre to much before 1100. It seems at least possible that she is a superimposed figure who was not named in the traditional lore. The fact that the names of famed kings' wives were rarely kept, and then only when they were the daughters of famous kings is telling here.[8] For the record, Gwenhwyfar is given several fathers in the literature, each equally unlikely.[9]

On a more positive note, the often opposing elements in the four British versions of the abduction suggest that Gwenhwyfar was considered to be Arthur's queen before the transference of the Arthurian material to the continent.[10] However, it is possible that their agreement here is a direct result of the overwhelming influence Geoffrey of Monmouth had on the development of the Arthurian legend. Until more information has been collected on this character, no clear idea of her nature or history may be given for certain.

Keu/Cei's role in the abduction is much simpler to determine. With the sole exceptions of the terse *Vita Gildae* and the heavily edited story in *Iwein*, he is always present. Further, the Welsh "Pa gur?" *Ymddiddan Gwenhwyfar ac Arthur*, and *Culhwch ac Olwen* indicate that Cei was originally a formidable warrior in Arthur's troupe. If, as the majority of the abductions say, Gauvain and others were away when Melwas/Urien came to court, Keu would have been an acceptable substitute for him. It is likely he was an original element in the tale and acted as Guinièvre's protector.

Arthur is the king and husband to the victim. In Irish lore the abduction of a powerful king's wife is a common phenomenon and thus an explanation of his role requires a review of the abduction theme in Irish myth. Typical abduction tales include a one-year delay between the kidnapping and the abductor's death or the surrender of the wife (see below). This is so in Chrétien and the *Vita Gildae*. However, in the Irish tales the king is usually the rescuer. In *La Charrette* and most of the variants, Arthur does not have this role. From a literary standpoint this is intriguing. From an historical standpoint, Arthur's role in the plot as it stands is inconsistent regarding the degree of his power and his representation as a warrior elsewhere. The author would suggest the Arthurian world has at one stage added Gwenhwyfar's abduction from another heroic age source.[11]

Any thesis that explores the Celtic aspect of *Le Chevalier de la Charrette* must also address the question of Lancelot. Did he exist in the British tradition before the birth of Arthurian romance in the twelfth century? If so, why is he not visible in Geoffrey of Monmouth's *Historia Regum Britanniae*, *The Pictish King-lists*, the oldest Welsh poems, or any other British tradition? Is he present in one of these works, but his name is so linguistically altered from something recognizable that one cannot distinguish him? To date, *no one* has linked him to any twelfth-century personage Chrétien may have wished to extol. Where did Chrétien get the information about Lancelot saving Guinièvre? Did he or Marie de Champagne invent the name? Lancelot does not rescue the queen in the other abductions— except for *Lanzelet*. Even then he is only one of many. That means that even if he has a history before 1100, Lancelot traditionally did not rescue the queen.

It would indeed appear that Chrétien simply invented Lancelot, but theories abound. Tatlock claims that Geoffrey's book contains *Anguselaus—L'Ancelot*.[12] He is Lleu Llaw Gyffes of the *Mabinogion*.[13] He is Lleog/Lleminog of *Preiddeu Annwn*.[14] Such theories are linguistically challenged, however, and the characters show no literary connections to Lancelot.

Take Rachel Bromwich's perception of the issue. In her massive undertaking, *Trioedd Ynys Prydein*, she states persuasively that "because of the absence of any convincing resemblance in the name forms, I feel no hesitation in rejecting the derivation of "Lancelot"<Elyflath<Eliwlat proposed by T. Gwynn Jones and also that proposed by R.S. Loomis in which he associates "Lancelot" with "Lluch Llauynauc" of BBC 94, 13–14 and so derives the name ultimately from that of the Irish god Lug."[15]

The examination will begin where Dr. Bromwich does. In a concluding remark following several well-researched and generally accepted Arthurian matches, Thomas Jones informs us that Middle Welsh *Eliwlad* is "a kind of rendering of Lancelot."[16] He gives no literary, historical, or referential support for this theory, nor does he explain the word change by oral or written means.

The author is in total agreement that Jones's argument is unsupported and weak.

In *Celtic Myth and Romance* Professor Loomis theorized that Lancelot was in reality the Irish god Lug descended through several men listed in the Welsh Arthurian poems.[17] He continued this belief throughout the rest of his career. The Welsh intermediaries, he said, could be found in *Culhwch ac Olwen*, "Pa gur?," and two versions of the same triad of *TYP*.[18] In Loomis's words:

> The puzzle may be explained by the fact that the person and the name were borrowed from some foreign people, probably from the Irish since the Welsh are known to have borrowed a few figures famed in Irish saga and enrolled them among Arthur's warriors, e.g. Manawidan ab Llyr in *The Black Book of Carmarthen*, and Cynchwyr mab Nes, Cubert mab Daere, Fercos mab Poch, Lluber Beuthach, Corvii Bervach, and Sgilti in *Kulhwch*.[19]

Thus, Lancelot's original name was Llwch, transferable to Irish as Lugh. His last name was originally Lonnbemnech but, for some reason Loomis does not explain, the linguistically related and culturally tied Welsh could not understand or even translate it. For Loomis, this accounted for the varying appellations the hero has been given over the centuries. However, the theory does not explain the otherwise unmentioned Lleog/Llemenawc of *Preiddeu Annwn*. It can be conceded that the first syllable of the character, *llem<llam* meaning "the bounding or prancing one," does have some affinity with the athletic Lancelot.[20] However, there remain difficulties with accepting this proposal. For one, such arguments rely heavily on linguistic evidence, an uncertain tool at the best of times.[21] Arthurian studies are hardly that, Old British was going through a period of dramatic changes during the mid- and late sixth centuries; most likely a great many names and places from that period simply disappeared. When the Cumbric language died around 1100, likely many more were lost.

Even if the etymologies of Jones or Loomis are correct and there is a connection to one of the legendary or mythic characters of Irish or pan–Celtic literature, this still proves nothing. The character Lancelot does not need to have been euhemerized; an etymological connection to a deity does not preclude him having been an historical figure. In many instances people have been named after deities of an extinct religion. Current religions occasionally have followers named after one of their deities. The name Bridget among the Welsh and Irish has been quite popular over the centuries, as have Thor or Freyr among the Germanic countries and names beginning with *Os* among the English.[22] In Arthuriana, the textual variant Arcturus has connected Arthur to Ursa Major,[23] yet no one would use this isolated case to make any connections between him and any divinities.

3. The Characters and Their Roles

Thus the two most prominent theories cannot stand up under scrutiny. Tatlock's theory, however, seems much stronger at first sight. Tatlock was building off of a comment the Viscount Hersant de la Villémarque made in an 1842 discussion on *Le Chevalier de la Charrette*. He had opened with a short commentary on a long-standing problem in French manuscripts—the *L'*. When this nuisance is applied to the Chrétien poem, the *L'* could very well mean that Lancelot was originally L' Ancelot, as several manuscripts read.[24]

Ancelot could possibly be a name found in the Insular sources, and Tatlock's Anguselaus seems the most likely target. Dr. Pope's *From Latin to Modern French with Especial Consideration of Anglo-Norman* is of great help here.[25] Dr. Pope suggests that the name Anguselaus would normally lose its middle syllable in translation from Latin to Old French if it were in a weak and unaccented position, which *gu* is. This change would leave Anselaus, a name corrupted into Ancelot more easily than either Eliwlat or Lluch.

However, it should be noted that the author here speaks of the alteration of words that occurred over a period of a thousand years. Tatlock speaks of an outright translation from Latin to Old French. Still, the adjustment of Anguselaus into Old French Anselaus and from there to Ancelot is linguistically plausible. From here, Chrétien's talent and the fame of his poems must have controlled the fate of the name. From a literary standpoint, *ancelot* in French means "servant," giving L'Ancelot "the servant."[26] Chrétien would have enjoyed the duality of meanings in the name, his hero was now both a king and a love slave, and the fact that several manuscripts have the form L'Ancelot supports the idea that this was his intended meaning.

Anguselaus' British form would be *Unguist*.[27] This name matches two figures in *The Pictish King-Lists*. The more likely candidate to have been drawn into the Arthurian milieu is the son of Forgus, who ruled in the early sixth century. Forgus succeeded in conquering Dalriada and reigning approximately thirty-one years.[28] He was a very powerful and warlike king and most likely inspired heroic stories that could then have been brought into Arthur's literary court. Of course this does not preclude other possibilities; Unguist could represent the cognomen of any British hero or king who existed between 400 and 1200.

With the possibility of Unguist/Anguselaus/Lancelaus/L'Ancelot one has a scribal solution. There are, though, two problems with the theory. As Professor Tatlock and others have made note, there was an Angus of Moray killed in 1130 who claimed to be the King of Scotland, just as Geoffrey's Anguselaus of Albany does. It has been argued Geoffrey could have been using the name of Anguselaus to introduce a humorous element in the story—he along with everyone in the English court were laughing at their contemporary's impertinence.

Second, no connection has ever been made with any thing or any one who is listed in the pertinent manuscripts. And while Goodrich's theory that Lancelot was a noble Pict (and therefore not of interest to the British) might be used to account for this phenomenon, it seems unreasonable to simply assume Lancelot existed within the Arthurian orbit before Chrétien introduced him. After all, several Picts, Irish, and even a few Germanic warriors are mentioned in them.

In a recent article, Dr. Lloyd-Morgan summarized the argument concisely; Lancelot did not have a past before Chrétien invented him in *Cligès*.[29] However, she does add a single, potentially damaging corollary to her conclusion. Tristan was not a prevalent figure, either. Dr. Lloyd-Morgan suggests the two may not have been common in Welsh lore because their themes both undermine beloved kings.[30] Thus, the very argument she uses allows for a reason why Lancelot was not a popular character while stories that would have been associated with him were circulating in Wales. The window is still open, and Lancelot may have been a part of Welsh lore at one time.

And it would seem odd if he were an entirely made-up character. If that was the case, he and Cligès would be the only non–Celtic figures in the first round of Arthurian romances. It also seems unlikely to this writer that Chrétien or his translator would have created him for a bit-part in *Cligès* and *Erec*,[31] and that this same invented character would then have been used at around the same time some twenty or thirty years later in both *Le Chevalier de la Charrette* and *Lanzelet*. If that were so it would mean that two men living in different kingdoms during the medieval period would have written independent variants of the same story and starring the same minor personage twenty or so years later. Such a scenario is highly unlikely, especially given the line of tradition we can see attached to other popular figures. The simple fact that Lancelot's education is by fairies in *Lanzelet* is evidence that the German version of the story was in an oral environment for an extended period of time.[32] One can safely say the Lancelot character had a predecessor before his inclusion in *Cligès* and *Erec* and therefore before 1160. However, as has been seen, finding a reasonable predecessor has proven problematic.

Proving that a saga figure lived at all is difficult. However, it is possible. Research on other heroic ages has shown that, if a figure did exist, he is to be located in the same period and general location as the central figure of the saga.[33] On the other hand, it would seem that fictional incidents can be attached to a character as soon as they die[34] or even within his or her lifetime. Professor Chadwick's philosophy on the matter has been borne out over the decades.[35]

The fact is that Lancelot is a mystery as a literary and as an historical character. It is difficult to say whether he became confused later with Arthur or was initially a part of the early version of the legendary king's band. He probably was not originally associated with saving Guinièvre from Melwas. There are no concrete or even tenable grounds in the Welsh oral sources to make such an assumption. He may, however, have been a Pictish or British king. He may have helped steal a cauldron under the appellation Llenlleawg, as Loomis suggested, but there is no tangible proof that he did. Whether or not any of this is so, the literary figure Lancelot probably existed in some form before 1100. Dr. Bromwich eventually followed Loomis in suggesting an eleventh-century *Lancelin* of Brittany as a prototype,[36] and the author would agree that this name is the most important clue about Lancelot's beginnings.

It can be assumed that the abductor, Cei, the abducted, and the hero (likely Gauvain or his Welsh antecedent) were in the sources of all the versions of the abductions.[37] One can also be fairly certain they performed the same basic functions there. This, as Dr. Bromwich has often pointed out, is remarkable.[38] Such a faithful preservation of a foreign culture's heroes with or without that region's stock features is, to the current author's knowledge, unique in ancient and medieval world literature, both oral and written. Yet there it is, present in French, German, and Italian, and later in Dutch, Spanish, Icelandic, Irish, and Scottish romances, with all the accouterments of Celtic literature. This presence is because *Glas* was probably a written source[39] that each progressive author felt a need to reinterpret, not remake. The abduction story, however, has more to offer an inquisitive scholar, as I hope the next three chapters will demonstrate. A penetrating examination of the first full-length version of the abduction will reveal elements in the story that could be historical, followed by a chapter devoted to certainly historical material. The aim of these chapters will be to establish a rough date for the earliest elements of the abduction in Arthurian literature.

4
Literary Tools for Supplementary Material

In the last chapter, it was seen that the material that made up the plot for the abduction of Arthur's queen came from Britain and that the characters in the story were remarkably consistent. This in turn suggested that narratives and individuals all derived from a common tradition, whatever its form and from whatever point the details therein began to mutate. Building on this realization, the author will be analyzing in this chapter the Chrétien version of the tale as well as other Gwenhwyfar/Guinièvre abductions to develop some idea of what that precursor may have looked like. It will also allow us to learn which works have British elements that are independent of any now-extant earlier version. Knowing this information will not only help to cement the theory of a common source well before Chrétien, but it will also be useful in beginning to determine when that source may have first taken a recognizable form.

The first of the pre–Galfridic versions of the abduction is in the *Vita Gildae*. Here Melwas abducts the queen and takes her to the Isle of Glass, with Arthur pursuing him at the head of an army. Once there, Melwas seeks protection from the monastery. Gildas successfully mediates the situation, allowing Arthur to have his queen back and saving Melwas from certain death. In gratitude, Arthur donates land to the monastery.

The *Vita Gildae* is ascribed to Caradoc,[1] a monk of Llancarfan who was a professional hagiographer.[2] Caradoc wrote for Glastonbury, one of the best monasteries in medieval Europe at fabricating history and sanctity for themselves. In Britain, it was second only to Canterbury in terms of prestige. It was here where "Arthur" and his "wife" were discovered in the twelfth century, and where the Glastonbury-derived source for *Perlesvaus* claimed the Holy Grail was kept. At one point, Glastonbury claimed that she had been founded by Christ himself.[3]

4. Literary Tools for Supplementary Material

Caradoc's rendition is fraught with improbabilities, which makes it clear that his *vita* was adjusted to serve Glastonbury's purposes as well. Foremost, it places Gildas in Glastonbury, whereas the earlier, anonymous *Vita Gildae* does not. And there is no question it was pasted into the story as an afterthought; Caradoc's version includes no other reference to Gildas living in Glastonbury. It is clear he is only there to serve a purpose: Arthur's gratitude at recovering his wife. The act of giving territory to Glastonbury was written up as a contractual arrangement at the back of the *vita*, while the antiquity of the document gave it a sanctity beyond question. The reality is that Gildas could not possibly have been to Glastonbury; it was not an abbey until the eighth century.[4] However, the nature of *vita* writing, and the odd twists to be found in Caradoc and nowhere else, shows that the abduction story itself was in existence well before he wrote.[5]

There is a gleam of antiquity in the story, though. Caradoc's statement that Arthur searched for the queen about a year is most enlightening. The period of time seems unnecessarily long and does have similarities to Celtic motifs. The one-year hunt for the abductor has numerous parallels in Irish myth.[6] It is an obvious sign of some aspect of Celtic oral handling.

The inclusion of a king as rescuer is a common device in saints' lives and legends, so it should lead one to believe that there is a serious divergence from the continental versions here.[7] And yet most of the other aspects of the plot are similar to them. In the *Vitae Gildae* Gwenhwyfar is still the victim, there is a removal to an island, and the queen is eventually restored to Arthur. That it predates Chrétien makes it all the more valuable; it means the story was independent of his influence. That the story was written in Britain means that it was probably independent of all French tradition.

Of the three abductions that could be prior to Geoffrey, that from the *Life of Gildas* is by far the most complete. The other two, *Ymddiddan Gwenhwyfar ac Arthur* and *The Modena Archivolt*, share a common problem for this comparison: they portray only one scene.[8] However, they both contain material independent of Geoffrey and Chrétien and are therefore worthy of study.

The first of these, *Ymddiddan Gwenhwyfar ac Arthur*, is found in two versions. Both involve mainly a conversation between Gwenhwyfar and Cei, and would appear to belong to a scene before the defeat of Keu (Cei) in *La Charrette* where Meleagant (here Melwas) is attempting to take Guinièvre (Gwenhwyfar) and the queen is warning him that Keu is more than his match.

Both works have enough dialogic similarities to be considered two products of a common original. How far back the work should be placed is a different matter. The height and prowess accorded to Cei throughout the confrontation points much more toward a traditional Welsh origin than most of the romances.[9] The placement of Arthur in Dyfneint, or Devon, could also be from native tradition before Geoffrey. The prominence of Cei and the probable absence of Arthur make it clear the dialogue was not based on the Caradoc version.[10] However, this work has Glastonbury influence: the location of Melwas in the "Isle of Glass" can only have been due to the church's influence.[11] Still, aware of the probable motivations of the original author, one can make good use of both pieces.

The other pre–Galfridic abduction—found in the Archivolt relief of an Italian church—is more problematic in nature. It is a picture of one scene, and from it one may gather that a certain Caradoc has imprisoned Gwenhwyfar in a castle. Meanwhile Arthur, Cei, Gwalgavius, and Isdernus are attacking it from both sides. Unfortunately the only hints as to date can be gleaned from the armor etched on the figures and the spelling of their names. Such is not a strong foundation. Caradoc and Isdernus are nowhere else connected with the abduction, and Arthur is active only in the *Vitae Gildae*. This is a great number of unknowns, for which there is not enough information to hazard a guess.

Together, these three versions of the Guinièvre abduction demonstrate a consistent plot. In it the common story may be seen. The protagonist makes a challenge and wins the queen. He is allowed to take her to his region without further threat of violence. Arthur's men and possibly Arthur himself rescue her and return her to Arthur's hall. In this respect *Le Chevalier de la Charrette* is clearly a fourth variant of the abduction episode. It is quite apparent that the material in the four versions goes back to a common oral and/or literary source. This source was undoubtedly to be found in the British literature prior to 1130, when Caradoc of Llancarfan wrote.

However, there are more versions of the abduction of Guinièvre, and Geoffrey of Monmouth can be said to lead this second collection for two reasons. First, he wrote the first internationally read Arthurian history. Second, that "history" had a tremendous impact on Arthurian literature throughout the Middle Ages. Yet the abduction contained therein bears little resemblance to what the author has postulated above as a prototype, and the chapters pertaining to Modred have no basis in Welsh literature. The kidnapping of Guinièvre in this version actually contains a dearth of historical, motifal, or nomenclatural knowledge regarding Dark Age Britain.[12] And, nothing that is new here appears later on.

There is not much detail in Geoffrey's narrative. Instead of the casual story pace one generally finds in Welsh tales such as *Owain*,[13] the events seem hurried, as in French *Yvain*. In Geoffrey's account, Arthur rushes from France to combat the pretender to his throne and fights two battles in two days, the last ending in his death. There is no mention of protocol or the specific

4. Literary Tools for Supplementary Material 41

weapons of combat, methods of fighting, or rights of inheritance that would slow things down or indicate a time and place of origin for the narrative. Geoffrey simply generalizes and passes from one event to the next too quickly! The only real hint one is given that his continental campaigns and the quelling of Modred's rebellion are not simply the creation of Geoffrey's mind are in his descriptions of heroes' deaths.[14] However, the author would speculate that even this was more likely included out of the morbid curiosity of his readers than any source material he might have had.

Geoffrey of Monmouth probably knew of Guinièvre's abduction and decided for whatever reason to use it as a plot device to explain the end of the Arthurian realm. His tendency to displace and rearrange segments of British history even as he claimed to be representing it is well known. It has been well established that Geoffrey was writing to further his political career, and in fact he was promoted to bishop soon after *Historia Regum Britanniae*'s publication. Because of this, one will be on safer ground avoiding Geoffrey, and any version of Modred's abduction of Guinièvre.[15]

Chretien de Troyes' La Charrette (c. 1185)

Hugh de Moville's Text (c. 1194)

Ulrich von Zatzikhoven's Lanzelet (c. 1200)

The traditional development of *Lanzelet*, noting only its influence by Chrétien de Troyes, even as the author claimed the use of an independent source.

In sharp contrast, Ulrich von Zatzikhoven's *Lanzelet* is a document that offers a wealth of Celtic material.[16] This supports Zatzikhoven's statement that his source was a *Welsche* book[17] and contrasts to the general opinion that condemns him as a German redactor of Chrétien. In addition, something more is known of Ulrich von Zatzikhoven's source than Chrétien's. Its owner was Hughe de Morville who was brought to Germany in 1194 as a surety for the rest of King Richard's ransom.[18] Hughe was a man of Cumberland or southwestern Scotland.[19] If Ulrich von Zatzikhoven's book is to be thought of as a direct translation and interpretation of Chrétien, it was at no less than one remove from the French poet.

Any direct correlation to *La Charrette*, however, must be viewed with skepticism. Zatzikhoven makes fifty-three appeals to authority and without exception each is in a section with traditional material.[20] Often these invocations are in sections for which *Le Chevalier de la Charrette* offers no parallel. Further, in the *Lanzelet* redaction Keii helps in the rescue instead of being the cause of the abduction. Bademagus' counterpart, Malduz, guides the heroes to Guinièvre, as opposed to holding her captive for the abductor. These and Chrétiens other variations of strongly Celtic roots make it difficult to believe that *Lanzelet* was based in any significant way on Chrétien's poem.

Lanzelet also offers hints of the societal structure of the culture from which it originated. In one episode, Lanzelet kills a man and his niece inherits the lands. Lanzelet then "marries" her and superimposes his person onto the land. This arrangement would have been highly unusual to Ulrich von Zatzikhoven and all of Europe's medieval culture.[21] Succession by the eldest son, primogeniture, had been the rule for several centuries by 1200. Males and descendants of males ruled the land, with women taking control only when there were no male clan members. Ulrich von Zatzikhoven could not have understood that such an arrangement would not have been uncommon in post–Roman Britain. Instead, he has the lovesick girl give Lanzelet her property. Lanzelet collects three kingdoms by seducing two more women in this manner.[22] For Zatzikhoven, it was the only reasonable interpretation of the facts.

Lanzelet, one may conclude, seems to have too many Celtic peculiarities that do not come from *Vita Gildae* or Chrétien de Troyes to be considered to be derived solely from either source.[23] In fact, the often contradictory actions of the characters Keu/Keii and Bademagus/Malduz and the absence of the romantic element in the main plot of *Lanzelet* argue for a great deal of separation between the two. Further, *Lanzelet* reveals a large amount of preserved heroic-age details in this supposed romance. Therefore, the author shall rely on it for confirming British elements in *La Charrette*. In the words of Hendricus Spaarnay:

> Though it is true that Lanzelet possesses the virtue of courage, axiomatic in a medieval hero, and is capable of loyalty, sacrifice, and liberality, he takes life much as it comes. He has no conscience in love; religion is as foreign to him as it was presumably to the author of Morville's book. His biography is an Arthurian romance in its most elementary stage.[24]

Diu Crône was written in 1200 × 1250 by Heinrich von dem Türlin. Despite its relatively late date, this document, too, possesses a great deal of traditional material original to the Arthurian milieu. In it Keii (Cei) is shown the same respect accorded him in the early Welsh tales. He is the one who most greatly laments the supposed death of Gawein.[25] It is he who later leads Arthur's army to meet with Gawein "as was proper."[26] It must be admitted that Türlin indicates strong influence from Chrétien elsewhere, but he is quite certain of Keii's prominence in Arthur's court despite that influence.

4. Literary Tools for Supplementary Material 43

Although Keii might be unpleasant and quite mannerless, he still had not lost the pride of nobility. Indeed, he was so brave that he wouldn't avoid any monster: He dared fight it no matter how large it seemed to him and whatever his chances of success. You should also know that Arthur was zealous of virtue and in his faultless youth had chosen such attendants as were free of deceit. How could Keii have remained one of them for a short time if he had been as evil as many have said? The truth is that he liked to scoff and spare no one. That was his chief failing.[27]

In fact, ramblings such as this indicate the preservation of Cei's personality in the world of romance. Later stories make him the dupe to be beaten by each new entrant into the Arthurian court. In fact he would have been bested by new entrants; it would have been necessary to do so in order to be allowed into the Arthurian household. Cei was like Glewlwyd the gatekeeper. It was his duty to make sure none but those who were worthy ever made it into the king's hall, just as the gatekeepers of old had done. Traditionally, the testing involved scoffing a potential entrant until he was able to prove himself. To the eyes of a medieval man, however, such activities would simply have been seen as bad manners, so that the author has here attempted to resolve the conflict he perceives between Keii's personality and the culture around him.[28]

Diu Crône also has an interesting scene reminiscent of that in "Pa gur?," and one that is thoroughly Celtic. In the latter literary piece, a gatekeeper makes Arthur prove the worth of all of his comrades in order that they might gain entrance. *Diu Crône* likewise has a scene where Gawein proves his worth to a gatekeeper. Also noteworthy is the repeated use of decapitation,[29] and Gawein's promiscuity,[30] though as will be seen these details can be thought of as common Arthurian motifs by the mid-thirteenth century. As Dr. Spaarnay put it nearly five decades ago: "On the whole, one gets the impression that Heinrich created very little out of whole cloth, that much of his material came from lost sources, but that he made his own combinations and exercised considerable freedom in the invention of detail."[31] Those lost sources were probably British, though there is no way of knowing where Türlin is cutting and pasting and where he has invented. For that reason, he will only be used cautiously.

In about 1205 Hartmann von Aue wrote a German adaptation of Chrétien's *Yvain* for a German lord who was probably attempting to emulate the French courts.[32] His *Iwein* largely follows the storyline and specifics of Chrétien or alters them to what should have been the taste of a German court. However, he does with one stroke show an indication of an independent Celtic source. Gawein alone is mentioned as Guinièvre's liberator.[33] Admittedly this is fragile evidence, but the more complete details regarding the

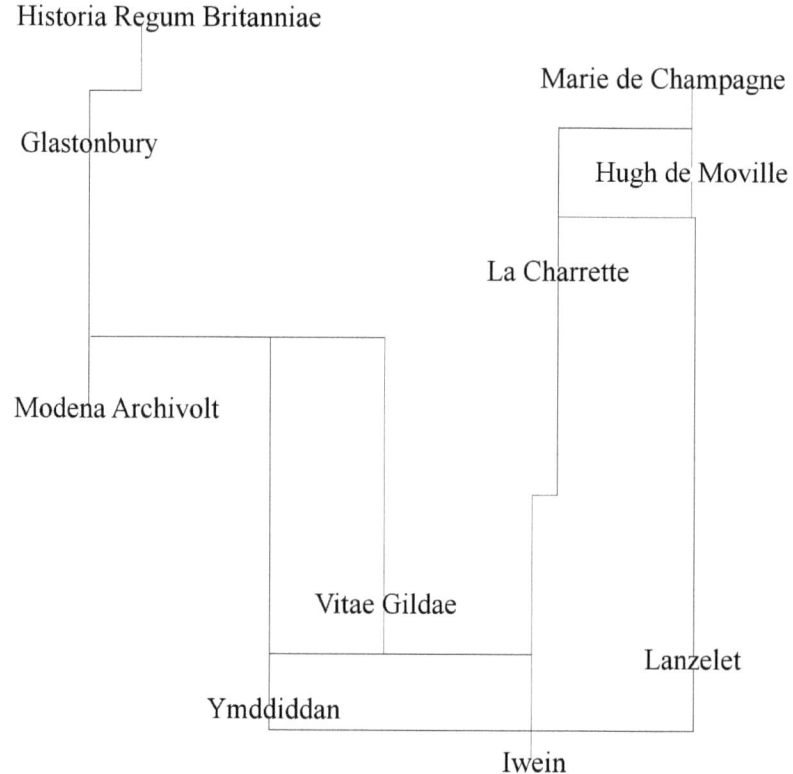

The traditional development of the common abduction story. There is clear indication of only two pieces of original work, that of Geoffrey of Monmouth and the work inspired by Marie de Champagne.

actual scene in which the queen is abducted lend themselves to the conclusion that von Aue had access to a version that was not influenced by Chrétien. Overall, however, the evidence is awkward at best, and this source will also be one to use sparingly.

From the above group of abduction versions that are known to have derived from at least one common source, four relatively safe assumptions may be made. First, the abductions of *Ymddiddan Gwenhwyfar ac Arthur*, *Vita Gildae*, *Modena Archivolt*, *Diu Crône*, and *Lanzelet* all contain many unique details of British provenance that are unknown in the previous extant manuscripts. This evidences at least partial independence from Chrétien and each other. Second, the consistency with which the independent elements of each version may be linked back to a much older British culture argues for a single common source.[34]

4. Literary Tools for Supplementary Material 45

Third, the diversity of detail in the abduction theme and the earliest dates for some of the abduction redactions are telling. They allow for the conjecture that the tradition of the abduction of Arthur's queen was an old one by 1100.[35] Finally, the consistency with which Gwenhwyfar/Guinièvre is made Arthur's queen implies that she was either a part of the oldest Arthurian tradition or that she had been attached to it before the development of the abduction theme. Again, this would have happened well before 1100. The date at which this prototype first emerged is an important one, and the question will be explored as fully as possible. In the next two chapters evidence will be brought forward to help prove it was in existence before 900. This evidence will be of an historical nature. It is hoped that the establishment of historical elements in the poem may reasonably allow one to chronologically link the abduction prototype to *Glas*. At the very least, doing so will increase the viability of seeing this literary tradition as possessing some qualities of historical value for a period well before the twelfth century.

5

Motifs and Details: Clues of Celtic Origins

Onomastic study has provided a useful tool in the search for Celtic origins in Chrétien; it has established a common tradition for the abduction legend. A survey of those elements in the other early abduction romances that possessed Celtic and probably non-motifal elements confirmed their independent use of *Glas*, the probably written British common source. Certain motifs and themes are also visible in the lines of Chrétien's verse. They are occasionally historical, but more often than not they reflect *Glas*' stay in an oral environment. To point these instances out, the author will survey both the Celtic motifs and themes in Chrétien's poem. This process should bring the reader to better understand the extent and nature of Chrétien's debt to the Britons. It is unfortunate that the study has never been done before.

The Arthurian hall, as Chrétien paints it, could very well have been ancient in Chrétien's day. The poet describes the structure in two passages — at the Cart Castle and the Castle of the Four Axemen. These are addressed one at a time.

The dining hall of the Cart Castle has three beds on which the two visitors, Gauvain and Lancelot, retire. The hostess also leaves for a room in another chamber to sleep. One can assume that the two guests are not being insulted as Gauvain is otherwise treated with the utmost courtesy. Why does the damsel make these warriors sleep in the dining hall and not a guest room? Certainly there were more rooms in the royal or noble castles of Chrétien's time that he should have mentioned.[1]

The other instance of a castle being described is the Castle of the Four Axemen, where a lady offers to shelter Lancelot in return for sexual favors. There Lancelot is again made to sleep in the hall of the castle.[2] What is more telling of the normalcy of this arrangement is Lancelot's surprise at not finding the woman waiting for him when he goes there to sleep.

A contemporary Norman castle would have had no need to regularly use the dining hall as a spare bedroom. These structures featured living quarters adjacent to the dining hall for exactly that purpose.[3] The dining hall Chrétien would have known was simply not designed to be a sleeping quarters for individuals of any respected station.[4] For the upper echelon of nobility to retire to the drafty dining room the servants slept in would have been considered both uncomfortable and degrading. The conveniences of private quarters were simply expected by visitors by that time. If one cannot state with impunity that the castles Chrétien describes are British and date to well before 1100, one may be secure in believing that they may have been.

It is a moot point that older castles of the lower nobility were in existence in the twelfth century. It is also known that many of them may have had dining halls that served the dual purpose of eating and sleeping, which is implied in the Arthurian poem. But again, the Arthurian world is a perfect one, without peasants or the inconveniences of lesser comforts. It should not be forgotten, too, that even royal halls of the Arthurian period had the dual use that Chrétien has depicted.

In *Beowulf*, the sleeping arrangement of the hero and his men is clearly described: the king moves to separate quarters while the guest and his retainers remain in the hall. This is more precisely articulated in *Hrolf Kraki's Saga*, where it is stated that the lord of the dwelling and his wife were to sleep in a separate chamber in the hall.[5] All other men, even such distinguished guests as Beowulf, then slept in the same room in which they had dined.[6]

Early Welsh tales rarely speak of the architectural arrangements of their royal dwellings. However, post–Roman archaeology in Britain supports the theory of dining/sleeping halls, though the agreement has been anything but uniform.[7] Beginning with Professor Alcock in Dinas Powys and Cadbury Castle, Somerset, many archaeologists have come to the conclusion that feasting halls were in existence and used to house warriors of lesser experience.[8] In Dr. Kenneth Dark's *Civitas to Kingdom*, the author reasons backwards in explaining why he believes they existed. English *stafell* (hall) may well derive from Latin *stabellum* (barn or aisled building). The difference in the archaeological record between these two is negligible, showing that the Germanic invaders likely used the same structures and employed an Anglicized version of its Roman name. They also seem to have used them for at least some of the same functions, such as feasting.[9] It seems only reasonable that the Britons, who had been much more thoroughly Romanized, would have made the same transition.

Dr. Laing has not only accepted the proposal but has produced an article, "Timber Halls: Some Problems," which surveys the various obstacles in detecting a hall on a site.[10] Though currently not accepted by all experts, the idea is accepted by most. The theory of halls is an established part of British studies in the post–Roman era. *La Charrette* contains them as well.

A second aspect of Chrétien's poem that is surprising is Lancelot's military behavior, in particular the way in which all his duels seem destined to end: decapitation. Lancelot beheads a man at the request of Jandrée just after crossing the stony passage. He does so again to Meleagant himself.[11]

The prescience that this is Celtic, even common in ancient and Medieval societies, is easy to verify.[12] Herodotus tells us that a Celtic warrior could not receive his share of the booty without a head.[13] Livy records that one general, Postumius, was taken to a temple by the Celtic tribe Boii where they decapitated him and made a gold-mounted cup of his skull.[14] In another instance, Livy writes that his countrymen had received no word of a particular battle until: "In conspectu fuere Gallorum equites, pectoribus equorum suspensa gestantes capita et lanceis infixa ovantesque oris sui carmine; ... some Gallic horsemen came in sight, with heads hanging at their horses' breasts or fixed on their lances, and singing their customary song of triumph."[15]

Irish myth contains the same theme of decapitation. All of Cú Chulainn's battles seem to end with a head dangling from its own hair. Such is the case with the warriors Nadcranntail, Loch, and many others.[16] Brân, two instances in *Peredur*,[17] and the elegy to Urien's head provides further evidence of the widespread phenomenon.[18] The Celts had a cultural fascination with the human head. It seems reasonable to believe that the head had some sort of mystical or religious meaning to the Celts even after Christianity.[19]

It may be argued, and with some cogency, that such things as decapitations were familiar to the twelfth-century mind and therefore that they are not uniquely Celtic. War has always brought out human's worst tendencies, and decapitation is a motif of both heroic-age societies and medieval Europe. On the other hand, neither the Greek nor German heroic ages have recorded such a fascination with that particular practice.[20] Achilles dragged Hector's entire body around Troy, and Sigurd's head becomes no man's trophy. It is very possible that this facet of the romances has purely Celtic origins

Another point that must be made concerns the sexual habits of Chrétien's heroes. Gauvain, Lancelot, and Perceval seem to be romantically entangled with many women, despite Andreas Capellanus' strict rules about loving only one woman at a time.

Interestingly, their exploits do not seem out of place when compared to the Celtic peoples' history, mythology, and laws. Herodotus was the first man to record their marital customs. Of the Massagetae he wrote that each man married a wife, but these wives were common to all.[21] Caesar was appalled at the promiscuity of the women, claiming that a female might share between ten and twelve men, mainly brothers, fathers, and sons.[22] Strabo went so far as to say the Celtic women were carnally active with their own sons and brothers, though he admits this is only hearsay.[23] Dio Cassius wrote that the Maeatae and Caledonians shared their women.[24]

These practices are similarly in Insular lore. In *Culhwch ac Olwen*, a woman is offered to the hero at the gate right after food, wine, and song.[25] There is a legend that Hercules was the progenitor of the Galatian family during one of his travels; he is said to have slept with the founding mothers of the various tribes. The compert stories illustrated in the births of Mongan, MacBeth, and SS. Kentigern, Ambrosius, and Dubricius all demonstrate the continuation of this practice among the British and Irish.[26] Several instances in *Tochmarc Emere* contain relevant examples in Irish myth as well; what we term promiscuity was a socially acceptable practice of the pre–Christian Celts. The law-texts only confirm what historians and myth imply. To quote Dr. Binchy: "The large numbers of sons begotten by kings indicate widespread polygyny among royalty."[27]

In Irish law, there was only one "form of matrimony that is fully legitimate and honorable," that of *cét muinteras*—a lifetime marriage with a woman who thereby acquired full status in her husband's family. There was, however, more than one legal form of marriage. In the laws of *Críth Gablach* one is told that *lanamnas* was a legal term for "neither permanent nor monogamous" marriage and a *dormuine* was a "temporary concubine." Binchy tells us this differentiation was common to most legal tracts, as was the concept of seven forms of marriage.[28] The temporary concubine was an established part of the Irish way of life. The coming of Patrick and Christianity obviously put pressure on the Irish customs. Because of these influences a series of modifications were made to marriage laws from the fifth century onward. However, the practice clearly persevered.

The Welsh laws also contain evidence that the taking of a wife could be both of a temporary or permanent nature:

> Whoever sleeps three nights with a woman from when the fire is covered until it is uncovered on the morrow, and from then on wants to leave her, let him pay her a steer worth twenty pence and another worth thirty pence and another worth forty pence. And if he takes her to house and home and she is with him seven years, he is bound to share with her from then on as with a wife with bestowers.[29]

Even when she was fully married as a *gwriag briod*, a woman might legally go outside the common bounds of monogamy.[30] One of the three cases in Welsh law in which a husband could not receive compensation for his wife was "if a man from afar from a strange country should fondle her before knowing the law of the country."[31]

All the evidence seems fairly straightforward when looked at as a whole and leads to a reasonably clear picture. The common man practiced a form of polygyny. More important, it was not at all uncommon for Celtic princes to arrive in foreign kingdoms and there beget offspring through limited and indiscriminate contacts with royals and any other women who might find them of interest. Considering the Celtic customs, perhaps we may also better understand what has happened in the poem being studied here, and increasingly in the tales that followed. A Celtic theme is being carefully hidden. Chrétien first leaves us a hint in *La Charrette*. In the moments when Lancelot watches Guinièvre and attempts to jump to her, the author makes a coy remark about Gauvain being occupied with the lady of the Cart Castle.

> A l'autre fenestre delez
> estoit la pucele venue, si l'i ot a consoil tenue
> mes sire Gauvains an requoi
> une piece, ne sai de quoi.[32]

The maiden had come to the next window, where my lord Gauvain had chatted with her for awhile in private, though I do not know what was said or the subject of their conversation.[33]

Lancelot is not totally free of this behavior, either.

> Il lore done, puis san va
> tant que de bas vespre trova
> une dameisele venant,
> molt tres bele et molt avenant,
> bien acesmee et bien vestue
> La dameisele le salue.
> Come sage et bien afeitiee
> et cil respont: Sainne et Heitiee,
> dameisele, vos face Dex."
> pios li dit: "sire, mes ostex
> vos est ci prés apareilliez
> se del prandre estes conseilliez;
> mes paritel herbergeroiz
> que avoec moi vos coucheroiz
> einsi le vos ofre et presant."
> Plusor sont quie de presant
> li randissent cinc cenz merciz,
> et il an fu trestoz nerciz
> et li a respondu totel:
> "Dameisele, de vostre ostel
> vos merci ge, si l'ai molthchier
> me soferroie je molt bien."

5. *Motifs and Details* 51

> "-Je n'an feroie autremant rien."
> fet la pucele, "par mes ialz."
> Et cil, des que il ne puet mialz,
> l'otroie li cuers le dialt
> quant itant seulement le blesce,
> molt avra couchier tristesce.[34]

Then he goes on his way until, late in the evening, he met a damsel coming his way who was exceedingly beautiful and attractive, elegantly dressed and adorned. This damsel greets him discretely and politely, and he replies: "May God keep you healthy and happy, young lady!" Then she said to him: "My home, sir, is all ready for your lodging, if you're prepared to accept it. But you'll be given hospitality on condition that you sleep with me: Those are the terms of my offer." Many people would have thanked her five hundred times for this favour; yet it leaves him quite miserable, and he gives her a very different reply: "I thank you, damsel, for your offer of hospitality and am most grateful for it. But, if you were agreeable, I could well do without the sleeping arrangement."—"By my eyes," says the maiden, "My offer depends on that!" then, as there is nothing else for it, he agrees to her condition.[35]

Can one believe that the territory Lancelot is passing through demands he stay in the Castle of Four Axemen? It is not practical; he is in friendly territory and will be for several more days. Besides, a medieval knight, especially the model for knights, should not have needed a comfortable bed every evening. It was not a necessity in Chrétien's romances, either. Later Arthurian knights often slept in forests. Perceval would do so in *Le Conte du Graal* and Gawen in *Syre Gawen and the Grene Knight*. Yet this is the sole reason Chrétien gives us for Lancelot consenting to the lady's conditions.[36]

Later in the poem, one finds the wife of Meleagant's seneschal making a bargain for sexual privileges with Lancelot[37] and then quietly accepting that she will never get her end of the deal. Why? Even Jandrée, who saves Lancelot from the tower where Meleagant imprisons him, gives us little doubt that she would consent to more intimate relations as well. Her attraction is useless, however, to both her and the plot of the story. Jandrée is described as repulsive, so that it does not raise Lancelot's stature when she finds him desirable.

All the above examples point in one direction, toward a different view on male sexuality than the one Marie wished to develop. Chrétien undoubtedly shows the reader a theme of Lancelot's devotion to Guinièvre. However, it is also clear he was dealing with a tradition that ran counter to that theme. If it was a Celtic tale (as seems most likely), then the hero was probably carnally active throughout. For Chrétien, these activities were not acceptable to his own moral conscience or to Marie's views on love and sexuality. To rectify the situation, he turned sexual adventures into opportunities to show the reader the hero's attractive physical qualities and ability to keep one love. However, the stitches in the patchwork remain in Chrétien. And, in the independent and more British *Lanzelet*, the hero is unrestrained by Marie's fetters and finds a great many lovers. Most likely this is much closer to the original hero's activities than Chrétien's hero.

Another action of Chrétien's characters is helpful in understanding his material; the phenomenon of the taunting knight who provokes a fight with the protagonist. This might well have its precursor in heroic tales as well.[38] In the prelude to a near-confrontation between Lancelot and a king's son in which the lady of the Castle of Four Axemen is present, the monologue of the overconfident prince is as follows:

> qu' adés vos en maing gié
> Un mui de sel avroit maingié
> cist chevaliers, si con je croi,
> einçois qu'il vos desraist vers moi.
> Ne cuit c'onques home veïsse
> vers cui je ne vos conqueïsse
> Et quant je vos truis ci an eise,
> mesque bien li poist et despleise,
> vos an manrai veant ses ialz,
> et s'an face trestot son mialz.[39]

And a poor escort indeed it is, for I'm about to take you off! I fancy this knight would have eaten a bushel of salt before he could protect you from me: I don't believe I've ever seen one from whom I couldn't win you. And since I conveniently find you here, though it may very well vex and displease him, I'll take you away under his very nose, despite all his efforts.[40]

One is a bit mystified when one finds the same man later admitting he was fortunate to have been saved from fighting such a knight as Lancelot. Such modesty is hardly a stock quality of the rash challenger motif prevalent in medieval tales. Yet it is something any true warrior might say. In addition, it is also a heroic-age quality.

Honor and respect toward one's adversaries was a cultivated aspect of the ideal warrior's personality in heroic-age culture. In *Taín Bó Cuailgne*, while Cú Chulainn is holding off Queen Medb's army with duels,[41] every warrior who is asked to fight him freely admits Cú Chulainn is more skilled.[42] Such modesty of speech can also be seen to some degree in *Mahabharata*[43] and the *Iliad*.[44] The heroic ages of the Norse, Japanese, Greeks, and other similar cultures demonstrate a like attitude. It is most definitely a heroic-age, and in this case probably Celtic, notion. In all the above cultures it cannot be mistaken for cowardice, though. Without exception, the warriors accept and even embrace death when it comes.

5. Motifs and Details

In conjunction with honor and respect, gentility was a praised feature in Chrétien's time. Chaucer's description of his knight being "meek as a maid" is as unforgettable as it is ironic. How odd it is that a man who had fought in so many campaigns and lived in the brutal climate of professional killers throughout his career should be described as "meek as a maid." The picture, however, is a part of a long literary tradition in twelfth-century Europe. The knight of great prowess who is cowed by the woman he admires is a common theme with Chrétien as well — in the personalities of Yvain, Alexander, Cligès, and Perceval. Marie must have rejoiced at the idea of having a great warrior be totally obedient to the woman he loved.

The British Heroic Age also contains a parallel in the contemporary evidence of *Y Gododdin*. In it the warrior Ywain mab Marro is praised as "Diffun ymlaen bun, medd a dalai; Breathless in the presence of a girl."[45] Later in the same stanza: "Rhag pebyll Madog pan atgoriai, Namyn un gûr o gant ni ddelai; when he used to come back to Madog's tent there used not to return but one in a hundred."[46] In a praise of Ceredig it is said: "cyn dyfod ei ddidd, gowychydd ei wybod; his refined manners were perfection."[47] The januslike qualities of the perfect warrior are expressed in praise of the northern hero Urien of Rheged as well:

Gnawt gweled ymdanaw   am teyrn gocnaw
Amdanaw gwyled   a lliaws maranhed
eurteyrn gogled   ar benhic
teyrnwd[48]

    Courtesy is usual around him,
    around the provocative chief.
    Courtesy surrounds him
    and plentiful wealth,
    golden chieftain of *the North*,
    foremost of kings.[49]

The two distinct qualities of ferocity in battle and timidity in the presence of a lady are treated as equal in importance. Further examples of the phenomenon are apparent in Irish legend. The *Taín Bó Cuailgne* portrays Cú Chulainn as the unquestioned champion of Ulster, but he is clearly not of the romantic mold. He sleeps with Aífe after making an oath with his bride-to-be Emer to remain faithful. Still, he shows a clear bashfulness around women of his native court. Conchobar's only solution to Cú Chulainn's battle-fury is to send naked women out to greet him.[50] He is also slowed in his approach to the Munstermen by the satirist Riches, who strips in front of him.[51]

Such a dual personality of terror in battle and courtesy in noble company is not characteristic of the typical Germanic hero of saga. It is not common in any other cultures to the author's knowledge — except in the Celtic literature and the literature of continental Europe, which had been influenced by the Celtic bards.[52]

The British hero was supposed to have a mildly "schizophrenic" nature. He was not to be a drunken oaf whose sole benefit to the king was his ability to go berserk against the enemy, as Adhil's warriors do in *Hrolf Kraki's Saga*. He was to be equally adjusted to the king's court and the terrors of the battlefield.

Another commonplace in Chrétien's poetry is that a knight is given free lodging wherever he may find a house. Erec, Cligès, Yvain, Gauvain, and later Perceval are all beneficiaries of this custom. Lancelot also enjoys this privilege; there is no mention of any payment for his stay at the Cart Castle or when he stays with Bademagus. For one intent on writing a fairy tale, these things only add to the dreamy background that makes the Arthurian world so memorable. The mere inclusion of money would bring the reader back to the world from which she is trying to escape. For the more historically oriented, it seems reasonable that a stranger knight might be offered hospitality by a regional ruler. However, Gauvain is posing as a merchant when he is offered a room in *Le Conte*. That does not figure into a perfect world and actually borders on favoring commoners. Literary experts would probably say that the intention of such a scene was to further the plot. While this might be true, the cultural repercussions that particular detail has on Marie's perfect world are immense and threaten to tear down the very world Chrétien was tasked with erecting.

There is, on the other hand, a connection to Celtic law and custom here. Most freemen had a contractual responsibility known as *biathad* in Ireland — "the general obligation of supplying hospitality to all persons, together with their appropriate company."[53] Further on in the same entry Binchy informs the reader that refusal to do so by anyone above the rank of minor householder or *ócaire* was punishable. The fine was the honor-price of the person refused.[54] Hospitality was considered an integral part of society. There was even a specially defined class of hospitallers, who were expected to situate themselves for common access and give food and shelter to anyone who asked. These were known as *briugu* and were defined as being "a rich landowner whose property is reckoned in the hundreds."[55] In return, such men were given the honor-price of a *Rí Tuaithe*, or king of a country.

The cultural tradition was an ancient one. It appears throughout Irish myth and legend, most conspicuously in *Togaíl Bruidne Dá Derga*. It was also extremely useful for several levels of society. Traveling bards and merchants made use of them, as did a king on his annual royal circuit. Local *briugu* would have made the movement of troops a convenient matter as well, reducing the need for supply lines in warfare. The reputation of the king who supplied his hospitallers should not be overlooked, either. It could only have added to a man's reputation for generosity.

The Irish were insistent that a stranger should not be left hungry or wet if he had no wish to be. One cannot doubt that those areas of Britain with little Roman intervention would have retained the same Celtic custom; Welsh law evidences its retention in Wales during the later Middle Ages. It may be that this Arthurian theme is due to influence from France or another continental culture. However, it is equally possible that its inclusion in the Arthurian romances is a direct response to native British influences. Closely related to this custom was the practice of putting a foreigner under a king's protection. Bademagus' speech to his son when he nears Lancelot after the Sword Bridge episode demonstrates this cultural aspect best of all.[56]

> Et si vos praing, cui qu'il enuit,
> Vers trestoz homes an conduit,
> Ja mar doteroiz de nelui
> Fors que seulement de celui
> Qui la reïne amena ça
> Onques hom si ne menaca
> Autre con ge l'ai menacié
> Et par po je ne l'ai chacié
> De ma terre par mautalant
> Por ce que il ne la vos rant
> s'est il mes filz, mes ne vos chaille
> Se il ne vos vaint an bataille
> Se il ne vos porra sor mon pois
> D'enui faire vaillant un pois.[57]

However indignant anyone may be, I place you under my safekeeping against all men. You need fear no man except the one who brought the queen here. No man ever threatened another as I threatened him. Because he did not hand her over to you, my fury almost caused me to drive him from my land. Yes, he is my son. But do not worry. Unless he defeats you in combat, he can never, against my will, cause you the least harm.[58]

Why does Bademagus show Lancelot such generosity? Is this a mere politeness? Is Chrétien just using Bademagus' words as a contrast to his headstrong son Meleagant, and as a balance against the highly emotional Lancelot? It is very possible; contrasts are an excellent tool in all forms of literature. On the other hand, why should Chrétien allow Bademagus, father of the enemy, to be looked on kindly? Why make the father support the man who has come to kill his son? Again, heroic-age ideals and Welsh and Irish laws give another possibility.

Whatever the Sword Bridge incident was[59] the successful conquest of the bridge challenge it obviously drew the attention and admiration of the spectators by its audacity, sheer bravery, and/or physical difficulty. The man who accomplished the feat commanded some measure of respect and delicacy. It would not be to Bademagus' glory to overwhelm Lancelot with men once he had made the crossing, as no bard would praise any but Lancelot and his courage against certain death. So Bademagus safeguarded himself from reproach by formally putting Lancelot under his protection. This reading fits the facts well. When it is heard in Bademagus' presence that Lancelot has died retrieving Gauvain, he promises death by hanging, burning, or drowning to the perpetrators of the crime. Curiously, when Lancelot is later found to be a prisoner off of the island and Meleagant the probable cause, Bademagus makes no such threats. There is no way of knowing if the hero is injured or not. Chrétien only tells us that Bademagus will hand over Lancelot if he finds him. Because Lancelot is no longer under his cloak of protection, Bademagus' honor is not at stake in seeing that he is taken from harm.

Heroic culture also helps to explain why Meleagant did not attempt to have his adversary killed or maimed while he was keeping him in a prison within the borders of his father's kingdom. Meleagant wanted to win Guinièvre, but to injure Lancelot physically while he was formally under Bademagus' protection would have meant dishonoring his father.[60] By merely imprisoning him, he hoped to win Guinièvre and avoid any unnecessary complications.

One other repeating element of the poem bears a strong Celtic influence: the cloak. It is an item of clothing with a long-standing use among the Celtic peoples. Diodorus Siculus noted that the Celts wore striped cloaks with a checkered pattern, which they fastened using a clasp.[61] The writers of *Culhwch ac Olwen*, the *Taín Bó Cuailgne*, and other surviving Celtic tales monotonously include it as well. It plays a key role in *The Boyhood Deeds of Finn*, where the hero grabs the brooch of a girl. Her cloak falls off and she is forced to return to Fionn, presumably to grant him a wish of some sort.[62] Dá Derga's men are described as each wearing "a short cloak to their buttock."[63]

The Law of Hywel Dda confirms that the cloak of the Celts survived after the Romans had departed. The statutes are clear that both parties in a divorce retain their cloaks, though all else is to be divided equally.[64] The damp nature of the regions that they inhabited called for its regular employment. The practice of wearing a cloak continues to this day.

It must be admitted that any coastal region, such as France, could be expected to have some similar form of protection against regular but limited precipitation. However, such clothing is rarely if ever mentioned in the Germanic tales, and it is entirely absent from the Roland romances, except as ceremonial clothing. The cloak's presence is of Celtic origin. It is also prominent in the Arthurian romances throughout Europe. Lancelot is more than once given a cloak by a woman,[65] as is Perceval.[66]

Of the remaining scenes and passages in *Le Chevalier de la Charrette*, two strike the author as particularly romantic and synthetic in comparison to the rest of the narrative. These are the bridges that lead into Gorre and the bed scene between Lancelot and Guinièvre. As has been seen in the previous pages, neither Chrétien, the *latimari*, the *trouvères*, nor the *troubadours* invented any particular detail or episode in the romances unless it made the action of the scene more contemporary. Neither the bridges nor the bed scene perform this function.[67] It seems most likely, then, that they are both the result of Chrétien's compromise between the sens of Marie and the original British tale.

What is to be made of the plot devices, the *pont espée* and the *pont evage*? Truthfully, they are too much the expression of romance to be seen easily as part of any pre-ninth-century historical or literary source. On the other hand, the two bridges do not have any known literary predecessors on the continent. They are too original to be a product of a romance movement that is based on the Celtic myths and legends. On closer inspection, however, several details argue for a Celtic and heroic origin.

The reader is told that Gorre is the land of no return and it is clearly difficult for a mortal to cross into it.[68] These two facts have led a number of scholars to believe the Sword Bridge is a passage to the land of the dead. In this respect, the crossing would be similar to the Orpheus or Heracles' journeys into Hades. Others have suggested it is the Celtic equivalent of the Bridge of Souls as outlined by Gregory the Great and Gregory of Tours in the sixth century. However, there are some problems with both these hypotheses.[69]

First, there is no earlier version of a Celtic warrior going to the Underworld. Cú Chulainn's trip to Alba has been called so, but it has few similarities to other Indo-European underworlds. He fights to get in or to leave; he only proves his worthiness as a student to Scáthach by crossing the Bridge of Leaps. He is allowed to depart when and as he wishes, and in fact the Albans seem pleased to be rid of him. Heracles and Orpheus can only enter by defeating Cerberus, and only by getting Hades' permission are they able to depart. The very location of Alba is too well defined to be magical. Alba is northern Britain, a nearby place to the Irish and one well known to the Irish traders throughout prehistory.

As a Celtic equivalent to a Christian Bridge of Souls, the pont éspée has little more substance. The first instance of a Christian otherworld bridge in the British Isles is found in *Fís Adamnan*.[70] This work dates to the eleventh century, making it chronologically anterior to *La Charrette*. The *pont éspée* is hardly a Christian adaptation. To cross a Bridge of Souls, one needs moral strength and virtue. Chrétien's hero has neither; he has instead the Celtic qualities of honor and courage. If Chrétien found a wonderful bridge in his source, it was not a Christian soul bridge. Lancelot's unchristian attitudes would have made it impossible for our ethical poet to allow him passage.

This *pont éspée*, then, is not some Bridge of Souls or the passage to the Celtic underworld. There are other possibilities, but they cannot be found in the work of previous scholars on the matter. Their conclusions may best be summed up by Dr. Laura Loomis: "As a Perilous Passage, the sword bridge, however amazingly elongated and strangely used, has little real analogy with the more incredible marvels of Celtic story. Moreover the form, the realistic quality of an actual sword used as a bridge, and its connection with the romantic episode of Guinièvre's rescue, remain unexplained."[71]

To begin, then, the Sword Bridge of *La Charrette* is two lance-lengths. Chrétien is telling his readers that Lancelot crawled over a sword bridge of sixteen to twenty feet. This detail seems suspect; jumping the distance of twenty feet would not be an outrageous feat and therefore one might expect the hero to forgo crawling when a display of athleticism would work just as well. Such a *faux pax* implies that Chrétien has modified part of this episode for his own purposes, which in turn argues that his original source for the material was Celtic. In this, there are two possibilities.

Cú Chulainn defeats Curoi in *Bricriu's Feast* by hovering around him in a swooping feat.[72] It is possible that the hero was said to have performed a similar feat. Alternatively, Lancelot's crossing could have been the sword feat. The heroes who did this marvel walked across the blade and were famed because they were so light of foot they did not cut themselves in the process. Both would have impressed an audience, and a British Guinièvre, far more than crawling.

Gauvain's bridge, the pont evage, is even more intriguing. Here the pride of *Erec et Enide* and *Yvain* is made a blundering failure as he nearly drowns crossing the water bridge. This is very different from the picture given of him in *Culhwch ac Olwen* as a man who never came home without accomplishing his quest.[73] But perhaps, as has been seen above, he was the original hero of the tale and Chrétien was asked to replace him with Lancelot.[74] Weston pointed out that Gauvain is a key figure in every Guinièvre rescue, while Lancelot is not.[75] That, and Hartmann von Aue's peculiar modification of Chrétien's *Yvain*, is an indicator that one is on solid ground with this possibility.[76] With this in mind, a closer look at the water bridge should reveal a great deal about the original version of the story.

Chrétien uses the term *pont evage* (water bridge) to describe Gauvain's

5. Motifs and Details

means of landing in Gorre. This difficult phrase is never further described by Chrétien, so one can make only a perilous guess as to its nature. However, Chrétien's evasive attitude toward the word leaves two options. Either there is here a textual problem with the word or he has again modified something that he did not understand or did not care to understand.[77] Invention seems more likely here. A textual problem has probably not occurred for reasons of consistency among the extant manuscripts; these all give the same term.

The episode — Gauvain's embarrassing situation, the ease with which Lancelot aids him, and Chrétien's mysterious reluctance to explain Gauvain's pont evage — is all inexplicable if one takes the phrase at face value. It is a bridge over water or one of water. However, if Gauvain's original position has been usurped by Lancelot, Gauvain would inevitably have become the foil of Lancelot, and Gauvain's bridge the invention of Chrétien or whomever took Gauvain from his position as the hero. The term "water bridge" would then be an irony and would simply mean that the "bridge" Gauvain took was through water, whether the sea or a lake. In other words, he either tried to take a boat (which must have capsized) or swam. Chrétien has not explained the bridge further because the joke is clear enough; Gauvain fails to cross it. Thematically speaking, getting all wet is his moral punishment for refusing to jump into the cart with Lancelot earlier.

To Chrétien and his twelfth-century French audience, a fabulous entrance was needed to justify Lancelot's instant respect in Gorre, so Chrétien made one. He could not have known getting past the *porthawr*, the gatekeeper he meets at the stony passage, would have been just as impressive to a British audience; he had no understanding of Celtic culture from which to draw such a conclusion. Chrétien then put the usurped hero in a similar position and allowed him to fail in order to highlight Lancelot's success. This counterpoint was done to perfection.

In this light Cei's personality and later role in Arthurian literature might be discussed. From Chrétien on, his role is well defined. Eschenbach put it best:

> Iche gihe von im der mæer,
> er was ein merkære.
> er tet vil rûhes willen schîn
> ze scherme dem hêrren sîn:
> partierre und valsche diet,
> von den werden er die schiet:
> er was ir fuore ein strenger hagel,
> noch scherpfer dan der bîn ir zagel.

I own that Keie was a critical observer. In order to protect his lord he displayed much asperity, sorting out impostors and dishonest folk from the honest — he came down on their behavior like a hailstorm, with a sting sharper than a bee's.[78]

If one may for the moment forget Keu's constant verbal attacks, one might see an alternative primary role for him. This other quality would align better with his character in "Pa Gur," *Culhwch ac Olwen*, and *Ymddiddan Gwenhwyfar ac Arthur*. He was Arthur's porter, the man at the gate whose duty it was to screen unworthies from the king's presence. This obligation often included being critical of newcomer warriors and forcing them to prove themselves mentally or through their physical prowess before they were allowed into Arthur's hall. Such is the situation Arthur finds himself in with the porter Glewlwyd in "Pa Gur?" and as Melwas finds himself with Cei in *Ymddiddan*.

To the uninitiated, the relevant passages in these works seem uncouth in the extreme, but the participants, indeed the original audiences, would have perceived Cei's words and actions as no more than fulfilled duties. Dr. Gowans has noted two of Cei's qualities and two verbal exchanges where this misinterpretation may have proved disastrous for Cei as a literary character. These are his boastful nature, his magical qualities, how he deals with a new unknown in the king's hall, and his offense at the englyn Arthur gives him upon delivering Dillus' beard in *Culhwch ac Olwen*. A brief summary of each will help to show the mental and cultural disposition behind them, and their incompatibility with the twelfth century.

Cei's brazen character in "Pa Gur?" is strictly heroic age in nature. Arthur boasts that Cei entreated his enemies as he killed them.[79] As demonstrated previously, boasting and pridefulness were necessary ingredients in the disposition of the heroic-age warrior.

Cei's magical qualities also link him to heroic-age society. In *Culhwch ac Olwen* the reader learns that Cei's father gave him the peculiarities of always having cold hands, of bearing fire and water better than anyone, of being peerless as a servant and an officer, and of being able to hide any burden that he happened to be carrying. Later on, the reader is introduced to more abilities: to be nine days and nights without water, to be of great height when he chose, to kill an opponent with every landed blow, and to use his hands as a source of great heat when needed. "Pa Gur?" adds that he can drink enough from a buffalo horn for four men.[80]

Most of the above attributes have clear analogues in the Celtic spectrum of literature. The cold hands demonstrate a nervelessness that is integral to any hero's repertoire. Many Irish heroes are said have heated hands.[81] Cei's ability to withstand cold and heat is one he shares with Cormac. His greatness as a servant and officer is something that bears a clear similarity to any of the great Celtic heroes. The statement that no man who takes a blow from him will live resembles similar statements made of Fionn, Cú Chulainn, and even Arthur.

An instance where Cei's actions would be readily misinterpreted is found in *Culhwch ac Olwen*. Culhwch approaches the gate of Arthur's hall and is advised the evening meal has begun. He is also told that the law of the court states no one but prince or craftsman may enter the hall after the meal is in progress. Culhwch does not say he is either, but insists on his entrance nevertheless. The gatekeeper approaches Arthur to tell him of the stranger at the entrance and asks him what to do. Cei reminds his lord of the hall's custom and with it the need to keep one's honor. Arthur, however, overrides him. He decides that the renown of being generous is the greater principle to keep. In this instance Cei is not being rude; he is instead protecting his king's honor. He continues in character; when Culhwch's identity is known and Arthur announces a quest, Cei is the first to volunteer.[82]

The second scene where Cei's behavior seems antisocial takes place following the episode where Cei has tricked the giant Dillus, shaved his beard, and killed him. Arthur greets him with verse: "Kynllyuan a oruc Kei, O uaryf Dillus uab Eurei, Pei iach dy angheu uydei; Cei made a leash from Dillus' beard, son of Eurei. Were he alive, thy death he'd be."[83] Cei leaves the hall immediately thereafter, and is not heard from again in the story. In today's society, Arthur's welcome would be accepted as a joke and probably returned with a smile or a retort of some sort. One wonders why Cei is so upset. But what Arthur has said is satire. To quote Gowans:

> Something which is conveyed very strongly in the stories of the Irish heroes is a horror of being satirised. Cú Chulainn is prepared to expend the last of his weapons to prevent it, and the power of the spoken word to cause more than mental harm is strongly attested in Medieval Wales, as well as an influential in the beliefs and folklore of cultures far beyond Celtic lands. The suggestion that Cei might have met his match would alone cause great offence, but in addition, the border between satire and what would now be seen as prophecy or curse is an indistinct one. In any society such a casual and flippant reference to the possibility of a leading warrior's death (especially a reference in verse) would be very foolish, and put Cei to shame in a far more subtle and dangerous way than the mid-river transformation of a herd of cattle.[84]

Cei was not a feeble wit to the Welsh. He was instead a character whose personality has been misunderstood over the centuries because he responds to situations in a manner consistent with the world he came from, but in ways that were awkward and undesirable in the world where Arthuriana reemerged during the twelfth century. The portrayal of Cei suffered accordingly with Chrétien and those who followed him. As a result, the great champion was made a foil to Chrétien's heroes and a parody of his Celtic self.

The most prominent theme of all, more basic to the plot than any one episode, even the Sword Bridge, is the theft of the queen. Is the kidnapping of Guinièvre a myth, motif, or historical possibility? A mythological source must be entertained, if only because of the preponderance of similar tales in Celtic lore.[85] However, Celtic myth has relatively few rescues by a lover; they are usually by the husband.[86] The exceptions to this rule all have unusual circumstances attached to them, which is why Dr. Cross felt comfortable in claiming there was no rescue by a lover in the original tales.[87] If one is to say it is based on myth, one must first deduce a reason why the role of the hero was early on taken from Arthur. Then, one must prove the abduction did not historically happen. This the present author would see as a formidable task.[88]

The possibility that Guinièvre has been imposed on an established theme is also reasonable. Any recurrent mythic element may find its way into a bard's repertoire, and then any group of characters might be inserted into the key roles. However, problems abound with this proposal. Chief among them is the inconsistency of the motif in the redactions. Certainly Meleagant could be Valerin, but the nature of both characters does not fit the motifal pattern. The abductor in the archetypal kidnapping is always a benevolent wizard or god,[89] and Melwas in the most ancient versions—*Vitae Gildae* and *Ymddiddan Gwenhwyfar ac Arthur*—is certainly not.[90] Further, the combination of Guinièvre and the abduction is one of the few instances where a character and a basic motif were passed to the continent in tandem.[91] It is the rare case where the main elements remained intact, implying that Guinièvre was always connected with the abduction, and thus that it was not a theme.

Finally, the option of history must be attended to. The only reason for the inclusion of this contingency is that the first two possibilities are tenuous, and the abductions of queens were common and an accepted part of Celtic society. This may be demonstrated in the myths and legends of Britain and Ireland. It is conceivable that a historic king of the fifth or sixth century could have had his wife abducted, though it is in no way probable or provable that this is the case here.

There is, then, more that could be Celtic in Chrétien's narrative than the names. The previous list, one of motifs and themes that fit equally (often better) in the context of heroic-age Britain and twelfth-century France, is unexpectedly large. Without all the above Celtic-derived material and any of the continental resources named in Chapter 2, Chrétien's poem is very much reduced.

While the idea is very possible that Chrétien could have either invented many of the motifal Celtic elements based on his own culture and the bards, *troubadours*, or *trouvères*, or accidentally created many aspects of sub–Roman British life, it only seems possible at first glance. If Chrétien took his information from the previously mentioned limited sources, or even if he were able to make lucky guesses, why are there so many distinctive characteristics of the British sub–Roman culture? How has he created an entire world that looks similar to post–Roman Britain as seen through the eyes of a twelfth-century poet? Considering the heavy influences of both classical and contemporary writers, should it be granted that he had the ability to create such a complete world along with his other literary abilities? Should one not assume he did the same thing with the Celtic sources he had access to as with his continental influences? Is it not likely that he followed them closely and reinterpreted only when he needed to deepen the emotional content of the passage or please his feminist patron? Is it not also likely that the lesser artists who preceded him made even less of an impact on the story?

One should not be alarmed at the proposal that the greatest French poet of the Middle Ages was heavily dependent on previous literature. It is well known that medieval writers thought of themselves as merely presenting older data for the better understanding of their audience. In this sense, Chrétien was no different from any other medieval artist. If a story had been original, the poet would have been forced to invent a source. To quote Geoffrey of Vinsauf: "And in the degree that it is more difficult so also it is more praiseworthy to treat such material well, namely, common and familiar material, than to treat other material, namely, new and unusual."[92]

This chapter has demonstrated that the Celtic influences on Chrétien were much greater than has hitherto been acknowledged.[93] Beyond the names and a basic plot, several episodes have elements that are very possibly Celtic and seem logical in an historical context. This finding suggests at least one source for the poem that was, in turn, historical or pseudohistorical in nature, *Glas*. To date, *Glas* has only been chronologically placed well before 1100, but the terminus may be placed much earlier. A study of the historical elements of the poem will reveal that date. It will also demonstrate the British point of origin for this tale and its oldest characters. In conjunction, these two proofs will allow for the possibility that the source of *Le Chevalier de la Charrette* and the other abduction tales could originally have been a part of the *Northern Memorandum* or a related text. In other words, it will give evidence that the abduction story is derived from a literary source that dates back to 900, and possibly much earlier.

6

The Sixth Century in Chrétien

Up to this point in the study, the author has discussed the influence of continental writers on Chrétien and the significance of the names and some motifs that Chrétien integrates into his work. This discussion has helped explain the origins and nuances of much of the romance, but many aspects remain that have been untouched by Celtic and French scholars alike. To resolve this dilemma the author will now inspect the poem by utilizing the knowledge derived from archaeological finds, law tracts, and historical documents as well as legends and the *vitae* of the Irish and Welsh saints. These resources will uncover the most important historical elements in Chrétien and will aid in the formulation of a more precise date for *Glas*.

The most likely places to look for historical materials are in scenes that betray Ovid and Andreas Capellanus' unmistakable influence. It has been shown that these two influences were inserted into the story by Chrétien in order to displace original matter that the sophisticates of Marie's court would have found displeasing. As a recent scholar has noted, Chrétien takes the supernatural and fits them into something recognizable and acceptable for his audience. In the case of *La Charrette*, scenes that were originally Celtic were replaced in favor of details that better suited Marie de Champagne's "romantic" designs.[1]

The first and perhaps the most blatant example of this is the cart episode. It seems particularly Ovidian, and most out of place in a hero tale. In it Lancelot, as a slave to the Roman poet's views on love, steps into a cart and knowingly degrades himself so that he might hear some news about Guinièvre.

As far back as Sir John Rhys' contributions, scholars have taken a skeptical view of the charrette scene. "How far the cart incident is to be regarded as the poet's invention, it is difficult to say."[2] It is too much a fairy tale for many, while others have pointed out the absence of mythic and romantic precursors for the act. It is, put simply, a motif that comes from nowhere. However, Chrétien gives the reader two vague hints of something more tangible and more useful to the current study when he writes that his cart was a *pilori* (pillory)[3] and that "en oren a plus de trois mile, n'ennavoit a cel tans que une; On every fair-sized town where now one finds over three thousand of them, there was at that time only one."[4]

Chrétien continues that this unusual cart making its way slowly into town was a vehicle of dishonor, the transport of the condemned. However, though Lancelot is in it he is not killed, neither is he put in prison. In fact, he continues to have the same accommodation as his companion Gauvain even after riding in it; clearly no shame fell upon him as far as his hostess was concerned, nor does Gauvain suggest to the reader that his companion has somehow been lowered by riding in it.

In fact, quite the opposite seems to be true; Lancelot is undoubtedly a man of some importance in the territories through which he passes, and the cart seems to have no impact on how he is treated. As was seen in the last chapter, he commands great respect at the Castle of Four Axemen and on Gorre itself, both events occur after the cart. What would make more sense would be if his transportation somehow reflected his high status. The cart as described by Chrétien does not. As there seems to be no literary precursor to Chrétien's scene, perhaps one of two historical prototypes can help explain the cryptic cart; it could be a war chariot or a high-status vehicle.

Le Chevalier de la Charrette uses the word *la charrette* to describe the vehicle, while *The Vulgate Version of the Arthurian Romances* uses *la carete*.[5] *La carete* and Chrétien's *la charrette* are identical words meaning "a four-wheeled vehicle."[6] The only four-wheeled vehicle known to Britain during the Celtic and Roman periods was the chariot, like those described in the tales about Cú Chulainn and his comrades.[7]

The four-wheeled chariot was an established part of the military of the pre–Roman Britons and Picts. Julius Caesar seems to have had trouble with them.[8] Tacitus records the same vehicles in the possession of the peoples of the North a century later.[9] Even though his biographical subject, Agricola, did not seem to have the same difficulty in dealing with the chariots, they were enough of a tactical obstacle to be mentioned even then.[10] Throughout the world, the chariot was traditionally an excellent tactical weapon for breaking through infantry formations. It seems reasonable to assume the Celts of Britain retained it as a part of their military arsenal through the end of the Roman period. This reasoning is especially so when one remembers how much the Romans relied on their legions for military supremacy and how much of a threat the empire was to British freedom.

This assumption may be verified as well; evidence shows that chariots were employed in Early Christian Britain. An example of a British king owning a chariot exists in literature. The Welsh recorded Morgan Mwynfa(w)r's "chariot" in the list of the *Thirteen Treasures of the Welsh*.[11] A *medieval* chariot has also been found in a recent dig near Edinburgh.[12] Together, these two examples demonstrate a continued familiarity by the British with the chariot through the early medieval period. Chrétien could not have known this, and even if he had, he knew that his patron did not want to be brought back to the sixth century and Arthur's time. Marie de Champagne wanted the Arthurian characters to be brought into the twelfth century. The fact that in Chrétien's time a cart was used as a transport for criminals was a happy coincidence for him; it was in perfect accordance with the sens of Marie de Champagne. And, it made the transition of his chief character from a heroic to a romantic figure a much smoother one.

The cart could have also performed a more peaceful function as a vehicle for high-status individuals. However, here the scholar is on less certain footing. Only two sources exist that confirm the existence of such carts: the Meigle Stone[13] and an episode from the *Life of Columba*.

The Meigle Stone is a Pictish stone with the same writing and decoration on it as others have.[14] As a group, the Pictish stones have been dated to sometime in the post–Roman period,[15] and therefore it is a contemporary source. The carving on it shows a second type of chariot, a two-wheeled vehicle that is demonstrably different from anything Irish or even Roman.[16] It also has a distinctive purpose: it takes people with money and land from one place to another. That is exactly what one would expect in reading through Chrétien's passage with a critical eye. The one flaw in theorizing that this model is what Chrétien meant is that the poem clearly says that Lancelot rides in a four-wheeled vehicle, not the two-wheeled transport of this alternative British form of locomotion.

The theory of a high-status, wheeled vehicle can also be supported by evidence from the *Vita Columbae*. In it, the saint is said to have ridden in a carriage (*currus*) with which he performed a miracle. The fable gives some providential details as to its structure, which indicates it was a four-wheeled chariot.[17] However, like the Scottish version, both the name and its purpose in the tale seems to indicate that it was used specifically for peaceful activities.

The episode from which it is taken has been compared to the stock incidents of Irish vitae, where saints often magically fix chariots. If the author had simply taken a motif and reapplied it, that would at first glance dull the force of the argument. However, one must remember that Adamnan was writing within a century of Columba and had as much access to Columban traditions as he had earlier vitae. Adamnan used oral and written materials that were contemporary with Columba's life. The reader should also keep in mind that whether or not the incident was borrowed, Adamnan's name and use for the chariot are unique. They show that high-status vehicles were in use by noncombatants.

There is, then, an alternative to the twelfth-century cart. The vehicle could be a heroic-age means of transportation. It would make practical sense and would explain both its unique quality and the attention it generates as Lancelot rides through the public area. The literature and archaeology indicate it was a noble method of traveling in luxury or war, though the literature and Chrétien himself favor a more warlike interpretation for the vehicle.

Following his first duel and his stay with the lady of the Castle of Four Axemen, Lancelot makes a detour in his mission to visit the tomb of one of his ancestors.[18] The consensus opinion has been that *Le Chevalier de la Charrette* is a poem designed to please Marie and that its sole purpose is to extol women and titillate one in particular. However, this solution begs the question, why is the "prince charming" of this poem procrastinating before coming to the rescue of the "damsel in distress"? This episode causes him to depart for Gorre days after Gauvain, so it is not something that serves Guinièvre in any way.[19] In fact, it temporarily relegates the heroine to a secondary importance.

On the other hand, the respect of one's ancestors is of ancient tradition. Any custom that demonstrated reverence was considered a noble and honorable way to conduct oneself, and a man of any culture would be duty-bound to follow it. The Code of Bushido, chivalry, and the cultures of Egypt, China, Babylonia, Greece, the Norse, and the Celts all insisted that a warrior felt an admiration for those who came before them.

It has been said that the cemetery scene is somehow a variation on the motif of the doughty warrior who shows the heads of his previous victims to demonstrate his own bravery and intimidate potential foes. This is done in *Erec*,[20] and *Lanzelet*,[21] and always leads to a duel. However, Lancelot fights no one until he leaves the cemetery and attempts the Stony Passage the next day. Not even Loomis could find a single undeniable element in the episode that might hint that there was originally a combat here. He could not give a single parallel to mythical source material for his opinion, either. The argument that the scene is motifal is flawed; the reader is probably looking at something Chrétien was not using to facilitate Guinièvre and Lancelot's passion or increase Guinièvre's stature. It was specifically designed to enhance the hero. Chrétien retained the scene anyway and converted it to his needs.

Chrétien creates a caricature of Lancelot in another scene, and this too holds some evidence of tampering on Chrétien's part. After spending a platonic night with a damsel who has provided lodging, Lancelot accepts his hostess' request to accompany him. As he rides toward Gorre on the journey, the lady looks down another path and

> Qant la damoisel parçoit
> La fontaine et le perron voit.
> Se ne volt pas que cil la voie
> Einz se mist en une autre voie.[22]

When the damsel notices the spring and sees the slab, not wanting the knight to see them, she turned to another road.[23]

Lancelot, however, notices the boulder and fountain and makes his way to them. This is the sole reason given why he leaves the other path. Conversely, when Lancelot and his companion arrive in the clearing the entire scene refocuses on a comb that is found on the grass near the boulder. The comb is evidently the central feature of the scene as it remains the locus of Chrétien's attention from the moment it is introduced to the exclusion of the stone and fountain. Chrétien has, for some reason he does not explain, only used the two objects to get to the romantic item. But the awkward transference of attention screams out that there is something here that has been hidden. The degree of romantic atmosphere in the lines that follow only punctuate such a conjecture.

The stone is the vehicle of the passage, as without it Lancelot would never find Guinièvre's comb. Its attributes and appearance, consistent in the Arthurian stories and always central to key episodes, prove that Chrétien's mysterious stone is not an anomaly and suggest it may well be ancient and Celtic. If the theory is accurate, it could originally have been either a kingship or a symbol stone. A review of the literature in which such a stone is mentioned will bear out the stone's nature.

The large stone is nothing more than a *perrun de marbre* (block of marble) to Marie de France.[24] However, Zatzikhoven terms it a "stone of honor."[25] In *Wigalois* its only quality is its selectiveness as to who touches it.[26] The French generically called them *perrons*. *Diu Crône* named one such object a "plot of land,"[27] though that plot is specifically associated with kingship. In British Arthurian lore, it was a *glas*, which means "blue or green or grey stone," though it seemed to have no particular value.[28]

In these romances, a coward could not touch it and only the most perfect could sit upon it. It was either laid upon,[29] or a sword was drawn from it prior to the hero's ascension to a throne.[30] Such an unusual rock is found in myth as well. Conchobar is brought forth on a prominent stone near a river.[31] He is from then on considered a man born to be the king.

The stones' attributes in the romances are easily connected to their function as a kingship stone. It is a screaming stone, a *lecc*, such as those found at Scone, Tara, Cruachu, Emain Macha, Mad Adair, Cráeb Tulcha, and Cothrigi. It was "an essential item of the inaugural furniture" along with an oak grove and mound — usually of an ancient nature.[32] It had the property that none but the rightful king could stand upon it. The perron in the comb scene of *Le Chevalier de la Charrette* is likely an allusion to an item of the inaugural ceremony. The perron episode might have been altered into its current state for whatever reason, but its purpose is still clear if it stands on its own; it was here that the hero was revealed as a king. Chrétien's statement that the maiden tried to lead Lancelot away from the path that contained the stone betrays much more than a maiden's whim and a woman's jealousy. It shows that behind this object, dismissed by Chrétien, was an insight into sub–Roman British culture.

There is, however, also the comb and fountain. As has been noted, the boulder that drew the attention of both Lancelot and the damsel is immediately replaced by the comb of Guinièvre and the fountain, which Lancelot uses as a mirror. Why these two objects and why does Chrétien so clearly switch the focus of his narrative from a ritual stone to a more romantic comb and water that is functionally a mirror? The answer seems obvious: to heighten the romantic aspect of the poem. Still, the skeptical reader will be rewarded for assuming that this part of the scene was merely altered by Chrétien, instead of being created by him. The fact that both the mirror and the comb are in the scene with the attention-getting stone allows the reader to consider the possibility that both might have served some purpose in a previous source. If so, this hypothetical source, *Glas*, may well have indicated the object of notice was a Pictish symbol stone and that the stone bore the most common pair of symbols found on them, the comb and the mirror. Chrétien, being unfamiliar with this foreign artwork, would have failed to understand what he was reading. He pieced the episode together as best he could with his own understanding of the world and while using the influence of Marie de Champagne as a guide. If the comb and the mirror were a part of the tale originally and the above conjecture is what happened, then Chrétien's rock was a Pictish stone.

It may never be known whether Lancelot originally saw a Pictish stone or a kingship stone. Perhaps it does not matter. The reality is one can see why the hero might have been lost in thought on seeing a kingship or Pictish stone, as both symbolized power.

The historical elements in the poem are all to be found in those places that are the most predictable; they are in the scenes where Chrétien has gone to an extreme in describing Lancelot's Ovidian response to Guinièvre. Although one can see the historical connections of the comb and the mirror, the cemetery, and the chariot, Chrétien's lack of comprehension in certain areas is understandable. One should have been surprised, on the other hand, if Chrétien had been cognizant of the customs and seen the meaning behind the symbolism buried in his poem. It comes as no shock, then, that Chrétien strayed from what is known to be true of the fifth and sixth centuries in reformulating the ancient story into *Le Chevalier de la Charrette*. Yet he has not strayed so far as to leave no evidence of where he began; elements of *Le Chevalier de la Charrette* are clearly historical. The symbol stones were not used after the ninth century and the tradition did not begin much before the fifth century. Nor is there any historical mention of kingship rituals such as that mentioned here, or chariots, much past the sixth century. Therefore, the ninth century is the latest possible date of origin for *Glas*, and it could not have been created much before the fifth century.

7
Conclusion

In the first chapter of this book I reviewed the current academic opinion of Chrétien's poems. It is believed that he evoked an entire world for Marie de Champagne based on classical and contemporary literature and his patroness' feminism. He took only the names and a rough storyline from the British. Six chapters later, that position is no longer tenable. To believe that anyone could create a world with such an uncanny resemblance to the post-Roman Britain reconstructable from Irish and Welsh myth, legend, law tracts, historical documents, and archaeological remains without materials based in that period is preposterous. Instead, it is clear that Chrétien did what he was obviously best at, namely forming the stories, themes, and patterns of others into a coherent whole. He had sources that gave him a sense of the period, and used them to please his patron and bring to life the era.

What do the parallels between the Celtic culture anterior to 900 and the details in *Le Chevalier de la Charrette* tell us? First, it is known that abductions were common in Celtic society, but the theft of a queen would have been an entirely foreign thought in medieval literature. Second, the correlations back to ancient Britain are so consistent that it becomes clear that the infrastructure was a British and ancient one, which the author has termed *Glas*. The other influences (e.g. classical and contemporary continental literature) are additions made by Chrétien. He may use an alternative work for many lines, but he always returns, and stays, with something Celtic. As has been seen, every scene of *La Charrette* apart from the evening with the vavasour before the Stony Bridge is bristling with distinctly Celtic items. This implies a very strong and, likely, very old tradition. D. D. R. Owen stated:

> Having said that Chrétien's imagination was free-ranging, I must qualify my words by adding that there were limits to its activity. As I have suggested, he was not happy when faced by the need to improvise important sections of his story, or extend its intrigue beyond what was in his source. This did sometimes happen, and with unfortunate results, as will be seen. He was certainly not less

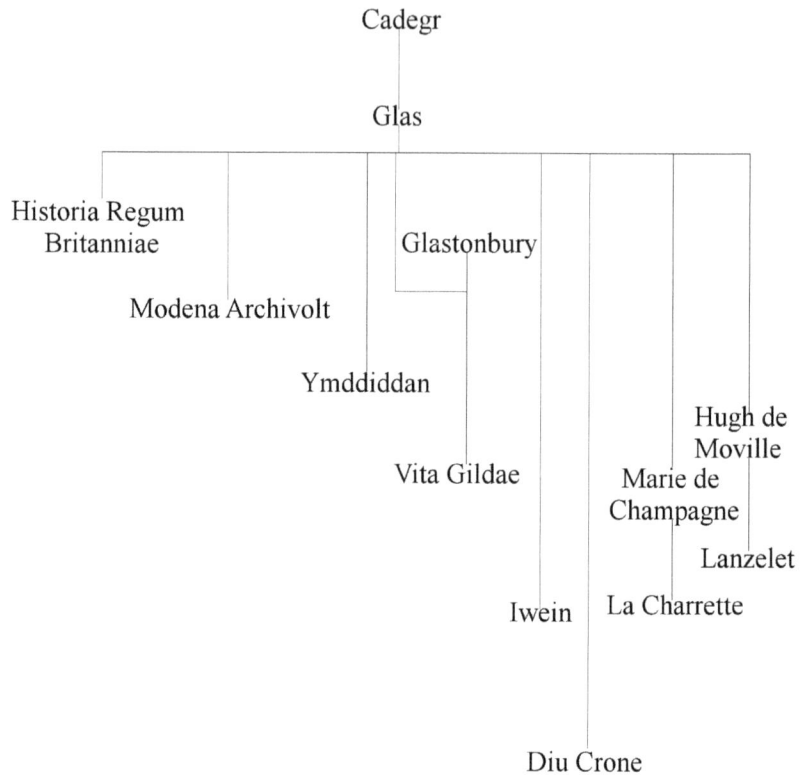

A revised development of the common abduction story. While it would be impossible to capture all of the nuances and interconnectivity of the primary abduction stories, the illustration shows a common reliance on a single source of information.

> inventive than most medieval poets, but inventiveness was not encouraged by the literary tradition. Authority laid a heavy hand on composition; and it was more the fashion to claim a source for one's work than to assert originality, except in the manner of presentation. Chrétien was no exception to this rule.[1]

Chrétien simply was not the type of author who could invent an entire world out of his imagination. Such authors were not supported in twelfth-century Europe.

Chrétien was not creating the world he portrayed; instead he was altering a Celtic story by inserting themes and thoughts that evidently came from his background and Marie de Champagne's wishes. Could one expect more from a man whose livelihood depended on pleasing a prechosen audience, one that wanted an aesthetic theme? Should one expect more, even if that man was the greatest French poet of the Middle Ages?

Conclusion

So what nonclassical, noncontemporary sources did he use? There were records and heroic poems in Britain before 800, as Jackson, Bromwich, Hughes, Dumville, and others have postulated.[2] There was also interaction between the Celts and French — directly through the Bretons and indirectly through various aspects of Henry II's kingdom. Further, evidence for an historical element in the poem studied here has been found to date earlier than 900, and possibly to the fifth and sixth centuries. What is to bar the idea that the heroic poetry pertaining to Arthuriana became removed and copied, or orally transferred, to a location in France? Its source would have been the *Northern Memoranda*, or a similar body of historical and pseudohistorical lore (see below). Chrétien could then be seen as using historical (in the twelfth-century sense of the word) texts, or materials on par with *Y Gododdin* or the Urien cycle. As has been seen, this suggestion agrees with the evidence at hand. Confirmation will be forthcoming in a critical study of *Le Conte du Graal*.

Part Two: The Holy Object

8

Introduction to Le Conte du Graal

The previous seven chapters have been devoted to the study of *Le Chevalier de la Charrette*. It has been determined that the poem's progenitor, *Glas*, was first formed between the fifth and ninth centuries. It was very likely created in the post–Roman period. It would have been a bardic poem of heroism dedicated to a British figure, most likely the progenitor of Gauvain. It would have survived and flourished in an oral environment for centuries and eventually been brought to its present state by Chrétien in the 1100s.

It has also been deduced that the less realistic portions of Chrétien's poem can be explained in one of three manners. The two traditional notions are that the less believable scenes are due to either a cultural misunderstanding or Chrétien's interpretation of the romantic ideals of Marie de Champagne. A third possibility was elaborated upon in the introduction to this book: many seemingly trivial elements in the poem were from or anterior to the ninth century in Britain. In the last three chapters this hypothesis was largely substantiated. The same objective is set for the present study of Chrétien's last known romance, *Le Conte du Graal*. The author will attempt to establish *an historical* basis for this tale as well.

Le Conte du Graal was written in the 1190s. As with all his Arthurian romances, here Chrétien injected his personal style and knowledge of the classics in his telling. He was also guided again in his endeavors. In the opening lines, he stated that he was given the *matìere* (material) by his patron, now Philip of Flanders.[1] In learning about his historical activities, it soon becomes clear that he had some very different motivations from Marie de Champagne. First, Philip had no fascination with courtly love. Chrétien's new patron was a man of religious appetite and strong moral conviction, and he was from a family renowned throughout Christendom for its fiber. Second, the theme of the poem was unique for Chrétien; it centers on the Christian religion.

As with his other Arthurian tales, here Chrétien proved to be both brilliant and a source of inspiration for other stories about Perceval and the grail he introduced to the continent. He is, therefore, central to any study on the subject. For this reason, it will be beneficial to this study to begin by exploring the two new underlying principles by which Chrétien was asked to work. That accomplished, the author will survey the four main theories regarding the origins of the grail ceremony. The explanation that each theory is able to provide will favor the conclusions that all are partially correct and that the Celtic elements make up the earliest strata of the story.[2] It will be found that each influence was introduced to the story individually through a process of progressive superimposition on an originally Celtic tale. Further, it will suggest that the original grail and the mystique surrounding it are a conglomerate of Celtic motifs. Following the hint that this provides, the author will attempt a comparison of other Celtic tales and historical material that pertains indirectly to Chrétien's *graal* and the ceremony surrounding it. This comparison will be made in the hope of gaining a better understanding of the object and the ceremony from which the poet would develop his graal. In conjunction with this analogous exploration, I will discuss later medieval versions of the grail story. This approach will prove valuable in showing certain general patterns for all early versions of the grail story, as it did in *Le Chevalier de la Charrette*. It will lead to a theory of why the different writers describe the grail and the ceremony surrounding it differently and will in turn help further explain the grail's original nature and purpose.

A chapter devoted to identifying the original roles of each of the major characters will follow a study of the grail itself. The most significant of these figures will be the Belatacudros figure, a British god of northern Britain. Details of his attributes and variations of his name will indicate that he was the prototype for the grail-king. This, in conjunction with the traditional view that Arthur and the people of the fifth century were Christian, will bring out a new wrinkle to the puzzle. The unraveling of this wrinkle will lead to a discussion of the nature and interaction of the Christian and native Celtic religions in sub–Roman Britain. In turn, the results developed there will preface a search for potentially historical Celtic material in the grail story. The author hopes to demonstrate here that the same link exists between *Le Conte* and ancient Britain as was shown to be in *La Charrette*. Further, the author believes that this process will serve to provide an overall picture of the grail story's genesis stemming from an original source, *Dysgyl*. It is hoped that the realization of these two objectives will help begin to define the historicity of the poem.

Unlike *Le Chevalier de la Charrette*, *Le Conte du Graal* introduces its chief character, Perceval, almost immediately. He is of royal blood and has been

8. Introduction to Le Conte du Graal   77

raised in an isolated village by his mother. The reader is first introduced to him as he is hunting animals for his household. Spying a group of Arthur's knights riding through his forest, he is enamored with them. They have no time for him, however, as they are in search of a kidnapped lady. They only stop to talk with the boy in order to get information from him. In a scene of levity, the knights instead find themselves answering all of his naïve questions and telling him of Arthur's court. After they leave, Perceval returns home and abruptly informs his mother that he has decided to become a knight of King Arthur. He rides off despite his mother's tears. Apart from one short delay, he proceeds directly to Arthur's court and there insists on being knighted by the king.

When he does arrive, a character called the Red Knight has just stolen the king's gold cup and dashed the wine it contained on Guinièvre. Keu alone has the presence of mind to respond to the boy's demand. He announces Perceval will be granted the boon of knighthood if he can prove his worth by killing the Red Knight. Unaware of the danger, Perceval runs right out and accomplishes the task, takes the man's honor, and rides away.

Riding along, he eventually comes to one of his uncles, Gornemanz de Gohorts, who teaches him how to ride, fight, and behave in a courtly fashion. Continuing on, he arrives at the castle of a cousin in distress. He rescues her, and then refuses her offer of marriage. From there he happens upon the grail castle where he witnesses the grail supper, but fails to ask the mysterious question that would end his kinsmens' suffering. He finds himself outside the castle the next morning. Soon thereafter he stumbles across Arthur's court again. It is at this point that *Le Conte du Graal* begins to become complicated in a way none of Chrétien's previous romances are. A lady known as the Ugly Damsel brings Perceval to shame by informing Arthur's men of what Perceval has failed to do at the grail castle. He leaves the court and goes in search of the grail castle for five years and visits no church during this time.

The Ugly Damsel was apparently only there to plead with Arthur's knights to lift a siege at Montesclare, however. Meanwhile, Gauvain is accused of murder by another visitor before he has a chance to respond. He rides out to defend his honor, leaving the reader to wonder what Perceval is up to and what becomes of Montesclare. Gauvain safely arrives at the home of the wronged man and becomes romantically entangled with a woman he soon learns is his accuser's sister. There is now a conflict of interests between Gauvain and the other knight—hosts cannot kill their guests. To solve the predicament, all sides agree the only proper thing for Gauvain to do is to take one year to hunt for the sacred lance that pierced Christ. Failure to capture and return with it will bring him back to the castle again for imprisonment. It is in this year when the tale ends, but in the meantime Gauvain manages to become lord of a castle, find a spouse for himself and one of his sisters, and anger another chieftain. In this Perceval arrives at his former host's castle incognito and fights Gauvain's intended opponent. The work stops curtly in the midst of the acclaim Arthur's court gives Gauvain on his return to them.

As a piece of literature, Chrétien de Troyes' *Le Conte du Graal* has attained international status. His characters are memorable and his plot was a prototype. His detailed descriptions of scenery and persons make the reader wonder if he had not seen the places and the fights in his poem. It is a masterpiece and a cornerstone of Arthuriana. It is, however, as a source that it will be examined. The author believes that it is also a reservoir of information about the late fifth and early sixth centuries. In this context it will help to elucidate the mystery of the grail.

9

Philip of Flanders, Life and Influences[1]

The "Phelipe de Flandres" who patronized Chrétien as he wrote *Le Conte du Graal* was from a family of some standing in twelfth-century Europe.[2] His father, Robert II, had gone on crusade. Robert's predecessor, Theodoric of Alsatia, had been given a phial of holy blood for his continuing aid to Jerusalem.[3] Philip's mother, Sibyl, also had a reputation for holiness. She accompanied Robert on his crusade and remained there at the Convent of St. Lazarus of Bethany.[4] A branch of Philip's family at one point produced several rulers of Jerusalem. Because of these Christian acts, the House of Flanders was considered a bastion of Christianity in the twelfth century, and its men were greatly admired.

Of Philip of Flanders' life specifically a great deal is also known. The future count, a second son, was born in 1142, and by 1156 he was next in line. At that time he married Elizabeth of Vermandois, gaining possession of her inheritance.

His character was quite powerful. His strength of faith as well as his skills in combat were acclaimed throughout Europe. He was also a good businessman, both in public and private, and is known to have protected the towns in his territory from economic oppression; they thrived as a result. Domestically he was just as prudent. When his wife was caught committing adultery he neither dissolved their marriage nor did anything that might forfeit him Vermandois. He wisely sent her instead to a convent.[5] He was not lacking in passion, either. The matter settled, he personally killed the lover.

Despite his good sense, Philip also made some embarrassing decisions. At one point early in his career he was considered for the regency of Jerusalem. Hoping to make use of the situation, Philip made the journey to the Holy Land under the pretense of seeing his mother. While there, he quietly visited the royal establishment at Jerusalem. Confronted with taking on the role, he turned them down flat. Instead, he spent the remainder of his time in the Holy Land attempting to marry the sisters of the ailing King of Jerusalem (his cousins) to a pair of his own men. Presumably this would have ensured that Philip would remain the dominant authority in Jerusalem even after the women had reached maturity. His actions were circumvented, however, and he left the city with nothing.

During his stay in Jerusalem, Philip was repeatedly asked to lead a force against the Muslims in order to strike fear into the enemy, but never did so. His perceived cowardice brought even more negative repercussions from his family and other forces throughout Europe. The Jerusalem voyage, intended by Philip and his family to vault him into the position of being one of the most prominent individuals in Christendom, ended only in his embarrassment.[6]

Unrepentant, Philip returned to Flanders and revolted when the young Philip Augustus ascended the throne in 1180. His refusal to accept the king went on for five years. When he finally did make peace, though, it was freely. He is known to have been a supportive vassal. In 1192 he went on crusade and died in the Holy Land.

Chrétien is known, by references in his poem, to have written between the years of Philip's revolt and his last trip to Jerusalem.[7] A more precise date than this is not feasible, nor is it necessary. Narrowing the years down that much allows the scholar to somewhat corroborate a theory that was originally developed by Helen Adolph.[8] The poem's consistent and often blatant parallels to Philip's historical actions and interactions have led to a nearly unanimous idea about the plot of the story among French experts. *Le Conte* is a mirror of Philip's life. Helen Adolph went through the main points of Philip's *vita*:

1. Goes to Jerusalem, always noted for riches but given religious importance.
2. Kingdom ruled by a sick man surrounded by enemies.
3. A cousin of the king is expected and finally arrives.
4. The king's sister mourns the premature death of her husband.
5. The cousin is offered a regency; rule of country.
6. Fails to live up to his relatives' expectations and is blamed for it.[9]

On pages 603–7 of Adolph's article, Philip's family tree is reconstructed and the events and qualities of each member listed. Further, it is compared exhaustively and cogently with Perceval's family as found in *Le Conte* to underline the point. In addition, the families of both Perceval and Philip are shown to inherit on the maternal side. There is also a political aspect to be seen in the dynastic struggles of 1180s Flanders with Perceval/Philip's real/perceived distance from Arthur/Philip Augustus.[10]

The influence Philip's life had on *Le Conte du Graal* should be readily apparent. The general reputation the counts of Flanders had, and the one Philip himself wished to engender, was one of an intensely religious spirit. This, as the reader will see, is an influence on the poem that cannot be overstated. However, Philip made mistakes of faith and morality—such as in the Holy Land and a revolt against the rightful king. Chrétien brings all these items to written form in the subtleties of his plot, with the full knowledge of the regretful and repentant Philip constantly in the back of his mind. It is Chrétien's use of Philip as a foundation that gives the poem so many details and scenes that have no parallel in Irish or Welsh myth, law, or motifs.[11] As Chapter 11 will show, it was the plot that Chrétien was directed to take, mimicked by the romance writers who followed, which changed the basic format of the grail legend into something barely comparable to its Celtic precursors. Such is probably the reason it has proven so difficult over the years to understand the origins of the legend.

The life of Philip was the key factor in the creation of *Le Conte*, but he personally had a part in making the Celtic information more readily available to his poet as well. Philip's alliance to Scotland in 1173–4 made the tie there stronger, as would Henry II's marriage to Maud and lesser marriages between the Norman and Scottish royal families. As a result of so many ties between Scotland and France during this period, it makes sense that Chrétien would have had access to a great deal of material from the region. And evidence of that is obvious from the start in reading the poem. Those place names he uses were newsworthy in the period between Henry II's marriage to Maud and the Scottish-Flanders alliance. For instance, in 1109 the Norman Count Alan Rufus took a well-known military tour to the Firth of Forth.[12] This probably caused the English name for the body of water, Scot's Water, to come into common aristocratic vocabulary. The name appears in Wace as *Escoce Watre* and once in Chrétien as *Cotouatre*.[13]

From 1110 until 1159 Galloway was in the hands of the Norseman Fergus, who was independent of and consistently hostile to the Scottish kings.[14] The boundary of this kingdom was the Nith River. It was notorious for its inhospitality to the Scots, and this comes through in *Le Conte du Graal* as Gauvain prepares to cross the Nith.

> Einz chevaliers n'an pot venir
> Qui ça alast ne chanp no voie,
> Que c'est la bone de Galvoie:
> qui ja an puisse retorner.[15]

No knight who has ever gone that way by road or field has ever been able to come back, for this is the frontier of Galloway, which a knight can't cross and then return again.[16]

The passage is all the more telling when one realizes that Gauvain not only has no trouble making his way through the region, but he is welcomed there with open arms.

The association of Gauvain with Galloway is quite ancient, as indicated in the name similarity.[17] In *Le Conte*, Gauvain's grandmother, mother, and sister are to be found in Galloway's borders at the Castle of the Maidens. Such a state of affairs implies a connection between Galloway and its eponym Gauvain that is supported by an early draft of *De Rebus Gestis Regum Anglorum*, c. 1125. Here Gauvain is specifically called the King of Galloway.[18] This tie is demonstrably old; the incongruous presence of his family in a region famed for its anti–Scottish sentiment in the twelfth century can be explained in no other way.

From 1124, King David of Scotland located his capital at Carlisle. It remained so until his death in 1157. David was raised by the Normans and was highly regarded by them for his prowess and manners. They considered him one of their own. His actions and location were known by the royalty of England, to whom he owed much of his power and with whom he maintained a friendly relation. Carlisle appears in Chrétien as *Carduel*, Arthur's capital.[19] The connection is undoubtedly valid; *Carduel* is the spelling for Carlisle in the *Anglo-Saxon Chronicle*, and in local charters.[20]

In addition to the place names, one rather unique oddity begins with Chrétien: the concept of the virgin knight. It is utterly foreign to the *Peredur* author and the generic Celtic legends, but may have its beginnings in the person of Alexander, King of Scotland from 1149–1165. Despite the urgings of his advisors, legend says he remained a virgin until his early death.[21]

In contrast to Marie de Champagne's influence, which was often flagrantly sexist, the inspiration of Philip was multifaceted. His house's prestige commanded a religious aspect, and his past and regrets about his decisions implied another. The friendly relations with Scotland allowed for much more diversity and in many cases offered Chrétien a number of intriguing names and places with which neither he nor his audience would have been otherwise familiar. He managed to combine all of his sources of information into a generally coherent and impressively entertaining whole, despite this obstacle. As will be seen next, the effort was so completely successful that no grail writer who followed would use any other format but the one the great poet had created.

10

Grail Theories

Que qu'il parloient d'un et d'el,
Uns vasiez d'une chanbre vint
Qui une blanche lance tint
Anpoigniee par le mieu,
Si passa par entre le feu
Et ces qui el lit se seoient,
Et tuit cil de leanz veoient
La lance blanche et le fer blanc,
S'issoit une gote vermoille.
Li vaslez vit cele chose avenoit,
Que del chasti li sovenoit
Celui qui chevalier le fist
Qui li anseigna et aprist
Que de trop parler se gardast;
Si crient, se il le demandast,
Qu'an li tenist a vilenie:
Por ce si nel demanda mie.
    Atant dui autre vaslet vindrent
Qui chandeliers an lor mains tindrent
De fin or, ovrez a neel.
Li vaslet estoient mout bel
Qui les chandeliers aportoient.
An chascun chandeliers ardoient
Dis chandoiles a tot le mains
    Une graal antre ses deus mains
Qui avoec les vaslez venoit,
Bele et gente et bien acesmee:
Quant ele fu leanz antree
A tot le graal qu'ele tint,
Une si granz clartez i vint
Qu'ausi perdirent les chandoiles

> Lor clarté come les estoiles
> Quant li solauz lieve ou la lune.
> Aprés celi an revint une
> Qui tint un tailleor d'argent.¹

While they were talking of this and that, out of a room came a youth with a white lance grasped by the middle; he passed by between the fire and those seated upon the couch. And everyone present could see the white lance with its shining head, and from the tip of the lance-head oozed a drop of blood, a crimson drop that ran down right to the lad's hand. The young man who had arrived there that night saw this marvel, but refrained from asking how this thing happened, since he remembered that warning given him by the man who knighted him and taught and instructed him to beware of talking too much. He feared that, had he asked, it would have been thought impolite, and so he did not enquire. Thereupon two other youths came, holding in their hands pure gold candle-sticks inlaid with black enamel. The lads carrying the candelabras were extremely handsome. At least ten candles were burning in each candelabra.

A damsel, who came with the youths and was fair and attractive and beautifully adorned, held in both hands a grail. Once she had entered with the grail that she held, so great a radiance appeared that the candles lost their brilliance just as the stars do at the rising of the sun or moon. After her came another maiden, holding a silver carving-dish.²

Chrétien's version of the grail scene thus has a lance, candelabra, grail, and silver carving platter. In every version of the story, the grail ceremony passes in front of the hero.³ Though most versions assign the grail a cornucopia quality, the procession itself causes anguish to the residents of the grail castle.

The entire spectacle that revolves around the grail has puzzled scholars for centuries, and it began with the French master. The redactions to Chrétien produced over the next sixty years seem to combine the strange beauty of the Christian Mass with the seemingly ageless, incoherent conglomeration that is Celtic Mythology. The grail romances have moral purity and religious fervor coupled with ancient kingship rituals. They show a fixation on an object held in a maid's hands, a barbaric concept of human life, and the symbolic importance of a dead warrior. The combination is striking and at times overwhelming. Theories as to the explanation of this wonderful object, the events of the ceremony, and the location of the grail castle have only reflected the various aspects of the grail's nature. It has been called Christian, Celtic, Greek, Jewish, or a universal nature rite. It is a beautiful example of the extinct "Celtic Christianity," or the invention of Chrétien's mind. The conjecture that Chrétien's ambiguous *graal* has provoked has been incalculable. However, there is an answer, and it is ascertainable with the knowledge available, as the author hopes to show in the following pages. This solution will best be facilitated by first reviewing the chief arguments of the major camps. Therefore, the following pages will be a summary and analysis of the most compelling points from each camp. This done, the flaws of each individual solution will be pointed out.[4] The author will then develop what is in essence a theory that complements them all.

The Christian theory has evolved mainly from focusing on the later romances, which are overtly Christian,[5] and the judgment that anything written for Philip's family must be have been of Christian origin. It now has few supporters.[6] The theory was often based on Christian phrases that superficially dot the poem,[7] much as the Norse sagas have similar and clearly later Christian additions.

There is pseudohistorical evidence that such a story as one finds in Chrétien could have been originally Christian, and quite old, however. Since the Middle Ages, Britain has considered itself one of the earliest Christian countries. The seeds that would later develop into some of the more amazing claims in Christendom had appeared as early as the 700s. At that time, the *Chronicle of Freculf* stated that SS. Philip and James sent twelve disciples to convert the island in the middle of the first century. Glastonbury later claimed that the leader of this mission was Joseph of Arimathea himself.[8] Such an assertion was only strengthened by extending that legend to encompass the most famed king of British lore.

It has been argued that Perceval seems to be a Christian character because of the general ambiance of the poem. The place he is raised is portrayed as a community in many ways comparable to a monastery. It is isolated from society and contains only the household servants and farmhands. There are none of the leisure activities associated with a royal center. However, the same or more spartan childhoods may be attributed to Fionn, Enlil of Babylonian myth, and the Tarzan of fiction, none of which are Christian or demonstrate strong Christian values. In addition, Perceval says he has kissed his mother's chambermaids,[9] not exactly the activities of an individual raised in an idyllic Christian community even if it is not anti–Christian behavior.

The manner in which Perceval is instructed also highlights the sense of Christianity in the poem, so the argument goes.[10] Early in his career, Perceval is taught by Gornemanz how to fight well, but warned not to kill, in accordance with Christian ideals.[11] As his experiences mature him, he comes to find a deeper form of belief in God. He begins to have an understanding of right and wrong, and a realization of his place of importance as a holy knight of God. On Good Friday pilgrims recall him to the faith from his wanderings. He spends the next few days cleansing his spirit along with his uncle the Hermit King. The reader is made to understand that when he has reached the proper level of understanding and demonstrated his devotion to God, he will be the next grail king. The religious views of Arthur's knights toward the grail and the reverence they hold it in indicate the object must be Christian.

Again, this is hardly strong evidence; heroes of any nation or faith know right and wrong and learn to understand their importance. They do kill, contrary to Gornemanz's advice, as did the holy men who went on crusade in the Middle Ages. The theme that faith is the necessary element in becoming a grail-king is a notion that can be attributed more to the life of Philip and his influences on the poem than to the values of Christianity.

The Christian ambiance of the poem is stressed to the point of nausea. Perceval refers to God and figures surrounding the Christian afterlife as he tries to figure out who the new figures are in his forest at the beginning of the poem.

> Par ma'ame,
> voir me dist ma mere ma dame,
> Qui me dist que deable sont
> Plus esfreé que rien del mont,[12]

By my soul, my lady mother spoke the truth when she told me that devils are the most hideous things in the world.[13]

Unable otherwise to describe their beauty when he has seen their armor, he concludes they are angels. Such a scene is intended only for humor and has no place in a discussion of the religious outlook of the grail.

There was a large volume of trade that took place between the East and West of Europe in the twelfth century due to the crusades. Because of this, critics who supported the Christian theory felt justified in using Orthodox as well Roman Catholic elements of the mass to explain the grail ceremony.[14] It is believed that Chrétien would have been exposed to Byzantine merchants or a returning crusader as a member of Philip's court. It has been further theorized that the unusual quality of the eastern ritual would have made it an exciting element of the grail ceremony. The use of evidence here by those who followed the Christian theory was extremely liberal and at times almost whimsical. There is no evidence that Chrétien made use of any eastern source here.

These scholars believed that the objects involved in the grail ceremony were to be found in the Byzantine rite, despite the weakness of their connection. There the blood of Christ was carried in a platter, the Lance of Longinus followed, and a bowl, which catches the blood from its tip, ended the procession of religious objects.[15] This, they claimed, neatly explained away many of the perceived pagan elements of the poem. Once the one major overt scene could be set aside, all the other anomalies of the poem seemingly fit into place behind the story of Christian origin. The Hermit King is clearly one who has found Christianity in the wilderness. He represents the easiest way of finding God, through penance and by avoiding the temptations of civilization. He is the one to lead Perceval from the ways of the world and to the path of religious observance. The Grail Keeper, known as the "Fisher King," is a name originally rendered from a literal interpretation of *Matthew*, "Follow me and I will make you fishers among men."[16]

However, none of it can seriously be connected to anything Christian. The grail ceremony does not strike one as particularly Christian. The grail and lance are kept in a castle, not a church or temple where they should be.[17] No aspect of Christianity satisfies the asking ceremony at which Perceval fails. There is none in the Roman Catholic Church, nor to the author's knowledge can anything like it be found in the Orthodox.

Beyond the clear divergences from Christianity, there are several less obvious nuances of the grail ceremony that also do not fit. A woman carries the grail of Chrétien, yet women were not included in similar Christian rites. Dr. Peebles believed this seemingly pagan detail could be shown to be one of a number of exceptional instances in which the general ban on women holding religious objects was overlooked. However, the small number of examples she could produce, and their limited geography, only weakened her argument.[18] A long line of conciliar decrees and episcopal edicts support the contention that women were not allowed to touch holy objects in ceremonies. The grail scene of later romances replaced the maiden with a youth or priest, apparently because those writers who followed Chrétien realized the discrepancy as well.

The lance, too, is most definitely not of Christian derivation in *Le Conte*. Chrétien says nothing of its part in Jesus' crucifixion. It simply precedes the grail and drips blood amidst mourning. Its literary connection to the Spear of Longinus was a later one. The first continuator was the earliest writer to give it a Christian quality.[19]

The castle where Perceval comes upon the grail also seems quite unchristian in its disposition. Chrétien's hero can only find it by chance even after he has been there. This implies the young man was either very bad with directions or, more probably, that the grail site had no set geographical setting. This castle is not a Christian one as mystic locations are the property of pagan religions alone.

One can be much less certain about the other, less tangible aspects of the world Chrétien shows us. However, certain details are not specifically Christian. The stone chair that splits as Perceval sits on it in *Didot Perceval*[20] and strange symbols such as the recurring combination of the colors white, red, and black are good examples. The Waste Land and the dead knight motif of later versions are also incongruent with Christianity.[21] Even the episode with the Hermit King indicates exactly how little the tale originally was Christian. That scene in *Le Conte du Graal* is borrowed from an episode in the life of the Irish hero Fionn MacCumhail,[22] and thus is a strictly Celtic element.

The reader may find in some of the discrepancies a recurring theme of things Celtic and naturally look to the history and literature of Celtic Christianity to explain the unique details of the grail story, but such an effort would be in vain. The phrase "Celtic Christianity" itself is a misnomer. It is true that the Insular Celts were isolated from the continent for centuries and did develop their own style of the Christian religion in the period. However, only two major questions were in dispute when the British were reunited with Roman Catholicism toward the end of the seventh century: the dating of Easter and tonsure. No record of questionable rites exists. The main force of the Celtic movement, the involvement of their art in their writing, was welcomed in the monastic tradition of Europe.

Nor is there any hint of unchristian activities such as those found in the grail stories in any of the literature deriving from the period. The fifth and sixth centuries were the Age of Saints, when every significant Celtic kingdom in Britain boasted a holy individual who could claim sainthood.[23] Numerous vitae were later written in which these saints were given credit for every conceivable miracle. Folktales, legends, and other vitae were all used to make each saint appear more holy than others. It is impossible to believe that a tradition of such beauty and significance as the one surrounding the grail would have been left unconnected with any saint, if the rite was indeed Christian. And yet, this is exactly what one finds. No grail, chalice, or cauldron ceremony or procession is included in any extant vita. This can only be because there was no such Christian object in Britain that became the precursor for the grail.[24]

These problems have led to the introduction of other theories. The possibility that Chrétien was Jewish has led Dr. Weinraub to the theory that the famed grail ceremony was a ritual celebrating the evacuation from Egypt, the Passover.[25] The comparisons he makes are numerous and intricate and have led to a speculation that, while never attaining the prominence of the Celtic or Christian hypotheses, has attained some degree of authority.

Circumstantial historical evidence is not wanting for Chrétien's Jewish affinity. Troyes, an important economic center, was famed for its renowned Jewish citizen and Pentateuch master, Rashi (1040–1105). The school he left behind was his legacy. In addition, there is testimony that fairs were held in Troyes concurrently with synods.[26] It is quite possible that the religious schools as well as traveling scholars contributed to an awareness of the Jewish religion in all of France, and especially Troyes. Chrétien would have lived in a city renowned for its Jewish learning and would have had easy and open access to the Jewish culture and customs because of that fact.

There is no dearth of textual evidence, either. Weinraub sees parallels to the Jewish religion in *Le Conte du Graal*'s general storyline. Moses' exile from Egypt is duplicated in Perceval's departure from his mother. The crossing of the Red Sea can be seen in miniature when Perceval crosses the grail castle drawbridge.[27] The Jews' inability to cross the Jordan because they have not been purified is duplicated by *Le Conte*'s hero, who cannot ford a stream because of his sin at the grail castle.[28] Moses' wanderings across the desert in which he comes to find himself are reexperienced in Perceval's meanderings through a large forest or desert for some years.[29] Moses' arrival into the Promised Land and fulfillment of his destiny is matched by Perceval's entrance to the grail castle.[30]

It has also been argued that the grail ceremony itself has numerous items that could be derived from the Passover meal. Upon Perceval's entrance to the castle, the grail king is found leaning on one elbow as was the custom of the twelfth-century Jew during the ceremony. The position was a symbol of freedom.[31] The dates, figs, and other foods served as part of the appetizer dishes of the grail supper are found in traditional Jewish meals. The main course that followed consisted of a flat round cake known as a *gastel*, pepper, and meat. In the second plate of the Passover meal, one was expected to make a sandwich of the bread and bitter herbs.[32] In addition, the grail platter is shown three times, as is the serving plate during the Passover supper.[33] But all this is not proof of a Jewish rite. Alternatively and more economically, all the food mentioned above would make for a typical aristocratic meal in Jerusalem.[34] The custom of leaning on one's elbow may have a deeper meaning for the Jewish people, but it is also a common habit for most people in any society when not seated on chairs and eating off of a table.

The two candles that precede the grail in some of the grail ceremonies are also easy to explain in the context of a Jewish custom. If Passover falls on a Saturday, the Lord's Day, a boy is to lead the servants with two wicks.[35] Similar contingencies allow for the variety of grail rites in the different tellings.

The grail maiden falls neatly into the Jewish pattern as well. Dr. Weinraub explains to his readers that the bearer of the grail, or main dish during Passover, could have been a Jewish woman in a twelfth-century French rite, as in Chrétien's scene. The modern-day Aleppo community follows the custom that the eldest daughter of the head of the household bears the chief vessel.[36] This is precisely what happens in *Le Conte*, where the grail maiden is the eldest virgin daughter of the grail king. In the twelfth-century ceremony, the Jewish girl was to take the plate away before the meal began to provoke the child to ask the key question, "Why?," just as Perceval is baited by the grail maiden.[37] This manufactured inquiry would then lead to the story of how the Jews fled from Pharaoh. The reader is told this ceremony is a common feature of Jewish societies. Apparently, it was often done in the grail ceremony, too. However, if the Jewish boy failed to make the query, the patriarch was to tell the story of the flight from Egypt as though it had been asked. If one were to make the comparison to *Le Conte*, then Perceval should not have been shunned from the castle because he missed his cue. Instead, the grail king himself should have made the explanation without being asked. In the story, the king does not explain what is happening when the boy does not ask, so he is made to suffer when Perceval leaves. But this is not what is explained to the reader; there the mistake is Perceval's alone.

After the grail procession, the king and Perceval both wash their hands, as participants in the Jewish festival are supposed to do.[38] Also to be found in the grail castle are four noteworthy items that pass Perceval, and the number four is a key figure in Jewish ceremony. Four questions are to be asked by the youngest child and four cups of wine are to be drunk by each person during the feast.[39]

Such is the Jewish solution to the puzzle. Dr. Weinraub may well have a valid point, the great French poet may have been a Jew by birth, and his writings could contain Jewish elements. However, he has only two substantial arguments: first, the strange foods served do resemble those of the Jewish feast, and second, the asking ceremony connection is at least given some form of precedent. On the other hand, the problems Dr. Weinraub's conclusions create are unsatisfactory. According to Dr. Weinraub's theory the important question is to come from a young member of the household, not a guest such as Perceval. Weinraub also overstretches the limits of his evidence by pointing out there are to be four questions asked. Perceval need only make one query. There is no expected guest in the Jewish ceremony, yet Perceval is just that. Dr. Weinraub also fails to explain the grail maiden's dual personality, the Wasteland motif, or Perceval's expected promotion to the kingship of the grail castle. The grail scene cannot be entirely a Jewish ceremony.

Inevitably, the Christian and Jewish theories cannot account for certain aspects of the grail story as found in the various romances. This has been the one problem that has consistently plagued all potential solutions to the mystery of the grail for centuries. In an effort to build a hypothesis that could account for these incongruities, Dr. Weston formed her own proposal. She believed the grail ceremony began with the first day of spring, which was the new year in agricultural terms. The year, symbolized by a person, would then progressively age and finally die just in time for the spring of the following year. The sacrifice, normally by drowning, would be the cause of great mourning and would be followed by the welcome of a new year.

One of the many problems with understanding the grail has been that its aspects seem to change dramatically between writers, but with Weston there was now an explanation for it. The festival outlined previously was widespread among ancient peoples, and it is one which nearly all agrarian societies observed. However, the details of that ceremony differed a great deal. So, to follow Weston, the grail writers who followed Chrétien probably had different details about the ceremony simply because they were adapting the tales to local variations of the nature festival.[40]

The Nature Rite is indeed quite ancient and widespread. Its first civilized record is in Babylonia, where it was associated with Tammuz. It was imitated in Phoenicia and Greece as the Adonis Ritual and in Greece as the Eleusian Mysteries. There is also evidence of continuity into the Christian period. Dr. Weston cited modern examples from all over Europe to show that it has continued to the present day in various, often more humane forms.[41] The rite is so universal, it may even be seen in the celebration of Easter.[42]

Weston makes several associations between this popular cult and the Arthurian romances. First, the grail symbolizes the feminine aspect of nature as a font of nourishment and a renewer of life. Second, the spear is a phallic symbol and the other necessary component for regeneration. The fact that it is dipped in blood when not used is evidence that this connection was recognized. Blood, such as that found in the bowl that precedes the lance, represented life itself to the medieval man of Europe.[43]

These are the chief components of the hypothesis. However, there are several secondary connections to be made. The grail king is clearly a part of the symbolism. He is the new year. However, at some subsequent stage the grail king was split into two characters: a castrated middle-aged king and his ancient father.[44] The castrated figure serves as the reason for Perceval's need to assume his office; the king's personal defect being the cause for the entire kingdom going barren. As he is the male element of the kingship and the land he rules, his absence from the equation is catastrophic to the land. Dr. Weston noted that the grail king's castle was near a lake in Chrétien's romance. She believed it was a remnant of the original story; it was where the old grail king was to be drowned.[45]

Another aspect of the fertility rite involved is seen in the grail maiden, the personification of flora. She is comely during the initial ceremony, but slowly loses her hair and beauty as the year wears on. She will regain her luster on the arrival of the youthful heir.[46]

However, Dr. Weston seems more preoccupied with the grail ceremony itself. What one sees first has clear parallels to the nature ritual. The mourning, the old man, the feminine and masculine elements of nature, and the need to ask the symbolic question in order to begin spring are all features of the Nature Ritual she describes. Much of what is not so obvious also indicates the presence of her theoretical construct. The grail seems to have three main manifestations, or levels of initiation. The first is the sexual, the forms of the cornucopia and lance. The second is the life-principle represented by the blood from the lance, and the third is the "holy grail."[47] The three grail guardians—the King of Castle Mortal, the Maimed King, and the Fisher King—each stand for one aspect of the grail.[48] They could also symbolize three levels of initiation, or three aspects of spirituality. The mysteries of the ancient world were not recorded and much of the details about them have been lost, but it does seem conceivable that they, too, had three levels of initiation—physical, symbolic, and ethereal.

Many details of the grail episode can also be better understood in light of this theory. It is commonly known that initiates were never allowed to reveal the nature of the mysteries of which they were a part. Much of the grail scene is explicable if the witnesses were, as Dr. Weston put it, "simple-minded participants." That is they would have seen the ritual feasts and were made to believe they had seen supernatural wonders.[49] Dr. Weston argued that the first-time viewer or initiate would have been made to believe the symbolism of the ritual as fact. That explains the floating candles, the memory of very old men looking only forty, and a cornucopic dish.

The Nature Ritual has some convincing points, but the hypothesis has serious flaws as well. At least one scholar has taken the time to thoroughly dismantle it.[50] Here it is only necessary to make three points.

First, her theory is flawed because no one would now claim that all religious systems originated from a common source. No one would argue that the Sumerian version had any direct correlation to the Chinese rites. Yet Weston's theory seems to do so, neglecting that all the regions of the world were agricultural until the advent of the industrial revolution. The seasons were vital to life and were therefore a prime candidate for ritualization. Because of that fact, the Nature Ritual has been independently developed in many different areas of the world.

Second, the theory is useless because if the Nature Ritual was a worldwide phenomenon with one common root, there would be nothing to draw from it. There are too many potential variations in the ritual to learn anything about how it would fit into the grail legend or to separate the contributions of the authors from local customs.

The greatest flaw in the armor of Weston's theory is its lack of tangible evidence.[51] Nowhere in *Le Conte du Graal* is there a sign that the grail king has aged according to a standard calendar. Nowhere in Chrétien's poem is there a link between Perceval's uncles and the three aspects of the grail she lays out. Neither is there a correlation between the two uncles in the more traditional Welsh stories, which refrain from using "grail" and "grail king" altogether. It is also true that the various redactions consistently portray Perceval's lack of action at the grail castle as the reason the kingdom surrounding it is in waste. However, if he was to represent the new year or the spring personified, there would be no need or practical desire for a first failed attempt. Indeed, his initial failure would have made him permanently ineligible for the position. Yet this is a fundamental element of the story. Weston's arguments are not able to explain fully the grail ceremony.

Another theory seems much more grounded and practical, that of its Celtic origins. Because of the similarity of motifs and the Celtic quality of the names in the poem, Villemarqué believed that the entire episode was originally a pagan tradition given Christian window dressings by Chrétien.[52] Variations of this theory have gained many adherents. The most prominent specialists on grail studies have advocated oral beginnings in pagan Ireland and/or Wales.[53]

The argument that the grail itself and all the unreality surrounding it are based upon Celtic myths is an old one, and to some extent it is undeniable. Irish culture was being brought to the continent in the sixth, seventh, eighth, and early ninth centuries by the Irish churchmen who were invigorating Western Europe with their enthusiasm, knowledge, and inventiveness. Inevitably a part of their culture made its way into continental Europe's culture.

In the eleventh and twelfth centuries, the unique position of the Bretons in the Norman world enabled them to become the new conveyers of the Celtic heritage.[54] They were allowed to travel or settle in any Celtic speaking regions because of their translating skills and loyalty. They were also able to retain ties with their homeland. As has been seen, evidence shows they spread the name of Arthur, at least, across Europe.

The most prominent indications that the grail story is Celtic are the names, which are evident in *Le Conte du Graal* and the works that followed and imitated Chrétien's last Arthurian poem. Perceval's uncle Gornemanz de Goorz, or Goort, is listed in *Culhwch ac Olwen* as Gonemans.[55] Loholt is the French version of Arthur's son Llacheu.[56] Pelles is related to the pan–Celtic god Beli/Bíle, as is Bron, who acts suspiciously like Brân.[57] In addition, there is the usual cast of Arthurian characters: Keu, Gauvain, Yvain, and Perceval. As a proper name, Perceval has no history on the continent before 1160, when it is associated with the grail.[58] However, the name is to be found in Britain in the form Peredur as early as the British Heroic Age. His *enfance* has been compared fruitfully to Cú Chulainn, Fionn MacCumhail,[59] and even to Pryderi with less success.[60] Perceval was long ago claimed as one of the Celtic examples of the Great Fool formula.[61]

The grail itself is an indicator that there is more Celtic material in the poem than just the names, however. Chrétien himself leaves the size of the object vague. Hélinand de Froidmont, a French poet who wrote in the last decade of the twelfth century and into the early thirteenth century, described graal as "scutella lata et aliquantulum profunda," which is a "fairly deep platter" of sixty or seventy centimeters.[62] As Loomis pointed out, a sacramental wafer of fifteen centimeters in length seems odd on such a wide receptacle.[63] He suggested that something significantly larger was originally meant to be on the platter. Alternatively, the graal vessel itself may be inaccurately named.

The term Chrétien used to describe this vessel was ambiguous. Loomis postulated a reason for the several interpretations of the term *graal* by romancers who followed Chrétien. The key to understanding the confusion was in translating Middle Welsh *corn*. Loomis' words sum up the reasoning best:

> What about the Welsh word *corn* when translated in the nominative as *cors*? *Cors* could have at least five meanings: horn, corner, court, course, body; few words in Old French were more ambiguous, and the meaning had to be guessed from the context. Though we have Anglo-Norman *Lai du Cor* and *Livre de Caradoc* magic drinking horns, Schultz says that in connexion with medieval table service that "only seldom do I find any mention of the drinking horn." Since this rarity would tend to eliminate the first meaning and since corner, court, and course did not fit the context, one meaning alone remained, body. This in the sense of Corpus Christi, the sacramental wafer, though it offered difficulties, was plausible enough since there were legends about the miraculous nutritive powers of the Host. Caesarius of Heisterbach, for example, tells (Book IX: Chapter 47) how a woman lived on the Body of Christ alone. Here, then, is a possible explanation of the graal and oiste, which sustained the life of the Fisher King's father in Chrétien's poem. The two Welsh vessels of plenty, the platter and the drinking horn, have been converted as a result of the ambiguity into the Grail and the Body of Christ.[64]

The source Chrétien had used had intended *dysgyl* (horn) but gave *cors* as an alternative. The word *cors* was a proper translation of the word, but Chrétien misunderstood the religious ceremony as Christian and interpreted the word accordingly.[65] Those who followed Chrétien rendered the word the same way in the same context, but interpreted it correctly in scenes where Chrétien's poem had not influenced them. This explains the recurrence of the horn in Arthurian lore. Erec employs one and Perceval conquers the pagan Castle of Four Horns in *Perlesvaus*.[66] *Corbenic*, Castle of the Horn, is the grail castle. Loomis' explanation also helps the modern scholar to understand the nature of the Holy Grail; it was the magical horn of Celtic myth and an important part of the rituals of those Celts who still followed their pre–Roman beliefs.

Unfortunately, the rest of Chrétien's poem offers no further evidence that might allow one to learn more about this graal. Chrétien never wrote of the second visit he surely envisioned. Luckily, many of those romance authors who followed Chrétien have also left indications of direct Celtic influence, and these authors gave the grail a plethora of new abilities and functions. Along with the grail's centrality to the Unspelling motif, the various authors assigned it the power of self-movement, of being ethereal, of healing the body, and of being the source of perpetual life. All the grail romancers who followed Chrétien gave it two more traits—it symbolized kingship and cornucopia (horn of plenty).[67] The qualities of self-movement and not being physical seem to belong to a body of characteristics that are universal for mystical objects. However, the ability to heal and feed are quite possibly Celtic alone.

The property of being a limitless food-giver is a telling one. Though cornucopias may be found in a Greek and Roman context, it is not found in the early medieval world. Nowhere is Alexander the Great or Charlemagne, Solomon or Julius Caesar linked to such a vessel. It was, however, a part of the living tradition of the Celts. The existence of such objects in Welsh legend is confirmed in *Tri Thlws ar Ddeg Ynys Brydain*, or *The Thirteen Treasures of Britain*, items 3, 10, and 11. These are the Horn of Brân the Niggard, and the Crook and Dish of Rhegenydd the Cleric.[68] In Ireland the Cauldron of Dagda had essentially the same qualities.[69]

Its cornucopic quality was Celtic, as were its peripheral functions as a life-giver and healer. As will be seen shortly, the cauldron owned by Brân had the former trait, and both are similar.

Both individual functions of the grail may seem to have a reasonable enough analogue in pan–Celtic roots. However, the entire range of extant Celtic mythology contains no single item that combines both the utilities the grail seems to have. This has always been perceived as a flaw in the Celtic argument. However, from Chapter 1 one can safely assume oral antecedents for a sizable proportion of Arthurian lore. The nature of oral transmission can easily account for the multiple facets of the grail in various romances.[70] The addition of attributes to essentially the same object in the Celtic oral tradition was a not uncommon phenomenon. It was possibly due to the nature of the bard's education, which involved memorizing motifs and learning to apply them to different heroes and stories.[71] The grail's attributes are a product of similar oral handling, hence its various properties and the many different combinations of those properties.

This oral transmission could also account for the many different versions of the grail ceremony, the castle, and all the Celtic figures associated with it. The constant flexibility of themes and characters in the work of the *latimari*, *troubadours*, and *trouvères* did not encourage unity, but it did support the haphazard process of sewing together various themes, objects, and characters into a more entertaining whole,[72] much as Chrétien did in his Arthurian poetry. It also explains the remarkable disunity of the grail plots. The grail legend is the most widespread and disharmonic of the Arthurian tales that came to the continent. Each retelling produced new qualities for the grail, the grail ceremony, and the grail company. This, say the proponents of the Celtic theory, is the reason the grail is a combination of a cup of kingship, a horn of plenty, and a healer of the sick and injured.[73]

The woman who transports the grail to and fro, traditionally the grail bearer, also makes sense in this context. Chrétien himself tells us very little about her, but all those who followed were more informative. She is the bride-to-be of the next grail king and is therefore associated with that kingship. She can either be beautiful or tremendously repulsive, depending on the state of affairs of the kingdom she symbolizes. These traits are shared by a woman known symbolically as the sovereignty.[74] The generic Irish name of goddesses in this aspect was Medb.[75]

In the Celtic model, the grail castle itself has some qualities that have been linked to the underworld, where undead beings exist in a castle or on an island. The comparison is readily visible; the titles "Chastel Mortel" and "Castle of Souls" in *Perlesvaus*[76] and "Schatel le Mort" in *Lanzelet*[77] are alternative names for the grail castle. The grail king in *Diu Crône* declares himself and his compatriots dead men.[78] For the careful observer the grail castle has some clear similarities to the typical Indo-European underworld, best exampled by Hy Breasail and Hades. In the main, these common traits are:

1. Living visitors must neither fall asleep nor drink its wine or mead.
2. The castle often vanishes from this world.
3. The castle is unlocatable except by chance.
4. The inhabitants of the castle are supernatural or have extended lives.[79]

These are not attributes of a Christian legend,[80] and seem foreign to the Nature Ritual and Jewish theories. They can most easily be imagined coming from an Indo-European source, and Celtic is the most likely.

Other elements of the grail saga are strongly Celtic. There is the white stag hunt to be found in *Le Conte du Graal*, *Didot Perceval*, and *Peredur*.[81] Probably the oldest form is the Breton tale *Graelant*, where the white stag fulfills a direct function. Here the animal is a catalyst. It leads the hero to a bathing pool into another world, where a fairy maiden has come to seduce him.

> A knight called Graelant is a vassal of the king of Brittany. The Queen falls in love with him, but Graelant rejects her advances and thus antagonises her. Henceforth he is impoverished, because the jealous Queen instigated the king to withhold the pay which was his due. Graelant goes off into a nearby forest,

where he sees a white hart which he pursues, and is thus led into a clearing where a beautiful girl is bathing in a pool. He seizes her clothes, and so has her at his mercy; nevertheless, she quickly consents to his love, for she had come on purpose to meet him. Before leaving her, she makes Graelant promise not to reveal her name or identity. She gives him a horse, and a servant who henceforth supplies him with all the wealth he can want. At the Feast of Pentecost the king hold a great assembly, at which he calls on all the court to join in asserting the queen's pre-eminence in beauty. Only Graelant refuses to do so, and thus he is provoked by the Queen's wrath into saying that he knows a fairer woman than she. The king decrees he must prove this seditious claim on pain of death. But now that he has named his fairy-mistress he can no longer find her, nor will she visit him, and so he has to submit himself to the king's judgment. As this is being passed, his mistress comes riding into court and confounds all with her beauty; thus Graelant is exonerated from his rash boast. The fairy leaves the court, but Graelant rides after her, until they come to a deep river. In attempting to cross it he is nearly drowned, but his lady has pity on him, and carries him across the water to her own land. Here the Bretons say he still lives with his mistress.[82]

The hero of the tale has been identified as the sixth-century Cornouaille king Grallon, or Gradlon Mor.[83] Similar sovereignty tales have been found for the founder of Vannes (*Gereint*) and one of many eleventh- and twelfth-century León kings named Guihomarc'h.[84] The various versions of the marriage of Sir Gawain provide an alternative variation on the motif.[85]

The theme of loss and recovery of sovereignty is also Celtic and particularly British. It is in *Erec et Enide*, *Yvain*, and *Perceval*, and more apparent in their Welsh equivalents.[86] Before Chrétien's period, the theme was in nearly every British tale. Gildas, *Historia Brittonum*, and *Armes Prydein* all mourn the loss of Britain and imply the return of sovereignty to the British people. Tales of the twelfth century still speak of London as the main seat of Celtic Britain. Even *Historia Regum Britanniae*, a document of psuedohistory and invention, contains this theme.[87]

In addition, one other episode revolves around the grail story as it relates to the Celtic underworld. There is the bizarre monster Pellinore chases throughout the later romances. It has the chimaera-like characteristics of being composed of the head of a snake, the body of a leopard, the hindquarters of a lion, and the feet of a hart. It has barking pups in its belly. It sounds much like an Arthurian version of the creature Gwyn ap Nuð pursues in British myth. That animal barked like thirty dogs, or had three heads like the beast at the Gallic altar in Oberseebach.[88]

The above Insular sources and some corroboration with the themes and motifs in the grail legend do provide evidence that Perceval's adventure was influenced by contact with a Celtic environment.[89] However, the author would not pursue the argument that the Perceval story involves a journey into the other- or underworld, as Loomis and other scholars have done. Oral literature is so unsteady that such a literal conclusion would be inappropriate. The evidence does, however, corroborate an argument for a Celtic infrastructure of the tale.

Strong as the case for a Celtic basis of the tale may be, it has had its detractors and the theory does have flaws. If one is to accept it, then one must also believe that Celtic bards and French storytellers were exchanging motifs and heroes. This is not improbable, as has been seen. However, making that concession does leave the theory without any means of proving the existence of an intermediate form between the original British version on the one hand and Arthurian romance on the other.[90] Such a flaw hardly lends itself to widespread support. Some scholars claim there is no relationship between Chrétien and the Celts is beyond criticism.[91] This may be an exaggeration, but it puts the problem in perspective. Some of the evidence that was at one time considered uniquely Celtic may well have been widely known or entirely universal themes in the twelfth century.[92]

Bewildering as the diversity of these four theories of the grail's origins may seem, they all hold some truth, though the degree of each is debatable. One cannot be sure whether Chrétien was or was not a Christian. However, the New Testament explanation of the Fisher King seems the most likely.[93] The resemblances in food content of the grail castle meal seem of Jewish derivation in Chrétien, and certain motifs can be seen as Jewish. However, Rashi or his school's influence may or may not have effected the great poet. The Celtic influence on the story is undeniable, but its extent is, at best, still an unknown. The Celtic names and several themes are a certainty, and the objects of the ceremony may be Celtic, but one can go no further at this juncture. The Wasteland motif could be Celtic, but may well have come from any agrarian society.

All the grail scholars, from Professor Nutt to Professor Weinraub, have been quite open about the plausibility of their theories and others. In addition, all have provided indisputable evidence that one piece of the grail story is derived from whichever source they postulate. Bearing this in mind, it seems impossible to resist the following conclusions. First, as the name of the hero, the grail itself, and the story are originally Celtic, that strata is most likely the oldest. Second, the episodes in the romances least concerned with christianizing the grail most likely represent the earliest strata.

Finally, the many forms of the incident found in the grail romances of the continent imply a great deal of alteration. This in turn suggests that fundamental changes were made to the story because of the individual tastes and abilities of the grail story's authors and their patrons. The example of the cor-

10. Grail Theories 99

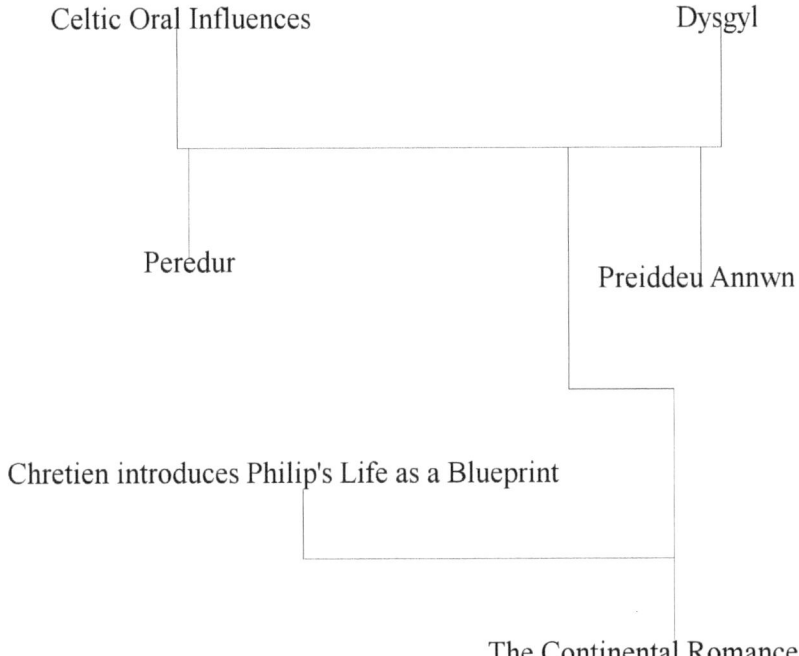

The progressive influences of the Grail Legend. There appear to have been at least three distinct sources for the ideas in all of the primary versions of the grail story. The influence of Philip of Flanders on the continent is made clear by the contrast between stories developing on the continent versus Britain. *Dysgyl* focuses on maidens and a cauldron, both non-traditional Celtic motifs. The additional stories in *Peredur* are Celtic in nature, though their inclusion does not necessarily mean they were a part of the oral body of Cltic materials.

roboration between the lives of Philip and Perceval, and Philip's other influences, much more restrictive than Marie, supports this conclusion. No one romance may be believed without strong complementary evidence from Celtic sources. The primary motive and plot of *Dysgyl* can only be guessed at through comparison to other grail versions and related material. This will be done in the next two chapters. However, the present author's hypothesis of how the grail story was transformed in the various states found in the extant redactions is roughly illustrated in the diagram above.

11
The Characters and Their Roles

In the last chapter the relative importance and constitution of each of the major grail interpretations were ascertained. It was determined that the infrastructure of the tale was Celtic. The theme of loss of sovereignty, the Christian, Celtic, and possibly Jewish motifs have been integrated into the plot successively at later stages. However, the basic nature of this Celtic infrastructure remains in doubt. The next reasonable step in better understanding the nature of the grail legend's precursor is to establish the role of all the main characters in the hypothesized original British version. The relative importance of the grail king, Arthur, Gauvain, Gonemans, Perceval's father, and Perceval will be examined thoroughly in this chapter.[1]

The figure of the grail king has been a mystery for centuries. Professor Loomis believed that he and Perceval's father were in effect the same person, Brân, split into two characters. He further believed that the tale's two themes, revenge and bespelling, had originally been interlinked. As they split, the character had to be divided in order to accommodate each of them. Perceval's father was allowed to die while attempting the former, while the invented uncle served to explain Perceval's function in the latter.[2] The volume and force of his arguments seem to have shut out or smothered many conflicting viewpoints. However, there is much to commend an opposing perspective.

The grail legend is the core element to this contention. No extant Welsh or Irish myth or tale contains a royal figure that is wounded through both legs and is waiting for the right initiate to enter his castle and ask the proper question. It would be unreasonable to believe this was ever the case. It is also unlikely that the eventual hero would not have been educated in how to successfully end the spell of the castle. Yet the harmony of all but two of the grail versions, *Peredur* and *Le Conte*, is perfect on this aspect of the story.[3] The uniformity presents a stumbling block to understanding the grail, but the knowledge developed in the last chapter about the evolution of the grail legend is the key to unraveling the grail king's character.

First, the grail king's consistent presence in the continental romances suggests that there was some prototype to the character in the hypothetical British source *Dysgyl*. Whatever the nature of the grail, he was connected to it. As has been hypothesized, he may originally have been the hero's father as well.

Second, the unanimous connection between the king and the grail castle requires that the two were fused by the last years of the twelfth century when Chrétien introduced it. The fact that so many other elements of the legend differ greatly suggests that the connection was sooner rather than later.

Third, Perceval's nonsensical question at the grail castle is useless to the story in any practical sense. There is no realism or any serious mythological precedent for it, suggesting that it was modified by Wolfram von Eschenbach (the first scholar to include it) and thereafter followed by later writers. This modification suggests that the original version of the scene was Celtic, as Loomis believed seventy years ago.

The name of the grail king figure, Pelles, was later to arrive in literature.[4] It emerges in the grail stories that follow Chrétien. The name is first to be found in *Perlesvaus*,[5] though not in the traditional role of grail king.[6] In later literature, the figure Pellinore (Beli Mawr) was given grail castle ties.[7] Another variation of the name can be seen in *Erec* as Bilis or Belin,[8] and to a pigmy monarch of the underworld.[9] These figures have no onomastic connection to Brân, as Loomis was loath to admit. However, there is a strong linguistic and literary connection among Pelles, Bilis, Belin, and the legendary personage Beli, known later as Beli Mawr. His is the name listed as the founder of a number of Welsh genaeologies.[10]

What was not known in the last generation of scholars was that Beli was the euhemerized version of a British god. In fact, his name was probably originally a part of the Celtic pantheon of gods. In regions of Ireland and Gallic France he was known as Bíle and Belenus. Archaeological evidence shows that he had an especially strong following along Hadrian's Wall under the name Belatacudros.[11] This figure is perhaps the most important for the present study.

Belatacudros was a solar figure whose primary duties also included fertility, though his appear to have been agrarian in nature, whereas Cernunnos was likely a Lord of Animals in that regard.[12] Like Cernunnos, he was associated with horns.[13] As has been seen, all these characteristics are at the center of the grail ceremony. It might then make sense why his literary descendent, Pelles, should be associated with these same qualities in their expanded forms of life, death, and renewal, which are universally integral in fertility worshipping.

The animal most commonly associated with Belatacudros was the bull, so it is unsurprising to find them buried in Arthurian romance as well. In *Perlesvaus*, Perceval destroys a giant copper bull.[14] And it appears again in *La Charrette*, a scene that occurs the night before Lancelot's crossing of the Sword Bridge. Here the hero is forced to fight a duel with a knight metaphorically associated with a bull. Upon his defeat, Jandrée appears and asks the boon that the beaten man be killed. No reason is given for Jandrée's request, nor does the scene seem to cause any consternation to the participants. The "bull" knight and Meleagant are the only two persons who die in the romance.

Loomis was also correct in believing Brân was to be associated with the grail king. He was wrong only in believing the influence was a primary one. An edited quotation from him will best point out Brân's connection to the grail literature.

> (1) In the *Didot Perceval* the Fisher King is called Bron.
> (6) In *Perlesvaus* Gauvain was present at a feast in the Fisher King's splendid castle, in company with twelve knights, "aged and grey-haired, and they did not seem to be so old as they were; for each was a hundred years old or more, and yet none seemed to be forty." Brân's followers ... passed eighty years in a great hall in the midst of abundance and joy; "none of them perceived that another was older by that time than when they came there."[15]

All of the latter details are consistently associated with Brân. Further indications of Brân's presence are simple to find. Perceval and Peredur are said to have multiple brothers, yet this conforms to nothing that is known of Beli Mawr or his progenitor Belatacudros. On the other hand, Brân does have several brothers according to British myth. Second, Brân's brother Manawydan and his father Llyr are both sea deities, suggesting he was as well before he was euhemerized. In the grail legend, the grail king spends all of his days on the lake. The reader is only told this is because the king has been wounded and can do nothing else. Certainly there is a great deal more a wounded man could do than fish, and yet his title is The Fisher King. The entire explanation sounds like the rationalization of an individual who did not have the cultural background to understand, and so found another way to make it all make sense. Thus the grail king is in reality the horned fertility god Belatacudros, who has acquired some of the features of the Brân.

Unlike the grail king, Arthur is much less of a shadowy figure in the romances. He is at first glance the centerpiece of the grail narrative. His is the court to which the hero comes and returns, it is to him that the hero goes to be knighted, and it is with his men that he proves his worth. One may note something else. As with all the continental romances, Arthur takes no active part in the quest for the grail castle. The only exception to this rule is the curious climax to *Peredur*. Arthur is clearly an unnecessary figure in the story as it can now be reconstructed.

11. The Characters and Their Roles

Gauvain is also an interesting character, but one who is hardly a necessary feature of the plot as we now have it.[16] With Arthur, he is in the final destruction scene of *Peredur* as cousin to the hero, but he is not really a part of the grail story elsewhere. Chrétien used him as a contrast to his hero.[17] He is the perfect knight and an excellent fighter, has beautiful manners, and is honorable. He is employed to show how even someone who is a standard of excellence in high society is still spiritually flawed, and how only a knight of God could approach perfect faith. Gauvain is, though, unnecessary to the plot. The three scenes in which he is the protagonist—the tournament, the encounter at his accuser's castle, and the Maiden Castle—contain very few Celtic elements and none with any historical character. On the other hand, all three scenes point out the strengths and weaknesses of the perfect knight as contrasted with the servant of God. Later writers would follow Chrétien's example, with the odd exception of *Diu Crône*.[18] One may safely conclude that Gauvain was not in the earliest Welsh literature pertaining to the grail.

Gonemans seems to be a character specific to Perceval's youth. In Welsh literature, his only scene independent of this function is in the list of Arthur's warriors in the composite tale *Culhwch ac Olwen*.[19] Even in the very late romances of *The Vulgate Version of the Arthurian Romances* and *Le Morte d'Arthur* he is mentioned almost exclusively with Percev022l. The only exception is the popular tradition that he was, as Gorlois, the one-time husband of Arthur's mother.[20] This adds no substantial data to his character.

Such a consistent correlation to Perceval makes it very likely to be an old one. The role that he plays as Perceval's tutor coupled with the Indo-European custom of uncles foster-raising their nephews makes this association a powerful one as well. Gonemans was probably a part of the story, in the role he invariably plays there.

The purpose of the hero's father is not so easily understood; the evidence points away from any certainty. As noted above, Perceval is the son of Efrawg in *Peredur*. In *Didot Perceval*, MS K of *The Continuations of Chrétien de Troyes*, *Li Chevaliers as deus espees*, and *Le Roman de Tristan en Prose*, the father is Alain.[21] In the *prologue* of Chrétien's version the character is named Bliocadran, while *Parzival* calls him Gahmuret. This shows confusion, and further study of the names warrants this initial judgment.

Welsh *Efrawg* translates as *Evrauc*, a corrupted form of the Latin for York, *Ebrauc*.[22] There was a chieftain in the Yorkshire area named Peredur, whose father was Eliffer. He lived in the last decades of the sixth century. It appears that the *Peredur* author may have connected his hero to this character, whether by tradition or otherwise. The author and the author's source for this hero apparently did not know Peredur's ancestry or confused it with his region of activity—in Latin *ab Ebrauc*—of York. It is very likely a Briton after perhaps 600 would not have known *ab* meant "of," and instead translated it or misread it as *ap*, "son of." His place of origin then became his patronymic in the Welsh form *ab Efrawg*—son of Efrawg.

Alain is a common Breton name and is found in *Culhwch ac Olwen*.[23] The Breton count Alan Fergant has a son listed there,[24] suggesting he may have been the inspiration for the Alain character, though his connection to the grail legend remains a mystery.

It is conceivable that Perceval's father was Brân. However, this theory has several flaws. Most important, the majority of the early extant grail stories either leave the father anonymous or name him Alain, a name that is clearly contemporary. The only early continental source that resists this trend is *Parzival*. As has been seen, he is there called Gahmuret. It is possible this name was stolen from Chrétien, who had a minor character named Ban de Gomeret. Otherwise that name is unknown in the record. Chrétien seems to have avoided the problem of Perceval's father altogether by beginning his poem in Perceval's youth, when he was already fatherless. Perhaps the original story did as well.

Like Lancelot in *Le Chevalier de la Charrette*, the question must be asked of Perceval, did he exist? If this question can be answered affirmatively, then when and in what capacity? Such questions are hardly necessary for the validation of the grail story as a literary source for the fifth and sixth centuries because the character Perceval may or may not have been superimposed on an earlier character. Nevertheless, an investigation of Perceval's historicity and chronological place seems compulsory to complete an onomastic study of the grail characters.

To begin with, there is the name itself. Pokorney made the observation that the word *Peredur* could be a corrupted, sub–Romanized form of *Praetor*, a Roman military title.[25] This would explain the name's first appearance within a century after the Roman departure in 410 and would allow for its latinity, antiquity, and Christian affiliation.

As to the original inspiration for the character, this has been generally identified as the King Peredur of Yorkshire, whom we have already met. He died in 580 according to the *Annales Cambriae*. It is believed he was later incorporated into the obit of the more famed king, Arthur, as is common with heroic tales.[26] Support for this belief may be found in the patronymic he is given in *Gereint* and *Peredur*, mab Efrawg. This, as has been seen, is a corruption of "from York." It is also to be found in the brother Perceval meets in *Parzival*.[27] In legend Peredur and his brother Gwrgi seem to have been inseparable. Finally, the historical Peredur probably fought against pagan Germanic peoples during a large portion of his career, just as Perceval fights against pagans in the grail romances.

However, the assumption has some fundamental flaws. Medieval Welsh bards, indeed the traditions of most ancient peoples, tend to associate lesser-known individuals with famed heroes.[28] This often includes connecting characters to heroes of Welsh tales haphazardly, as has probably been done regarding Perceval and his father.

Peredur was a fairly common name in the North during the sixth century if the extant records are any indication. Besides the man from York, there was a Peredur Arfau dur listed among the men who fought at Catraeth.[29] Peredur son of Cadwy and Peredur son of Morudd are also named for this period.[30] This gives three definite figures of the mid- to late sixth century, with a possible fourth. Any or all of these persons could have been the stimulus for Chrétien's Perceval. So one might ask a more provocative question: why were at least three kings in northern Britain during the period 540–600 named Peredur? Further, why was at least one other noteworthy personage so called?

In this era, when each generation has hundreds of thousands of people with the same given name, one may find it difficult to see why such a question is so important, even if the name was a corrupted form of a Roman title not used in a hundred years. The author must stress that it is. The pool of known individuals whose floruit was between 540 and 600 is approximately four hundred people. In this, four are named Peredur, a name not occurring in records before or after that for some time. After a watershed around 600, the name virtually disappears until after 1000. Someone was the motivation for the popularity of the name, and the author should like to propose that it was a Peredur that predated the namesakes who are known to us. This, as was seen in Chapter 1, was a time of radical changes in the British language, and no poetry and little legend has survived from that period to this day. If there had been a Peredur of note from that period, there very well would have been no record of him historically.

Of course, it is also possible that conventional wisdom is correct and the Peredur of romance did not develop from a British heroic figure. However, if this is so what was the reason for the popularity of the name Peredur in the latter half of the sixth century? The theory that there was an earlier inspiration is simply the easiest and most reasonable given the data at hand.

It has been seen in this chapter that there are grounds for believing a Peredur may have existed as one of Arthur's *teulu*. On the other hand, the tendency of heroic age literature to add originally foreign persons into the orbit of the most popular king makes it quite possible that he was not.

From the above discussion it may also be seen that a pre–600 hero, probably named Peredur, was associated with a pagan practice involving the god Belatacudros. This connection was likely in *an historical* or a pseudohistorical source. In this scheme Gonemans served as the hero's tutor. Gauvain either originally had a similar tale attached to him or was a late and artistic addition to Peredur's story. Arthur and Peredur's father were likely late arrivals to the tale. The absence of these latter two characters in the two following chapters will serve to reinforce the theory of their absence in *Dysgyl*.

12

Literary Tools for Supplementary Material

In the previous two chapters, it has been determined that the grail story as it may be reconstructed is a Celtic narrative. It involves a Christian hero, the Celtic god Belatacudros, Gonemans the tutor, and possibly Gauvain. The longer it existed, the more Celtic motifs, Christian and possibly Jewish influences were superimposed upon it. When it came into the hands of continental authors, they also made their marks on the story. Chief among them was Chrétien. Despite all that has been determined, little is yet known concerning the source or sources of the grail story. The definition of this source will be the objective of the present chapter. I'll now review and discuss the independence, in part or whole, of the various early redactions of the grail story of Chrétien. This study will entail reviewing the various episodes of *Dysgyl* as are found in most of the earliest and most reliable versions.[1]

The hero-to-be is raised in seclusion until he is sent to or learns of Arthur and his court. Deciding that is the best place for him to be, he sets out and finds the king without difficulty. There he learns that the Red Knight has stolen a cup from Arthur and is threatening the kingship. The hero kills the knight and takes his armor, sending the cup back to the court. With its return, he restores Arthur's honor. He himself does not go back, but rides on and finds two uncles who each give him advice and training in arms. Next he comes upon a besieged maiden, whom he rescues. An assortment of varied adventures follows, culminating in the kingship of the grail castle in the Chrétien tradition, or the destruction of its possible prototype in *Peredur* and its related texts. Amidst this motley barrage of adventures are several episodes with little or no value. Some of the most memorable are the incident with the maiden in the tent, Keu's defeat by Peredur, and the scene with the crow, its blood, and the snow matching his beloved's hair and face. Episodes such as these do not appear to be used to serve Philip's interests in any way.

Peredur itself has been called a group of confused "reminiscences of French and Anglo-Norman texts."[2] Considering the scholarly view that twelfth-century Arthurian influences were fluid, however, such a concrete opinion is now considered obsolete. It is more likely that *Peredur* was the result of *latimari* working in Wales but with access to north British, French, Anglo-Norman, Welsh, and Breton sources. With all that information and so many literary minds at work in a small area, it likely was bubbling with activity.

A debate as to the year of composition is still under way.[3] The dating of the manuscripts and the "proper" story's contents remain points of contention.[4] Even the story's conclusion is not generally acknowledged; it is either Peredur's marriage to the empress, as in *Peniarth 7*, or the destruction of the witches, such as one finds in the balance of the manuscripts.[5] The textual history is so difficult that scholars have generally avoided any oblique statements regarding it, so that nothing can be learned there, either. However, some points are generally accepted about the tale.

Four manuscripts feature *Peredur*. These have been dated from no later than the early fourteenth to the late fourteenth centuries. The orthography is a different matter. The most recent, *The Red Book of Hergest*, has traces of twelfth-century spellings.[6] This realization indicates both that the find represents a copy of an original and that this story has a manuscript history dating from the same century as Chrétien.

Until comparatively recently, Chrétien had been called the source of *Peredur* and the other Arthurian stories in the *Mabinogion* because of the romantic aspects and the general differences that all three have in contrast to the more traditional British stories. As Dr. Mac Cana has recently pointed out, however, such observations carry no weight.[7] There are sections where the *Peredur* author does agree with Chrétien, but there are many when he does not and by the nature of the material its source must have been Celtic.[8] The representatives of this latter group are to be found in the episodes involving Angharad Law Eurawg, snakes, giants, dead men rising from a tub, an Addanc, and a grail ceremony featuring a man's head.[9] These are all unknown in other grail romances, and in continental works in general, yet they are here present and occupy a large part of the story's plot. *Peredur* is, without doubt, independent of Chrétien; if it cannot be claimed it is free of continental influences.

Didot Perceval was another early redaction of the grail story. It was written between 1190 and 1212,[10] possibly by Robert de Boron. The manuscript history is difficult as there are only two versions ("D" and "E"), and these are often widely divergent. However, it does imply both are degenerate versions of their common original. The differences between them are normally attributed to Chrétien's influence on "D." "D" is much shorter and less coherent; indicating much of the original tale was lost in the manuscript tradition. "E" looks as if a later copyist tried and failed to resolve the conflicts between the original story and the poems of Chrétien de Troyes and Wauchier. In any event, "E" is generally considered the less corrupt of the two.[11]

As the extant manuscripts have it, *Didot Perceval* is a mediocre literary piece because of its consistent inconsistencies and limited creativity. As a text for better understanding Chrétien's matière and with it *Dysgyl*, however, it is a stroke of good fortune. The original author was not an innovator. The fact that details and, on occasion, episodes are dependent on no known sources has led many scholars to the conclusion the *Didot Perceval* had access to traditional sources.[12] In fact, at one time it was considered the source for Chrétien and those who followed. But this cannot be true because of the degeneration of the names found in Chrétien. On the other hand, there is a good deal to show that the story was also influenced by a version that predated Chrétien.

Episode "C" describes a stone that splits and causes all the enchantments of Britain to cease. The stone is comparable to the mound Pryderi relaxes on prior to his kingdom's disaster. The episode is found nowhere in Arthurian literature before this point, though it has been seen to be a part of the Celtic kingship cult in Chapter 5.

Episode "E" revolves around Perceval's visit to the Chessboard Castle. It is entirely absent from the other earliest versions of the grail legend on the continent but does have a parallel in *Peredur*.

Episode "H" describes Perceval's fight at a ford with an Urbain. Just as the hero is gaining the advantage, he is attacked by nine crows and chances to kill one. It is here that one learns the birds are his opponent's mistress and her maidens. This transformation can only be found in two other sources. These are the *Vita Merlini* (1130s), where Morgan does so, and *Breuddwyt Rhonabwy* (1200s), where Owain and Arthur's soldiers fight as birds. It should also be noted at this juncture that nine women with one male leader is a peculiarly Celtic combination. More will be said on that later.

Several scenes in *Didot Perceval* have no precursor on the continent, and do not appear to have been Celtic motifs. On the other hand, they definitely make the most sense in a Celtic context; they fall in line with their customs alone. This again suggests that source for the information there was British and either prior to Chrétien or his source without many of the Philip-influenced changes and cuts. In any event, *Didot Perceval* is a tenable source for Celtic information independent of Chrétien.

Parzival is chronologically the next version of the romance. It was begun in or after 1200 and was completed by or during 1210[13] by Wolfram von Eschenbach. Wolfram was widely held by his contemporaries to have been the greatest literary mind of his era and has been called "one of the greatest poets of all time."[14]

Wolfram von Eschenbach claimed to have had a written source whose author was a Provencal singer named Kyôt. This Kyôt is said to have translated the material from an Arab manuscript and wrote it down himself. If Wolfram's story was true, it would give what he wrote a great deal of credibility. However, a survey of *Parzival* and its French precursors makes it evident that his chief source was probably *Le Conte*.[15] There are also several instances where Wolfram gives what could be information directly from Welsh sources. The revenge motif, which has no continental Arthurian antecedent, appears in the form of Lahelin. He is introduced as the thief of Perceval's inheritance.[16]

Other details are noteworthy. The place-name Sanguin used by Chrétien is given a (presumably) closer rendering as Sabîns, the Severn River.[17] In addition, he takes great pains to explain that Keie is a worthy man, as in *Culhwch ac Olwen* and "Pa Gur," despite Chrétien's attitude toward him. The life of his father, here Gahmuret, seems to be drawn from whatever source the *Peredur* author used.[18]

The clearest example of Wolfram's independence from Chrétien is Gahmuret's episode with a dark lady. At the moment he takes her virginity, he is declared her husband and lord.[19] This is paralleled in ancient Celtic society and is Pictish and matrilineal in nature.[20] In these cultures, the women owned the land. Upon marriage, men were allowed to govern it. And, in all Celtic societies, the simple act of sex could be a form of marriage.[21] On the other hand, sex and marriage can hardly have been an expected combination in the high society of thirteenth-century Germany. There a sexual relationship might well be secretive, marriages were arranged, and inheritance was strictly ruled by the laws of primogeniture.

The latter half of Book 12 and the three that follow it are without literary antecedent and seem to finish, coherently, the poem that Chrétien did not. In these sections Gauvain's episode at Castle Marvelous bears the most unmistakable signs of celticity. There the testing bed of *Le Conte du Graal* is made to move like the couch in Cu Roi's castle.[22] Later Gauvain notices a magical pillar inside the castle, much like the one found inside the hall of Lug. These are not isolated incidents; they denote a consistent interaction between the romances and Irish and Welsh myth that is not in Chrétien. They also argue for another source independent of him, and our only clue as to that source is Kyôt.

In the nineteenth century, opinion prevailed that Kyôt was the alternative source that Wolfram employed in beginning and finishing the poem. However, the thinking of scholars over the past fifty years has been to disbelieve Wolfram's words and attribute them to the same etiquette of noncreativity that inspired Chrétien's prologues. The fact is, Kyôt is named as a Provencal, but we are told he wrote in French. Worse still, Kyôt's source is said to have been an Arab manuscript. This would suggest that the Arthurian legend had a good foothold in Muslim culture by 1200, less than a decade after it was introduced onto the continent and into a society that had no fascination with Arthur or Christ, and from which no extant works on the subject have emerged. Wolfram's claim is, to say the least, highly unlikely. There are other problems. Kyôt is described as a singer, yet the source Wolfram used for *Parzival* must have been massive and literary, not lyrical. The only known entertainer of that era and by that unusual name had interests widely separated from that of the Holy Grail. The Kyôt referred to in *Parzival* can not be reasonably seen as Wolfram's source and was possibly the butt of a joke.

Perlesvaus is another of the French romances composed in the wake of Chrétien's poem. It is a prose romance that was probably composed between 1191 and 1212 or 1220 to 1225.[23] The author is unknown, as is the story's relationship to the other grail versions. However, four points have generally been agreed upon. First, the author begins his tale where Chrétien left off and attempts to finish the story. Second, the tendency toward brutality in the book is not the product of an unsound mind, but of a man aware of his audience. Its popularity supports this conclusion. Third, the story was heavily influenced by Glastonbury. Finally, it antedates the *Vulgate* version. *Perlesvaus* has Perceval for the hero, while *Vulgate* introduces Galahad, a figure entirely unknown before then.

These last two points are crucial. If *Vulgate* appeared before *Perlesvaus* this romance would be useless for better understanding the genesis of the Perceval story. *Vulgate* is a poor composite of previous romances, and its publication marks the end of useful literature in the current author's historical studies. Second, as Glastonbury is known to have affected *Perlesvaus*, grail specialists have been loathe to place any confidence into the romance. As has been seen, the monastery is known to have fabricated stories for its own ends, and this romance was clearly written some time after it had begun to bring the Arthurian legend into its orbit.

Along with the author's blatant influence by Glastonbury, much of *Perlesvaus* is doubtless to be found in the pages of Chrétien and possibly two of his continuators. However, there are indications that another source existed, and that it was British in origin. In *Perlesvaus*, Guinièvre dies prematurely on hearing of the death of her son. This represents an alternate tradition, and one which is very likely more accurate.[24] The grail castle is described as "Castle of Souls" and "Castle of Four Horns,"[25] one an epithet for the fortress in *Preiddeu Annwn* (below) and the other an accurate description of the grail castle, as Chapter 9 demonstrated.

There are also some scenes do not belong in a romance created entirely by monks or under the influence of Chrétien's work. The action of Perceval's ally King Gurguran is a case in point. Upon learning that his son is dead, he boils the body: "et quant la char de son fil fu cuite, il la fet detrenchier au plus meneument qu'il pot, et fet mander toz ses homes de sa terre, et en done a chascun tant com la char dure; And when his son's flesh was cooked, he had it cut up into the smallest pieces possible, and summoned all the people of his land and gave each one a piece until all the flesh was gone."[26]

Such actions do not sound Christian. The cooking and eating of one's son would not be invented by any sane churchman to further the holiness of Glastonbury or Perceval. It does, however, sound like a possibility in a newly or nominally converted region. It is also possible the image was intended for use as propaganda, whether against pagans of the fifth century or Muslims of the twelfth.

And again:

> Il fet aprester une grant cuve et amener emi la cort, et fet amener les xi chevalier[s], et lor fet les chiés couper en la cuve et tant saignier com il pourent rendre de sanc; et puis fet les cors oster et les chiés, si que il n'ot que le sanc tot pur en la cuve. Aprés fet desarmer le Seignor des Mores, et amener devant la cuve ou il avoit plenté de sanc.
>
> He bade that a great vat be made ready and brought into the middle of the court; then he called for the eleven knights to be led forward, and had them beheaded in the vat and left to bleed as much blood as they could. Then he had their heads and bodies thrown out so that only the pure blood remained in the vat. Then he called forth the Lord of the Fens to be disarmed and led before the vat with its great fill of blood.[27]

This action is done in Perceval's presence. Both of these scenes in no way served the purpose of raising Glastonbury or Perceval's prestige, and thus were probably not invented by any author of the twelfth or thirteenth centuries. The actions are neither in Chrétien nor those who followed him, suggesting the original source for this information was British, regardless of how exaggerated the actions might be.

The previous group represents all the grail romances believed to have been written around 1200. However, Heinrich von dem Türlin's *Diu Crône* may also be considered a useful work in spite of its later composition (1200–1250) and conglomerate nature. To quote Spaarnay:

> On the whole, one gets the impression that Heinrich created very little out of whole cloth, that much of his material came from lost sources, but that he made his own combinations and exercised considerable freedom in the invention of detail.[28]

Such invention can be seen in the various creatures that appear throughout the book. However, distinct elements in his romance suggest a source other than those that had previously been written in the Arthurian milieu. For one, Türlin resisted the motifal personality of Keu as a boaster — he treats him with respect. The author allows him control of Arthur's army[29] and speaks as if to save his reputation.[30] Türlin's kind words for Keu betray an antiquity to be found in the oldest Welsh poems.

Also contained in Türlin's prose is a scene reminiscent of "Pa Gur?" It includes an indolent gatekeeper who plays the role of Glewlwyd and Gauvain who plays Arthur. In this instance, Gauvain is denied entrance into the castle.[31] One more quirk in the plot has been touched upon earlier. Instead of the hints that Gauvain was once the protagonist of the story, he is so in *Diu Crône*. This element of the romance either predates the other grail stories or was the creation of Türlin based on the degree to which he is a part of the other grail romances.

Two other redactions of the grail phenomenon should be mentioned here. The first is the four *Continuations of Le Conte du Graal*, and the other is the *Vulgate*.[32] Both are later versions and are generally agreed to have drawn nearly entirely on extant grail redactions. Specifically, the *First Continuation* (1191–1200) includes Gauvain as the main character, which may or may not indicate a British source, and a more Celtic description of the grail castle. It also includes an entirely unrelated romance of the Breton hero Caradoc.[33] All the other continuators continued to reuse Celtic motifs, occasionally adding foreign characters. The third has Perceval mending the sword broken in Chrétien.

The *Vulgate* was written between 1215 and 1230. It is possible, but not certain, that the sections similar to *Lanzelet* derive from tradition.[34] The only new developments one finds are the extended Lancelot/Guinièvre adultery as one finds it in Malory and the emergence of Galahad as the grail hero. These are progressive changes and have no British precursor.

As the present state of knowledge and understanding of the grail romances stand, six show clear influence from a British source. They are consistent enough to give a general idea of what the story may have looked like before Chrétien wrote. The hero is taught horsemanship, swordsmanship, and general manners by his maternal uncles. He is sent to Arthur's court and proves his worth there with the Red Knight.

From this point there are two separate versions. At one extreme is the conversion or death of pagans, and the destruction of various pagan objects culminating in the murder of nine witches at Caer Lloyw. This one is most clearly articulated in *Peredur*. At the other end of the spectrum, represented by *Le Conte*, is the hero's moral development from a naïve boy to the highest standard of Christian knighthood.

The common original of such varied stories would seem difficult to visualize. However, in Chapter 8 it was seen that Philip's life was the basis for the adventures of Perceval in *Le Conte*. It has also been seen that Chrétien was the starting point for all the continental grail romance writers. Unfortunately, *Peredur* is an orally based tale and is only loosely organized. For this reason, it is difficult to make out much of the original meaning of the ceremony with it alone. The conclusion of *Peredur* possesses two clues as to its significance: the locating of and destruction of nine witches and their cauldron.

Nine is a universally important number, though its connection to witches here is specifically Celtic. It is first witnessed in a Paleolithic drawing at Cagul, "The Tablet of Larzac" and the writings of Pomponius Mela. The destruction of witches or pagan priestesses compares directly to *Preiddeu Annwn*, "Pa Gur?," and the *Vitae Samsoni*. *Preiddeu Annwn* shows that the primary function of this coven was to maintain a cauldron.[35] The cauldron is most fully understood by its description in *Tri Thlws ar Ddeg Ynys Brydain*. A brief description of each of these stories and objects will prove useful in forming a better awareness of the grail.

The work of Pomponius Mela is from the first century. He recorded nine witches living on the island of Sena off France's coast.[36] The artwork in Cagul adds to this. It is pre–Roman in origin and portrays nine women dancing around a male figure who has horns coming from his head. It is apparent from the picture that the women are worshipping either a pagan deity or a personification of that deity.

The archaeology of Larzac produces more data in the form of a lengthy inscription buried with a woman who lived during the first century.[37] Few things are certain as to the nature of the writing or the people who wrote them. However, they were clearly familiar with a Celtic religion, and the ten persons involved seem to have formed one coven.[38] These individuals were involved in an intricate set of relationships described in familial terms and most likely represented nine sorceresses and one male master.

Preiddeu Annwn is the first British poem with this motif; it is a part of the pseudo–Taliesin collection. The work has been dated to between the ninth and twelfth centuries by Dr. Marged Haycock and to 850–1150 by Professor Sims-Williams,[39] both on purely linguistic grounds. The poem itself is cryptic, focusing on praise for Arthur's raid to the island of Annwn. However, several things may be pointed out that have a bearing on the current discussion. First, the nine women listed here are called priestesses, and not witches. This implies respect for them and with it a more intimate knowledge of their activities. Second, the women watch over a cauldron. In the course of the poem, one learns that Arthur and his men have destroyed the cauldron and presumably killed the women as well. The cauldron has the quality that "Ny beirw bwyl llwfyr ny ry tyghit; It will not boil the food of a coward, it has not been so destined."[40] A magical cauldron has already been associated with the grail legend; perhaps its literary predecessor was a standard object in a coven's ceremonies.

A second native British piece that has the nine witches motif is "Pa Gur?," to be found in *The Black Book of Carmarthen*. Sims-Williams dates the poem to 1100–1160 based on the language of other, better understood selections in the manuscript. The work itself is largely a monologue by Arthur to a gatekeeper, Glewlwyd. In it is contained a list of deeds by the members of his band. Chief of these is Cei, who is credited with killing the nine witches of Ystawingun.

Brittany also made a contribution to this theme. Books 26 and 27 of the *Vita Samsoni* consist of a conflict between a sorceress, called *theomacha*, and the saint. Before Samson commits her to God, she reveals that she is one of nine sisters led by a mother and that they all hide in the forest and practice their "pagan" religion. The information from which this anecdote and the life itself derive is considered to be nearly contemporary. The anonymous writer claimed to have received his knowledge through the nephew of the nephew of Samson himself. Because of this, the name-forms, and a lack of ninth-century priorities, it has been dated to the early seventh century by some.[41] All that can be certain, though, is that it dates to no later than the ninth century.[42]

The *Branwen* tale has the cauldron motif touched upon in *Preiddeu Annwn*. It comes in the same manuscripts as *Peredur*, and therefore the manuscript dating of thirteenth to fifteenth centuries and the orthography of pre–1200 for *The Red Book of Hergest* applies here as well. On historical grounds, the dating has been quite varied, but no earlier than 1050.[43]

The pertinent details are that during the course of a fight between the Britons under Branwen's brother Brân and the Irish under Matholwch, the British destroy a special cauldron. It is able to return the dead back to life at the cost that the resuscitated are mute. The former quality we have seen as one of the grail's attributes. The latter would explain what the romance writers have often said about the age and silence of the inhabitants of the grail castle.

Finally, there is the cauldron of *Tri Thlws ar Ddeg Ynys Brydain*. It is called the Cauldron of Dyrnwch and will only boil the food of a brave man.[44] This is almost exactly the same quality as that already noted for the cauldron in *Preiddeu Annwn*. The list itself may well be quite old, including as it does primarily heroic-age kings and no man who lived about 650.

The early stories listed previously, Pomponius' testimony, and the two archaeological remains together reveal a great deal despite the limited amount

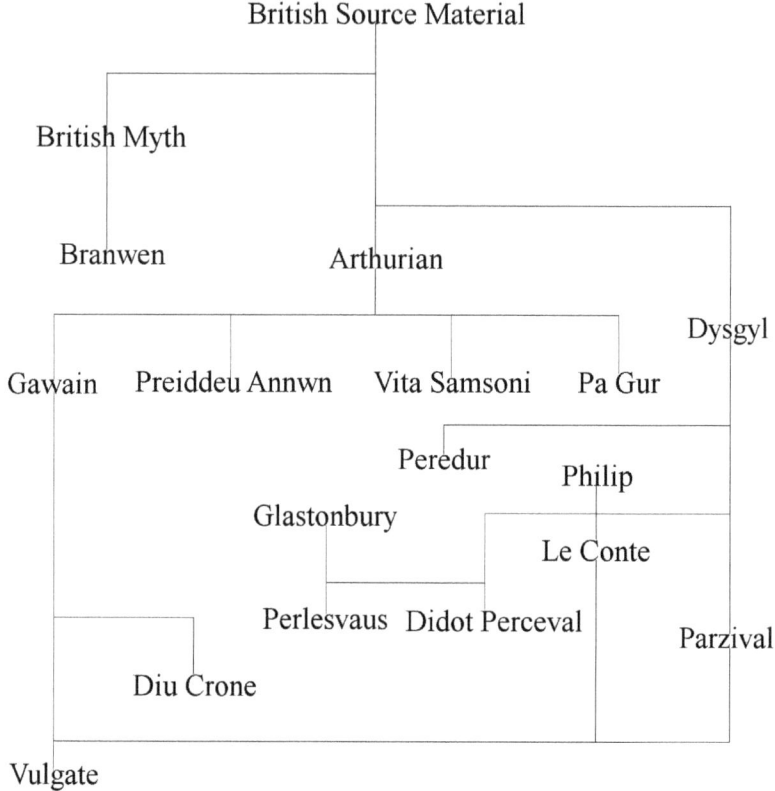

A traditional view of the development of the common grail saga. Note the assumption that all materials were developed from a large, undefined body of British materials and seem to have branched off into three distinct approaches to the subject.

of information each source has to offer. First, it may be determined that a group of nine priestesses, with a leader, formed cults before and well into the Christian era. Second, *Preiddeu Annwn* tells us that the maidens were the keepers of a cauldron. The third lesson one takes is that the cauldron's function was to cook food, but it will only for non-coward. A peculiarity should also be noted. The theft or destruction of the cauldron and the killing of the priestesses is associated solely with characters of the fifth and sixth centuries, Arthur, Peredur, and Samson. This is an observation that will be returned to in the next chapter.

This survey of the various elements of the final, largely unintelligible scene in the *Peredur* narrative explains much of what may have been the background for the story. A brief history of *Dysgyl* should serve to clarify this literary strand of the legend.

12. Literary Tools for Supplementary Material

At some time well before 1200, the story of the theft or destruction of a cauldron, normally associated with Arthur or one of his men, was now specifically attached to Perceval. Beginning in 1191, Chrétien would modify the story to match his patron Philip's life, and the continental writers who followed him would do so as well. This included mistranslating "horn" into "the body of Christ." It also involved changing the original cauldron, or medieval Welsh platter, into the Holy Grail that held the blood of Christ. The raid on a coven of witches was softened into the hero's acceptance into a holy fellowship. Added in was something that could only have come from Philip's poet Chrétien, that all Perceval had to do to win that honor was ask a question. That was all Philip had needed to do.

Still, though, the hints remain of a non–Christian origin. As has been seen, magical horns permeate the grail legend, as do cornucopias and the property of healing. In *Perlesvaus* and *Didot Perceval* especially, the destruction of pagan centers of worship are prominent. *Peredur* has all the details, but the story itself is confused and the episodes are probably misaligned. It is probably for that reason alone that *Peredur* has not been considered the primary source for the grail legend. That is unfortunate, as it has held the key to the mystery behind the grail all these centuries. See family tree illustration of *Dysgyl* on the previous page.

13

Religion in Fifth and Sixth Century Britain

The contents of the last five chapters represent the sum of mainstream arguments and ideas regarding the nature of the grail and *Le Conte du Graal*'s author. Scholars have determined Chrétien was either a Christian or a Jew writing for a Christian audience. Chrétien's patron desired to see the highest Christian ideals observed, and this Chrétien catered to admirably. The genius in the lines is the result of the master poet himself. The grail story as Chrétien found it was the product of an old source. It has also been seen that many of the grail romances that followed him were influenced by his source as much as by him. This common source is best represented by *Peredur*. As has been seen, variations of the climactic scene there only involve three characters and one group — Peredur, Gwalchmai, Arthur, and witches/maidens — and they belong between about 500 and 600. The dating of the source of *Peredur*, on the other hand, may only be determined at well before 1200. How much before 1200 is yet to be explored, but as the figures involved in the destruction of nine priestesses and a magical cauldron all fall in the century before 600, and clearly the tale involved religion, it seems the best way of furthering our knowledge of what may originally have happened is to examine the historical context of post–Roman Britain. The process should produce results that will supplement and perhaps add to our earlier findings.

Christianity was not a cornerstone of British society when the legions left forever in the fifth century; it had only recently become an accepted part of society. One may recall that the lowly officer Constantine was chosen as emperor, presumably out of a long list of higher ranking candidates, because of his religion just as much as his name. Without a doubt the Celtic beliefs were still quite strong in the early fifth century; most British temples survived for some decades after the Romans left, indicating continued public use.[1] The most cited evidence for the strength of the Celtic religion into Christian times is the construction of a Nodens temple in 364. Dr. Ross has also shown a distribution of votive shafts, wells, and sanctuaries associated with the Celtic religion, all dating to the fifth century.[2] There is also less easily covered but equally strong evidence for a pagan rural revival from the late fourth century and the early fifth century in Britain.[3]

In fact, Christianity was not as thoroughly entrenched in much of Europe as is generally believed. Pagans held prefectures in Italy into the 380s, and the Germanic tribes in Britain would not turn to Rome for religion until the close of the sixth century. Many areas on the perimeter of the Roman world were pagan or partially pagan when Emperor Honorius issued his refusal to help the British people in 410. With this in mind, it is clear that understanding where and how deeply affected the Christian regions were will prove invaluable in the current study.

Historically, it is uncertain how or at what point Christianity was introduced to the island. However, the religion did exist on some scale before the year 313. Christians there suffered with the rest of the empire until Galerius issued his Edict of Toleration.[4] Thereafter, the followers thrived. By 410, Christianity would not have existed for an entire century as an officially recognized religion, yet the Roman Empire had a Christian as its leader.

Within another century it was widespread, and there is evidence of its existence in every major British kingdom. Christian signs are more focused in the modern counties of Cumberland, Yorkshire, Devonshire, and Wiltshire— the remaining British areas where Roman control had been strongest. Conversely Gwynedd, Dyfed, and Lothian were not so romanized and show a more limited Christian influence. The resulting period of christianization became known as the Age of Saints. Many of the *vitae* speak of the conversion of natives and kings during the sixth century.[5]

The politico-religious situation inside Celtic Britain during the fifth and sixth centuries was thus an unstable mixture of Christianity and Celtic paganism. However, throughout the period Christianity can clearly be seen to take the ascendancy. After 600, there are no records of pagans amongst the Britons or Picts. On the other hand, the worship of Celtic gods, in one form or another, persisted throughout the Middle Ages. The "devil cults" of Britain during the next few centuries bore two striking resemblances to what is known of the Celtic cults. First, archaeological evidence points to the worship of a Celtic horn-god named Cernunnos. He survived as the "Old Hornie" of vernacular Middle English and was worshipped by black magic groups during the medieval period.[6] This figure is now known as the devil in modern parlance. Second, the sabbaths of the "dark religion" are identical to those of the Celtic holidays.[7] Clearly, the "cults" of ancient Britain maintained a continuity through the fifth and sixth centuries.

With the knowledge that both Christianity and Celtic cults were active around 500, and that no archaeological record of cults exists after 600, one may make some general conclusions about them. First, the state of the worshippers. There are three possibilities. The adherents of the Celtic religion could have been socially and economically inferior to their Christian contemporaries and therefore their record is nearly invisible. It is also possible that their sites were isolated and have yet to be found by modern archaeology.

Second, and perhaps more important, one may use the knowledge of continental history to hazard a guess that Christianity was a passive force behind the military suppression of the remaining pagan sects. This conclusion has a surprising amount of support. Here the *Vitae Martini*, written by Sulpicius Severus with first-hand access to the original material[8] will serve as a guide.

Traditionally, Martin began his career as a military man and only went into religion when called by a vision. Once there, he actively converted pagans and destroyed pagan properties. Sulpicius himself lists five instances where Martin personally destroyed pagan shrines.[9] He also tackled rural pagan remnants by establishing village churches. Martin was not an isolated zealot. Several instances of other persons taking part in similar acts confirm it was not uncommon. Praetorian Prefect Cynegius destroyed a number of temples.[10] Augustine noted the congregation at Colonia Sufetana overthrew a statue of Hercules.[11] It is also known that Victricius and his successors established rural churches in order to provide a more thorough Christian training.[12] Inevitably, the church condoned all forms of conversion.[13]

Conversion was made one other manner: political force. In the 480s and 490s, Clovis claimed Christianity as his religion and allied himself to the Roman church. For that, the bishop gave him the authority to conquer any non–Christian or Arian kingdom that he chose to attack. Clovis made good use of his blank check and acquired much of what is modern France in service to the church.

According to legend, only two figures commanded equal power in early Britain — Arthur and Gwrtheyrn. Whether or not one of them was responsible for silencing Celtic cults, the fact remains that men in the fifth century may well have had that power and that such activity would accord well with political events on the continent. It is also known that Britain and Gaul were economically and culturally tied throughout the period, so that events on the continent could have affected what happened in Britain.

As has been seen, *Peredur* has the most historically likely storyline for the grail story. In conjunction with what has been deduced here, we might again approach one of the more important questions about the grail. What

13. Religion in Fifth and Sixth Century Britain

of the final scene, where Peredur, Arthur, Gwalchmai, and the rest of the *teulu* destroy the nine witches and their cauldron? The author of *Peredur*, it has been said, looks "as if he were throwing in his hand."[14] While this may be true, it is also possible that the intended original audience would have understood the story fully given the previous episodes that are in *Peredur*. The three figures may early on have been associated with the destruction of pagan centers of worship. It has been seen that *Perlesvaus* and *Didot Perceval* give Perceval's accomplishments a story form, though in their essence they give him the precise role that has been attributed to Martin and several lesser known individuals on the continent.

One might also hypothesize that the hero of the story represents a captain or chieftain who reduced pagan sanctuaries in the fifth and sixth centuries. It should be noted here that *Culhwch ac Olwen* assigns Gwalchmai the killing of the Black Witch who lived in the North. There is no reason to believe this was not a traditional story long before it was in the tale. In the *First Continuation*, Arthur is also recorded as warring against a Brun, for what that is worth.[15]

The scenario worked as follows. One man (presumably Arthur) gained a period of ascendancy and used his power to demolish Celtic temples and expand his territories much as Clovis had. Alternatively, the continental practice of local extermination was brought to the island and soon became established there as well. If the anti-pagan campaign was due to Arthur's actions, it may be dated roughly between the last quarter of the fifth and the first third of the sixth centuries. If the activities were more vigilante in nature, they might have taken place at any time between the turn of the fifth century and about the year 600. After that, the practitioners of the Celtic cults were forced to conduct their rituals in secret, which is why no archaeological evidence of them exists after this time.

14

Motifs and Details: Clues of Celtic Origins

The preceding chapters have outlined the main characters of *Le Conte du Graal*. Several have well-defined roles that are integral and consistent throughout the different redactions of the grail. Together, they corroborate the theory of a stable prototype and tie together many seemingly detached fragments in the grail legend. The examination has also helped to articulate a plot with a more carefully defined objective than any one extant grail romance contains. However, elements of the legend still remain unexplained and detached from that objective. These leftovers are divisible into two groups. The first collection is one whose motifs and materials are congruent with both pretenth-century British and twelfth-century French culture. Second, the purely historical elements of the poem make up a small but significant portion of the poem. This chapter will survey the former of these divisions in order to lay the groundwork for a written source for the grail legend. In the process, it is hoped to show that many of the motifs and themes could be either from Chrétien's medieval world or Britain from the fifth to the ninth century. In every instance they seem more natural in the latter context. The concepts of marriage, hospitality and protection, and the dark-age hall and Celtic testing bed are all found in the rhymed passages of Chrétien. These are only the most conspicuous of many such examples.

The most obvious clue that something hitherto unseen lies beneath the surface of Chrétien's poem is found in the marital rituals of *Le Chevalier de la Charrette*. However, the traits of the custom are clearer, and examples of the phenomenon more abundant, in *Le Conte*. In *La Charrette*, Gauvain is given one insinuated partner, and Lancelot, several. In the grail poem, Gauvain pursues two women, and Perceval, one.[1]

It can also be gathered that the form of temporary union that is to be found in Chrétien is strictly Celtic. Sexuality had no place in Philip's biography and confession. Nor is the Ovidian concept of love complemented by heroes running around and indiscriminately finding new lovers. Lancelot, Gauvain, and Perceval's relationships are best explained as temporary Celtic marriages such as those outlined in Chapter 4.

Another scene that has an analogue to *La Charrette* is the perilous bed. After entering Galloway and gaining entrance to Castle Marvelous, Gauvain is warned not to sit on a particular bed inside the castle walls. In typical Arthurian fashion, Gauvain finds the bed and promptly lies on it. There follows a brief series of tests. First, the bed cords give out a shrill noise and bells ring. Then the entire hall gives out a noise and the windows fly open. Bolts and arrows follow, and many of them pierce Gauvain. The ordeal concludes with the attack of a lion. Gauvain survives it all[2] and is promptly named lord of the castle. Only then is it revealed that the inhabitants there are his kin.

Gauvain's bed test is preceded by a strange noise that seems to have a direct correlation with the kingship ceremony. Lia Fail, for instance, was said to let out a scream when the chosen ruler of Ulster sat on it. Many kingship stones had this tradition. The only real change is that in this instance it has been moved from the last to the first element of the story and is used to warn the hero of the impending danger. Chrétien had no way of knowing the significance of the scream and so was left to do his best to make sense of it.

In the Cart Castle of *La Charrette*, Lancelot is given a similar, odd test. It involves a flaming pendant attached to a lance. The result is the same, though. From a subject of mockery he is thereafter treated as a respected individual. It is unfortunate the scene has been so obscured by Marie's interests, or more might have been learned of it.

Both testing scenarios have three key elements. The beds are testing objects, designed to measure the suitability of the potential lord. For Gauvain this involves tests of strength and courage, while Lancelot only throws away a flaming lance that has landed in his bed. Second, they let out a loud noise. For Gauvain this precedes the actual test, while the lance makes the noise as it comes in the air. Finally, sovereignty. This is bluntly stated in *Le Conte*, while in *La Charrette* Lancelot's prestige merely rises dramatically. These were all aspects of the kingship ceremony in the Celtic kingdoms for centuries before the Romans and presumably for centuries after they had left. In this comparison the only loose end is the fact that Lancelot is not made a ruler. But the theme of the poem he was in was Ovidian love. Lancelot gaining a kingship while his love awaited would only have demonstrated selfishness.

The parallels exhibited in these customs are intriguing, but the consistency between sub–Roman architecture and Chrétien's poetry provide a more striking correlation. As much as in *Le Chevalier de la Charrette*, the grail castle allows the careful reader some connections to the standard sixth-century hall that is described in the literature and archaeology of the British people of the sub–Roman period. Some scholars have held that the famed building is an underworld structure of Celtic myth,[3] but this cannot be. The underworld castle they compare it to has a habit of spinning, is permanently in a state of spring, and contains glass walls and walking dead people. The inhabitants participate in a neverending feast. Chrétien's castle has none of these qualities. Instead, the structure that Chrétien describes is another clue that the reader is being shown a little bit of ancient Britain. Chrétien explains it as:

> An la sale qui fu quarree
> Et autant longue come lee
> En mi la sale, sor un lit,
> Un bel prodome seoir vit.

into the great hall, which was square in shape, as long as it was wide. In the middle of the hall he [Perceval] saw a handsome nobleman seated on a bed.[4]

Later one finds the grail king lying on one elbow

> De sesche busche cler ardant,
> Et fu antre quatre colomes.
> Bien poïst an quatre cenz homes
> Asseoir anviron le feu,
> S'aüst chascuns aeisié leu.

of dry logs, flaming bright between four columns. Four hundred men could easily sit around that fire, and each would have a comfortable spot.[5]

The previous descriptions closely match the details given of Heorot in *Hrolf Kraki's Saga* and the royal Palace of Connacht in Irish myth; it is the quintessential home of the heroic-age king.

Further indications of antiquity are evident in the grail castle as Chrétien shows it. As the grail king reposes in the hall following the evening meal, he tells Perceval:

> Amis,
> Tant est del colchier mes anuit.
> Je m'an irai, ne vos enuit,
> Leanz an mes chanbres gesir;
> Et quant vos vandra a pleisir,
> Vos colcherez ça dehors.
> Je n'ai nu pooir de mon cors,
> Si covandra que l'an m'an port.

My good friend, it's time to retire for the night. If you don't mind, I shall go to bed into my apartment in there; and when you please you can do so outside them. I have no strength in my limbs and so shall have to be carried.[6]

Chrétien tells his reader that the grail king is to sleep in a small room next to the hall. Perceval is to lie outside the entrance of the king's room to sleep. This suggests an addition to the hall that is well described in both *Hrolf Kraki's Saga* and *Beowulf*. It is a building with one long narrow banquet hall and a hidden sleeping chamber for the chief at one end. Archaeologists have found several examples of this type of dwelling in sub–Roman forts, most conspicuously present at Castle Dore and Yeavering.[7]

The hall being described by Chrétien was a product of a time when there were few stone buildings. There was not enough wealth for separate rooms for visitors or other dwellings for new warriors. These types of buildings only survived as long as a war chief's career, so that there was no point in building anything elaborate. The feudalization of much of Europe and gradual improvements in the political, military, and architectural sciences antiquated such structures long before the twelfth century.

By Chrétien's time the dinner hall was only a small part of a larger and more defensible building. It can hardly be assumed that he was, in describing a castle that was to represent Jersulalem itself, speaking about anything contemporary.

Alternatively, the hall that Chrétien depicts may be only the main part of a building whose other features are not useful for his plot. It's also possible that, as with the real Jerusalem, what Perceval sees is meant to underwhelm his sense of the majesty that place is supposed to hold. The simplicity of the place is intended to make it seem somehow less important. There are even features that appear to belong specifically to the twelfth century, such as the drawbridge that is raised on Perceval's departure.

However, such explanations do not stand up well under scrutiny. Chrétien is all about making his world perfect, and the grail castle is at the center of the world he is describing; why make it look so poor? The drawbridge is a plot device — it does not allow the hero to reenter once he is told what his mistake was. Otherwise, it is and would be entirely absent from the story. On the other hand, the food that is served there is clearly a part of making the grail castle seem like a place of tremendous wealth and culture, perhaps even giving it a supernatural quality.

The preceding comparisons between elements of the poem and aspects of the post–Roman British culture are useful for two reasons. First, they verify the story as a product of British source material. Second, they allow for an alternative and often better explanation of some *Le Conte* scenes, suggesting a source that is not only British but also very old. The episodes pertaining to Perceval and sovereignty only strengthen that possibility. In the first, Perceval arrives at the outskirts of Arthur's court in the last moments of a dramatic scene. The Red Knight tells Perceval his story.

> ...Or va donc tost et si revien,
> Et tant diras au malvés roi:
> Se ik ne vialt tenir de moi
> Sa terre, que il la me rande,
> Ou il anvoit qui la desfande
> Vers moi qui di que ele est moie.
> Et a ces ansaignes t'an croie
> Que devant lui pris orandroit
> Atot le vin dont il bevoit
> Ceste cope que je ci port.

Go there quickly now, and come back again. And you can tell this good-for-nothing king [Arthur] that, if he's not willing to hold his land from me, then he must give it up to me or else send someone to defend it against me, for I declare that it's mine. Here to convince you is the evidence; for just now I seized under his very eyes the cup I'm carrying along with the wine he was drinking.[8]

As the Red Knight continues, one learns that he has approached the king and taken his cup, and now bears it as a sign of the king's dishonor.[9] In any ancient society, the theft of a royal article would be an act of unusual courage and audacity, but the Red Knight seems to have gone unpunished by Arthur or his men. In fact, he considers the theft a direct challenge to Arthur's kingship and, by the tone of the court as Perceval enters, so do the members of Arthur's retinue. The cup may easily be seen as a symbol of the kingship. In this regard, *The Ecstasy of the Phantom* has already been noted as using just such an object for just such a purpose. According to the myth, after Lug has confirmed Conn and his descendants in the kingship of Ireland, they vanish leaving the king behind.[10] To follow the myth further, the personification of Ireland, Érin, gives the king the cup, and she is symbolically married to Conn. That the Red Knight stole the cup from Guinièvre is significant, because she may well represent the same symbolic marriage of Arthur to his kingdom.[11]

After bragging of his loot, the Red Knight sets it down on "un perron de roche bise; a slab of dark grey stone."[12] Again, we have already met such a stone, also associated with kingship. Here it appears again in a challenge to sovereignty. To summarize, a man strolls into Arthur's court and takes his cup of sovereignty from the personification of his kingdom. Then he sets it on the stone which decides the kings of the kingdom and waits for Arthur to come out and challenge him for his honor back. If no champion appears, the Red Knight will be the rightful king.

A second example of the kingship cup may be seen in Perceval's question, "For whom is the grail?" it sounds much like the rationalization, by a later continental poet, of Érin's question to Lug, "To whom shall this cup be given?" In all the romances apart from Chrétien, Perceval does return to the grail castle, properly asks the question, and does win the kingship, just as Conn is given his.

There is one additional Celtic kingship element in the grail legend; both *Peredur* and *Perlesvaus* inform the reader that the grail maiden can be either hideous or beautiful, depending on the state of the kingdom she represents. This metamorphic woman is also common throughout the Celtic world. She appears in *Ecstasy of the Phantom*, *The Adventures of the Sons of Eochaid Mugmedón*, *Lugaid Láigde*, *The Weddynge of Sir Gawen*, *Dame Ragnell*, *The Wife of Bath's Tale*, and *The Tale of Florent* with one or both qualities, but always she is associated with kingship. The Breton lais also have several women associated specifically with kingship.

To the author's knowledge, neither the cup, the stone, the woman, nor marriage of sovereignty appears in European literature apart for those influenced by the Celts. That particular motif is uniquely Celtic.[13] That they should appear so clearly in the extant grail literature allows us to better understand the mysteries behind the grail. If, as has been seen, the precursor of the grail was an object used in Celtic "fertility cults," then there was no need for a sovereignty of the grail castle. The culture that performed ceremonies with nine maidens and a cauldron had no need for kings, it was matriarchal. It follows that the sovereignty theme, being so prominent in Celtic literature, was probably added on to the original story at some stage prior to Chrétien. It is a Celtic literary layer to be peeled away along with the Christian, classical, and contemporary influences.

Another example of this Celtic layering may be found in the motif that Arthur's recruits are often unrelated and always unknown. The phenomenon has little to do with the society of medieval France in general or Philip in particular. Generations of knights were commonly a part of the same household in twelfth-century Europe; men knew each other and other knights throughout a large breadth of territories. However, such was not the case in heroic-age society, which has been seen as a culture that reorders civilization away from the traditional blood-ties and orients a man's sympathies toward the war-band. H. M. Chadwick observed that it was "at one time a regular custom for young princes to set out from their homes, on reaching manhood, and to seek the court of some foreign king with a view to marrying his daughter and thereby acquiring a share in the sovereignty."[14]

There would have been other reasons why young men would be unrecognized in a teulu (war-band) such as Arthur's. A blood feud or man of *ronin* status might bring men in from afar.[15] If Arthur was as famed a warrior in his time as the legends about him indicate, he would have been the most attractive lord in Britain around 500. As a result, the number of foreigners who were his men would have been that much more than the norm.

It should also be apparent that any new and unknown member of Arthur's court is not allowed much respect in either romance or legend.[16] This, too, was a part of Celtic tradition. A novitiate served a sort of probation when he joined a band. During that time, he was not only expected to learn how to fight and survive the battlefield, but also to prove his loyalty to his new lord. In more stable time, the Irish called the youthful man's status *fer midboth*. By law, a male did not achieve full adult status until either is father died or he was about twenty-five. Much the same was true in the war-band. By that age a youth would have proven himself and would have been given enough land to be self-sufficient.[17]

Adventure quests are also very Celtic, not a twelfth-century invention.[18] One may find it in the voyages of the Celtic saints, the folktales of Fionn MacCumhail, and the Breton lais. The first instance of the adventure quest is in *Preiddeu Annwn* and "Pa Gur?"; they were only continued with the troubadours, Marie de France, and Chrétien de Troyes.

The vague topography and otherworldliness that characterizes Arthuriana are not French per se, either. They are also found in the Fionn and the Ulster cycle.[19] In fact, most of Ireland's mythic and legendary characters were artificially set to historic dates and given a rough chronology many centuries after their legends were established. This suggests a great deal of Irish lore at one time had an obscure quality to it.

It has been seen that much of the grail saga, and *Le Conte* in particular, contains many elements that have been borrowed from the pan–Celtic pool of motifs. In many cases, this may well have been the first layer that was grafted onto the original tale. In others, the details make more sense in a post–Roman British context than in any other and suggest that the grail story is much older than its earliest suggestion in British literature. An extension of these observations will be forthcoming.

15

The Sixth Century in Chrétien

While Chrétien's patron changes between the poems under study here, the material he uses in *Le Conte du Graal* does have similarities to his earlier romance, *Le Chevalier de la Charrette*. As has been seen, *Le Conte*, much like *Le Chevalier*, has several details and episodes that correspond to British culture well before the twelfth century. This is particularly so with the nine priestesses who care for the cauldron and Belatacudros.

In Chapter 13, many of the elements of the pre-ninth century to be found in *Le Conte du Graal* were discussed and the manner by which they found their way into Chrétien's poem theorized upon. There were also components that had no Norman connection and yet indicated a location in Scotland. Gauvain's association with Galloway was one of these, and the presence there of his female relatives suggests a traditional bond to that region for this character.[1] Professor Ritchie long ago discussed several other connections to be found there. This link is indeed curious, and one should be well rewarded by asking oneself how Chrétien could have to make Gauvain a Scottish hero.

Northern British history was officially collected for the purpose of recording during only two periods. The first was ninth-century Strathclyde, and the data compiled then was largely brought to Gwynedd and used in the *Historia Brittonum*, *Annales Cambriae*, and *Y Gododdin* texts. The second occasion, and the more likely here, was in 1114 at the behest of David, early of Cumbria, for the purpose of establishing the claims of the Glasgow bishopric. It is said that David collected all the information from the sources of the Kentigern *vitae* and *Historia Brittonum*. In addition, he added all the traditions that the elders of Cumbria could verify.[2] Unfortunately, no documents from those proceedings have come down to us.[3] However, some of the sources he accessed must have dated back to at least the seventh century, if not earlier.[4] This means that the source from which Chrétien obtained the name Gauvain also may have contained information that dated to the seventh century.

A study of the influences on Chrétien's plot revealed it was based on

Philip's life, and a study of those who followed him showed his lengthy and powerful influence in this regard. Of the grail romances only *Peredur* is not demonstrably patterned on Philip, and for that its plot and motivations have been the basis for the common reconstructed original. Analogies to the scene there have been found throughout the Celtic world. All have seen the "grail" as something entirely different from a Christian object. Instead of a grail ceremony with the blood of Christ, there was a magical cauldron and a cornucopic horn. The grail king was not Pelles, but his inspiration Beli or Belatacudros, the horned god. Instead of Perceval as the man destined to rule as the grail king, Peredur's destruction of a coven of witches was heralded. A closer look at the key analogies to *Peredur* uncovered that all the heroes associated with killing the witches or stealing their cauldron seemed to date to about the sixth century. This in itself suggested a recurring historical pattern taking place within a short period, not a literary motif used over centuries.

It was not far to see that *Peredur* made good sense with other facts. A discussion of the religions in Britain during the same period brought out that Celtic cults were still publically acceptable through the end of the Roman period. It also showed that they became invisible during the next couple hundred years until they revived later in the Middle Ages as secret organizations of witchcraft. The most reasonable conclusion was that something happened between about 400 and 600 that did not destroy the Celtic beliefs, but forced the faithful to go into hiding. The outright destruction of many covens was the simplest reason why this might have occurred. That conclusion had the support of both Insular legend and continental historical parallels.

The internal evidence of *Le Conte du Graal* is intriguing and, as in *Le Chevalier de la Charrette*, again points to an origin before 900. Chrétien has reformed data that was current with elements of much greater antiquity. He has omitted the scenes with the nine priestesses and changed the cauldron and horns into a Christian ceremony to suit Philip's aesthetic needs. He probably did not know what they represented, and did not care. He has altered, borrowed, misunderstood, and recreated the story in the image of his patron. He has also retained enough of the ancient material for there to be a hint of the story's origins.

16
Conclusion

Chrétien de Troyes' *Le Conte du Graal* is an intriguing document, more so because it served as the basis for every continental grail romance that followed it. But much has been learned through it in the previous pages. Perhaps a summary will best put this into perspective.

The plot itself is twelfth century. The chronology, familial relationships and actions, and overall development of the main character are demonstrably a reconstruction of Philip of Flanders' life up to his departure for the crusades.

One can hardly believe that the destiny of a young man was to ask a question any curious visitor should have asked. It seems even less believable that this question would magically cure his grandfather and qualify himself to become a king. Such things have no parallels in Celtic mythology or literature, but they fit comfortably with Chrétien's style and purpose. This question is a twelfth-century accretion.

The grail and the rest of the ceremony surrounding it are very much Celtic, indicating this was the grail's original nature. The Christian and possibly Jewish details of the ceremony and the story were superimposed by Chrétien for his patron.

Many of the customs that the characters of *Le Conte* adhere to are often demonstrably of British origin. In the few instances where such items may be dated, they were in use no later than the ninth century.

The chief actor, Perceval, is without doubt the French version of Peredur. Several men of that name lived in sixth-century Britain, and there is no record of it as a personal name again until the late twelfth century. The inspiration for the original character was possibly a man from the fifth or late sixth century who was associated with killing priestesses and destroying their cauldron.

Together, the grail romances show there was a prototype of much greater historical value that can be partially reconstructed. They and their Celtic ana-

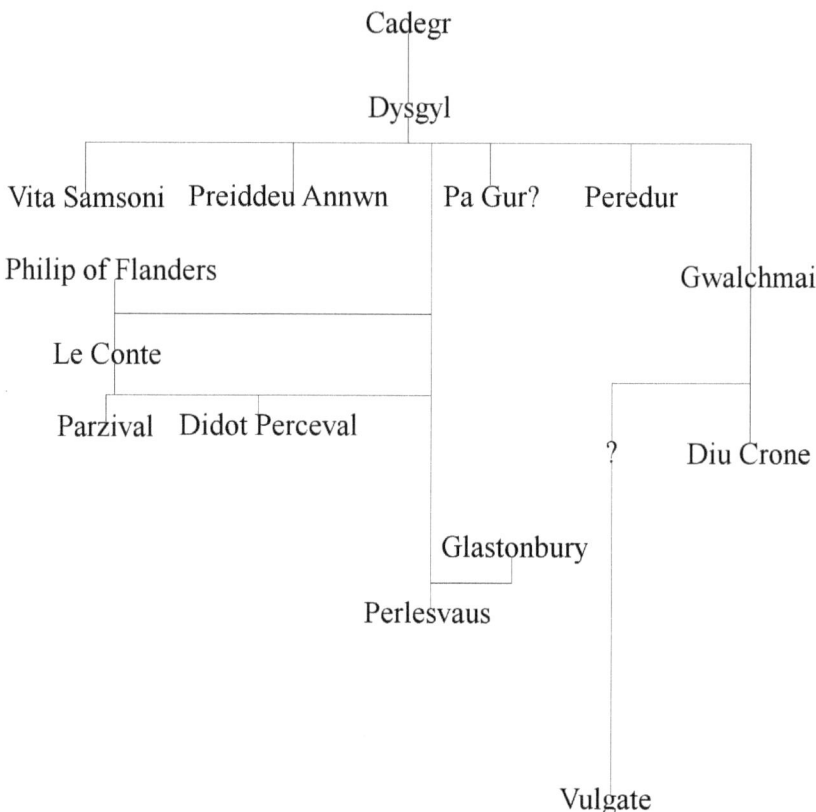

A revised development of the common grail saga. While the assumption of a large body of British materials remains, the illustration demonstrates better the interconnectivity of the several grail versions as well as the additional influences on the material.

logues reveal that many Celtic cults functioned as covens of nine women, presided over by the god Belatacudros or a male who symbolically acted like him. They were agricultural in their interests. These covens were destroyed by the sixth-century persons Peredur, Cei, Arthur, Samson, and possibly Gwalchmai.[1] Their activities were erratically recorded, as was everything that happened in Britain during this time. Some of these were written down relatively soon after they had occurred, as happened with the *Vita Samsoni* and possibly *Peredur*. Alternatively, some actions were remembered in a strictly oral environment, as has apparently happened in "Pa Gur?"

One might ask why there is no better record of the event than *Le Conte*, *Didot Perceval*, *Perlesvaus*, *Peredur*, and *Diu Crône*, and why this base of information conflicts in so many ways. The answers are familiar to those who have studied the gray areas of world history. There is little surviving information for the fifth and sixth century in Britain, and it too conflicts. The fifth century among the British was a time of floundering culture and economy, with kingdoms only just emerging. There was no interest in writing a history. In addition, Britain's wet climate made it difficult for the manuscripts written there to survive. Because of this obstacle, even less was remembered. As a result, there is only one chronologically based history of the Arthurian period, that of Geoffrey of Monmouth. He wrote six hundred years after Arthur died and is a classic example of the pseudohistory that plagues study of the period.

All this said, how far can the grail legend be used as history? Chrétien's purpose and influence must necessarily leave the reader skeptical. In determining the historicity of a literary work, three aspects must be scrutinized: external validation, historical context, and transmission.[2] Both prototypes will be examined separately. External validation is impossible for *Glas*. Truthfully, the abduction of a queen would hardly have been important enough to warrant mention in an annal. There is so little information from the period it is unsurprising that Meleagant's version of events has not survived, either. There is, however, some historical context. Celtic legend abounds with abductions, and a heroic-age abduction would have served a very political motivation. As to transmission, that is impossible to determine from the moment of creation until the time it reached Chrétien. However, enough information has been collected to suggest a most likely scenario.

Probably, there was an historical abduction, though whether it was Arthur's queen or Arthur or Gauvain who saved her is unknown. It would have taken place in the fifth or sixth centuries. Recollection of it was formed into a narrative soon enough after the event that some of the nonmotifal elements of the story would have made sense to an audience. This was then remembered in oral form, with Celtic motifs being added to it such as the hero's childhood. However, the plot itself seems to have remained very consistent through the centuries, and the abductee is always the same, while the abductor was normally Melwas/Meleagant. This suggests a relatively short time in an oral environment. In the early twelfth century, the story first emerged in the extant written record. Chrétien himself says he was given a written source for the story, and nothing that has come out in the previous pages warrants another opinion.

Dysgyl lacks direct external validation; none of the cults who were persecuted survived to tell of their destruction. However, the primary information from the *Vita Samsoni* confirms there were covens in sixth-century Britain and that they were being destroyed. Historical context is less difficult to see. A wide variety of otherwise unrelated literature attests to the existence of covens in Britain who worshipped Celtic gods and were destroyed by sixth-century figures. These activities are more thoroughly confirmed on the continent, where such behavior was openly condoned by local religious leaders.

Transmission in *Dysgyl* is also difficult to determine with any precision. However, as the historical context for the activities of the source were over by the year 600, so too was the reason for creating the story. The long list of Celtic motifs in Chapter 13 and the confusion of the name Belatacudros make it clear that the story survived in an oral environment at one time. But again, the hero of the tale is consistent throughout the early romances. This indicates it was not long without a written form, though the nonprogressive manner of *Peredur* suggests it was there long enough to confuse the original storyline beyond recovery. Again, Chrétien speaks of a written source, and Philip's alliance to Scotland in this period and Gauvain's undoubted connections to Galloway are strong evidence to believe him.

The fact that the men who wrote the romances were not historical authorities should not impede the scholar, either. The *Bible*, *Iliad* and *De Excidio Britanniae* were written with religious motives, yet they have all been employed to establish historical fact. The original versions of the abduction and grail romances were more than just literature. They can be added to the short list of primary sources for the Arthurian period. The fifth and sixth centuries did indeed have more sources than the traditional Gildas, Patrick, and archaeology. The annals of Ireland, Wales, and Gaul, Procopius, and many other continental historians verify several chronological sequences. The genealogies help with bloodlines and the locations of princes. The early saints' lives have been used in conjunction with each other and other sources for locating kings and battles, pinpointing customs and materials. They, too, have been used to build chronological sequences. Like the histories, annals, geneaologies, and vitae, *Glas* and *Dysgyl* are often suspect, but they are potentially valuable sources of information and must be used as such if any more of British history is to be unraveled. This investigation has been a first step to that end.

It is not claimed, however, that *Glas* and *Dysgyl* are historical documents. Such literatures for the sixth century are like the cries of ghosts—always howling but never seen. What is claimed is that the poems are useful for historians of the sixth century.

How much importance should be given these historical elements? Analogies alone can answer this. The *Iliad* has very little historical information, and yet Schliemann was able to find Troy from only the lines of the poem and a very basic grasp of archaeology. In the post–Roman period, the Taliesin poetry has been used to outline Urien's kingdom and locate several other important contemporaries. They have also aided in improving the under-

16. Conclusion

standing of the political atmosphere relative chronology of late sixth-century Britain. *Y Gododdin* is used as a sounding board by archaeologists against which they compare their own finds. *Glas* and *Dysgyl* may similarly serve historians in British studies. Further, other properly examined literary sources may be used to flesh out British history.

Part Three: Tristan

17

Introduction to the Tristan Legend

In the previous two segments of this work the abduction of Arthur's queen and the grail legend were studied in turn. Several of the conclusions that were drawn in examining the former story not only showed strong indications of being based on some historical event, but a couple key points were also employed in developing a better understanding of the latter narrative. Taken together, they both point toward a previously unconsidered grail solution — that the grail story was the history of Philip of Flanders superimposed on a series of legends about the destruction of at least one Mother Goddess cult.

More broadly, they evidenced that the approach itself was valid. Carefully analyzed and compared with similar stories and their parallels, the romances regarding Arthur can be used to form a better understanding of the Arthurian era. And, if the history could be pulled out of medieval romances, there was then hope for the less corrupted tales associated with other legendary kings, mythological characters, and the myths themselves.

In the midst of the grail solution and the barrage of possibilities that are a result of it, the reader would do well to remember that the Arthurian corpus contains the largest body of literature in the world — greater even than the *Bible*. The abduction of Arthur's queen and the "holy" grail saga make up only a fraction of that corpus. A good many of the remaining stories have been shown to contain a multitude of Celtic motifs, names, and recognizable objects that could indicate something more historically substantial.[1] These are all worthy of study from the same standpoint.

The fact is that the only reason the two Arthurian romances were used was because they showed the greatest potential for learning about the Arthurian world and most easily allowed the author to elucidate and then lay out the approach. In both cases, the stories had a strong Celtic background that gave some indication of their early form and development. The most influential and likely the first continental writer on both subjects was known as well. Chrétien de Troyes was the most successful Arthurian writer, and possibly the best. Because of his talents, his background, his readings, his patrons, and the circumstances around which they commissioned him have all been the subject of innumerable studies. To put it bluntly, all the necessary raw materials had already been developed and needed only to be properly organized to bring the author's approach to fruition.

Many other legends have shown promise for helping to better understand the period, though tackling them is not as alluring and would not prove either as straightforward or as rewarding. *Owain/Yvain* and *Erec/Geraint* are also traditional stories that were explored by Chrétien. Welsh references suggest several narratives involving Cei (Kay), Gwalchmai (Gawain), and even Arthur might have developed from historical anecdotes. Drutwas, Modred, and a dozen other minor characters may well have had tales attached to them at one time as well, as evidenced in the various and isolated clues extant in the native and earlier continental literature. These will have many episodes that may or may not have been based on an historical event. Much of the information to be found out about these figures will have little historical value, but as with the stories that have been scrutinized in the chapters here, some few may have episodes or details that are useful in that regard.

Possibly the remaining hero with the largest body of extant literature about him is Tristan. As a character, Tristan is deeply rooted in Welsh and Irish tradition. Joseph Loth, Heinrich Zimmer, Gertrude Schoepperle, Rachel Bromwich,[2] Oliver Padel, and dozens of other prominent and well-respected scholars have made this point beyond any reasonable doubt. That alone should make the story worthy of study in the same vein as *La Charrette* and *Le Conte*.

In its essence, the tale of Tristan is a life story of its leading character, from his father wooing his mother to his own sad death by a woman who wanted a part of him she could never have. The version of the tale that makes the most sense is as follows. Rivallon is a ruler in his own right who learns of the renown of King Mark. He goes to the other man's kingdom, either for personal honor, in order to seek a bride, or as an ally. He proves his worth almost immediately through his martial abilities and his wisdom in council. Parallel to earning Mark's respect, he falls in love with Blancheflour, Mark's sister, who happily returns his love. The three are content together, and Rivallon remains in Mark's kingdom for some time.

Rivallon gets word that his kingdom is being attacked, and he is forced to return to defend it. He takes Blancheflour with him. Over a span of several weeks, she becomes pregnant and they marry. Rivallon continues his campaign against the invaders, but dies in defeating them according to everyone

17. Introduction to the Tristan Legend

but Eilhart and the *Prose Tristan*. A short time later, Blancheflour dies of a broken heart while giving birth to Tristan.

Tristan is raised unaware of his heritage, as his father's most trusted man rules the kingdom and raises the boy as his own son. He learns all the finer arts of the upper crust of society under his own tutor. When he approaches adulthood, he reclaims his patrimony. At roughly the same time he is introduced to his uncle, Mark. Mark is taken with Tristan's culture and bearing. Tristan decides to live in his uncle's kingdom. He leaves the rule of his own kingdom in the hands of his foster parents and begins his training as a knight. One day a giant named Morholt visits Mark as an envoy of an Irish king. He reminds Mark that he is a vassal and demands the standard number of boys and girls as the year's tribute. He also offers Mark the option that his people can offer a champion to fight him if they believe he can be defeated.

In response, Tristan challenges the giant to a combat, over his uncle's pleas about his youth and inexperience. Tristan persists, and the battle is agreed upon. The fight is protracted and often one-sided, but eventually Tristan defeats Morholt with a stroke to his skull. In the process, he himself suffers a wound by the giant's poisoned sword. The wound makes him sickly, and it is thought that he might die. No physician that Mark calls upon can help him counter the poison, and he grows weaker. Realizing that nothing can be done for him in Mark's kingdom, he requests a ship from his uncle. As chance or his navigation would have it, he lands in that part of Ireland where Morholt was from. There his malady is made known to the palace and either the wife or daughter of the king recognizes the kind of poison he has been given. Informed, and knowing how to cure him as an expert, the potionist nurses Tristan back to full health. She does this without ever realizing that Tristan is the killer of her relative. For his part, Tristan thanks her for his life, and realizes he needs to return to his uncle before he gives away his identity.

Once back in Mark's kingdom, he praises the beauty of the Irish princess Isolt. Tristan is received with all of the pomp of a returning hero. As a reward for his continuing contributions to Cornwall he is made the heir, much to the chagrin of several nobles. From this point on, the nobles who had not wanted Tristan to become the heir set about to set he and Mark against each other. They begin their campaign against him by pleading with Mark to marry so that he can have a son of his own. They become insistent, and he realizes he cannot put them off anymore, so he either tells them he will only marry Isolt, or the owner of a golden hair that happens to catch his attention (which happens to have been Isolt's).[3]

Tristan arrives in Ireland and presently learns a dragon is decimating the population. A reward — the hand of Isolt — has been offered for killing it. Tristan tracks down the dragon, defeats it, and cuts out the beast's tongue.

He goes someplace quiet to rest and soon passes out because of either the battle fatigue or the tongue's poisonous qualities. His absence allows for the cowardly court seneschal to cut off the dragon's head and return with it to the king. The seneschal immediately demands his reward of Isolt's hand in marriage.

Isolt is disgusted at the thought of marrying the seneschal, a man she knows to be a coward. She finds the dragon's corpse and searches the area in hopes that there might be something that would disprove the seneschal's claim. Tristan is found and taken back to the princess' chambers. There he is healed a second time and bathed so that he might be more presentable. To show the young warrior her personal gratitude, Isolt takes his sword to clean and sharpen. Picking it up, she sees a noticeable divot in the blade. She compares it to the sword piece that was taken out of her uncle's head, and it matches. Confronting Tristan, she threatens to kill him. Thinking quickly, Tristan reminds Isolt of his practical use to her. His usefulness in getting her away from the seneschal convinces the young princess to spare his life.

Healed and at the court of the Irish king, Tristan defeats the seneschal's challenge by revealing the dragon's tongue. The seneschal insists that he killed the dragon, forcing Tristan to defeat him in combat as well. His claim proven, the king awards Isolt to him. Tristan tells the king of his plan to return to Cornwall, and he is given permission to leave.

For her part Isolt's mother understands how difficult it will be to marry a man she has never met. She pulls Isolt's handmaiden, Brangain, apart and gives her a love potion mixed in with some wine. The drug is to be given to the newlyweds on the night of their marriage. It is designed to ensure that Isolt will be happy with him. During the voyage, Brangain is somehow negligent, and the young pair find or are given the bottle that contains the love potion. They share in the contents and are instantly infected with its concoction. They fall instantly and inexorably in love with each other.

Thereafter begins a long and secretive love affair, always hidden from Mark and always hedging toward disaster. Their first trial comes on Isolt's wedding night; the lovers know that Mark will realize she has been with another man. To obfuscate him, Brangien changes places with her mistress and is replaced with the queen in the middle of the night.

The ploy works perfectly, with Mark having no doubts that he has been with Isolt. For her part, Isolt becomes concerned that her servant will one day give her secret away, dishonoring her and sending Tristan to his death. To ensure that never happens, she arranges for Brangien to be executed. She hires two men and has her servant abducted. They find themselves unable to fulfill their contract, however, when they realize the innocence of the woman. Isolt realizes her mistake only when she believes her friend is dead. On learning that Brangien is alive she rejoices. Brought together again, Brangien proves herself to be utterly loyal to her mistress. The two are reconciled.

In every version but Eilhart, an Irish warrior and member of Isolt's father's court uses a rote to trick Mark into giving up his queen. Learning that his lover has been kidnapped, Tristan saves her with a trick of his own. He returns her to Mark immediately.

During the early romance, Tristan once sends a message to his lover using floating wood inscribed with his name or a symbol to let her know it is he. The romance of the scene and the intimate knowledge required of each other make the episode memorable.

At one point the lovers are caught lying together and kissing as Mark comes in on them. Mark reacts mildly, censuring the couple and not allowing Tristan to be near her. Publically obeying him, they find a way to meet privately; they have trysts by the moonlight and continue their affair.

A dwarf learns about their meetings and comes into the employ of those who wish to get rid of Tristan. He convinces Mark to wait in a tree overlooking their usual spot so that he might see his wife and nephew continuing their relationship, despite his condemnation. When the lovers come to their designated spot, they individually see the shadows that their king and the informer cast. Sharp enough not to look up, they both guess who is in the tree. They immediately adjust their behavior toward each other; their conversation becomes innocent and their attitudes reflect how they should behave toward each other. Believing himself to have been unobserved and their actions to be honest, Mark is impressed and repentant toward his loyal nephew and obedient wife. The next day Tristan is given more latitude with Isolt than ever before.

Still disbelieving, the dwarf lays a second trap for the couple. They will ask Tristan to be a messenger to a faraway king the night before he is to go. The dwarf predicts that Tristan will need to spend the night with Isolt, and he plans to catch them. When Tristan and Isolt go to bed, the dwarf spreads flour around the knight and his lady. Tristan recognizes the trap immediately. When he believes it is safe, he jumps from his bed to the queen's in order to avoid leaving any evidence that he has been with her. He is unfortunate in that the strain of making such a leap forces several old wounds to burst open. The resulting blood in both beds is evidence enough to convict them of being lovers. They are caught and charged with cuckolding the king. Mark sentences them to death immediately.

On the way to their executions, Tristan comes across a religious building. Requesting to enter it on the pretense of making his peace with God, his jailors allow him to go. He moves to the back of the building, to a window overlooking a cliff. With a heroic leap, he jumps from a window and safely out of the reach of his captors. He makes his escape before the guards know he has bolted.

Meanwhile, Mark has been in a separate group with Isolt. He comes across a group of lepers who inquire as to what is going on. Upon learning of the circumstances, the group requests that he give his queen to them. Mark agrees to their proposal, commenting that time spent among them is a fate worse than death. This allows for Tristan, still free and tracking her, to rescue Isolt without confronting his uncle. Hunted by their king, they escape into the wilderness.

For some time, the pair hides in a large forest and live on the game Tristan can hunt and what few berries and nuts that Isolt comes across. They are often near starvation, but they both believe that their pain is well worth the bliss of being together and neither thinks of going back to their old existence.

Their exile ends when Mark catches the pair taking an afternoon nap together, fully clothed and with a sword between them. Convinced of their innocence once again, he allows the queen to come home to him. Isolt is welcomed back as his queen, with all of her privileges and honor restored. Tristan leaves the kingdom at Mark's request. Oddly, he does not return to his own kingdom. Wandering aimlessly, he comes upon a region that is under attack. He offers his sword and acquits himself well in this new king's service. Soon he is leading the entire army to victory. Pleased with his abilities, the king and his son offer Tristan the princess, a second Isolt, of the White Hands. Alone, realizing the horrible mistakes he made with his old lover, and understanding that he has to make a new life for himself, he feels as though he has no other choice but to accept the offer and make the best of his new situation. He marries the woman despite not loving her. Still in love with the first Isolt, he does not engage in carnal pleasures with his wife. This becomes a problem when her brother learns of this. The conversation between husband and brother leads to one last meeting with Isolt. Seeing the Cornish king's beauty and love for him, the latter man accepts that Tristan could never love his sister as much.

Defeating another invading army, Tristan is badly wounded for a third time in his life. He sends the prince of the kingdom with a message to Mark's queen and tells him to use white sails if he has brought her and black sails if he has not. Isolt comes with him, but by the time they return he is too weak to look out the window to see whether or not his salvation is coming with him. His wife, jealous of what he and the other Isolt had been to each other, tells him the sails are black. Heartbroken that his lover has failed him and blaming his own mistakes for her refusal to cure him, he dies of a broken heart. Devastated that her own selfish jealousy has killed the man she loved, Isolt of the White Hands dies as well.

The story is a simple one, a story of star-crossed love wrapped in a romantic triangle and set in one of the most picturesque and chivalrous backdrops in all of literature. However, a study of its usefulness as an historical source will not be as straightforward as any literary analysis. Several issues specific to the subject complicate a study of Tristan. These must be spelled out, examined, and dealt with each in turn before the legend can be considered as an historical source. It will be the function of the rest of this chapter to lay out the issues confronting just such a study, and the rest of this section to gain a more full understanding of them.

In both of the previous stories, one continental author was clearly the first to write on the subject, and that one author spawned dozens of imitators over the centuries. Though each of those who followed added their own details and had to meet the demands of their patrons, and though several of them managed to infuse their interpretations with additional Celtic materials, that one individual was pivotal to the direction the continent took in developing the stories. It was the information and plot that Chrétien supplied that became the basic framework for everything that was to follow. Because of his overwhelming influence, an in-depth study of his personal and professional history was essential to understanding both of his poems and the changes that he had imposed upon the Arthurian stories they were based upon in transitioning them from Welsh legend to courtly romances.

The Tristan body of literature does not have this advantage. The first non–Celt to write a full extant story on him was probably Thomas of Britain, though Marie de France was a contemporary and Béroul's primacy has been strongly suggested.[4] No scholar has formed a widely agreed upon development for the story, either, which means that working out who was first and who used whom as a source is still a hypothetical exercise. It tends to change from expert to expert.

Not that determining a relative chronology could be of help in any event. If it was believed that Thomas of Britain was the first writer, it would not make the situation any better without more research and discovery. Almost nothing is known of Thomas, and there are only ten fragments from six manuscripts that are extant from his writing.[5] All told, only a fraction of his story has survived, and any attempt to fill in the blanks must make heavy use of those adaptors who followed him. Those adaptors, reasonably, had motivations of their own. For that reason and more direct evidence, they cannot be wholly trusted.[6]

Another issue is the lack of Welsh literature pertaining to Tristan. Both of the above Arthurian stories had several early British versions, dating before and roughly contemporary to Chrétien. Conversely, there is no full story associated with Tristan and Isolt in the Welsh literature. The *Mabinogion*, for whatever reason, contains no tale about the pair, nor has anything more than a couple of poorly understood and isolated stanzas survived in the poetry of the early Middle Ages. Without a more substantial body of material, there is no way of knowing what plot and specific information Thomas might have started with, nor any way of determining where he might have altered the story.

The nature of the early redactions only complicates matters. Thomas of Britain, Béroul, Gottfried von Strassburg, Eilhart von Oberg, the *Prose Tristan*, and the *Madness of Tristan* write essentially the same plot with most of the same details; the only variances found in them seem to revolve around the personal values of the authors and the specific instructions those authors were given by their patrons.[7] Even the names of most of the characters only differ slightly as they transition between languages and regions. Their uniformity gives the reader very little diversity to work with and very little indication that those who followed the first writer had access to any materials they didn't find in his work.

On the other hand, Tristan appears to be an old character; he is present in the earliest portions of the Welsh Triads. Uniformity of plot on the continent and antiquity of the primary character together suggest that either the supply of information regarding the tale was cut off after the first transmission or that such a dramatic change in storyline and names took place at some point that those who followed either could not see a connection back to the native story or saw nothing of interest in it any more. The former option is not supported by the facts—such as the detail that the great boom of Arthurian literature was yet to come. The latter will be supported throughout the book.

A study of the Tristan saga will need to address these issues. However, the manner of approach will be the same as was employed with *Le Chevalier de La Charrette* and *Le Conte du Graal*. The characters will be examined to achieve a better grasp of the story's plot and the original functions of its characters. The several early authors and versions of the Tristan story will be studied in the hopes of better understanding their interrelationship and whatever Celtic sources they may have drawn upon. The results of those two assessments should reveal some information as to the nature and dating of a common Tristan source. In the process, the concerns named above should all be addressed.

The next few chapters will show beyond any reasonable doubt when it made its way to the continent and how it was initially treated. A closer examination of the characters and their consistency will suggest one source from which the others took their ideas. A chapter on Thomas will show that the circumstances of his patronage provide a potential date of formation and plot that predates and supersedes all others. A look at the motifal aspects of the

17. Introduction to the Tristan Legend

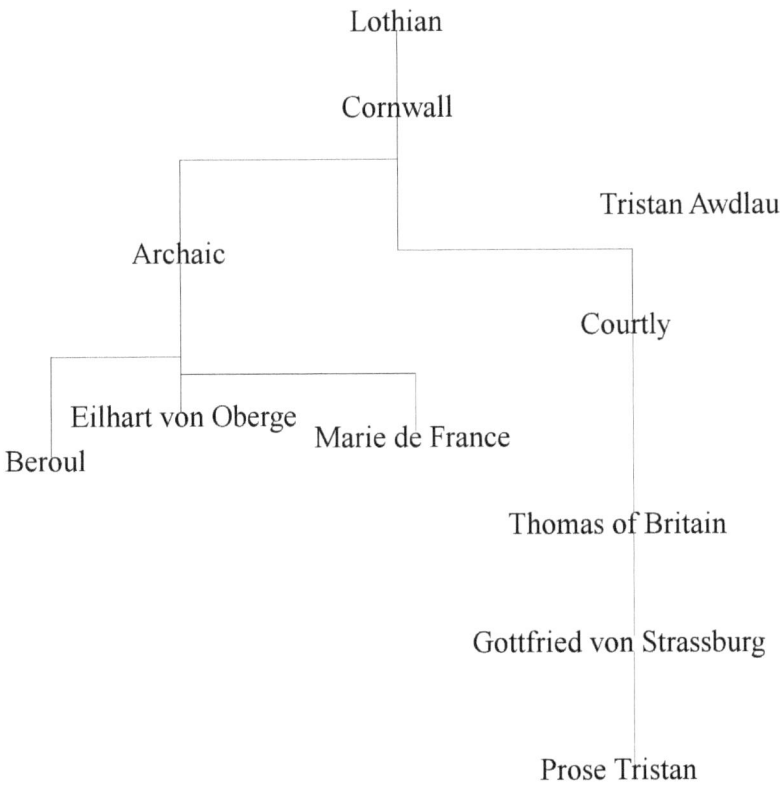

A traditional view of the development of the Tristan legend. This is distinguished by the separation of the archaic and courtly approaches to the subject.

story will help to peel away those layers of the story that were added on later. Finally, a chapter devoted to any nonmotifal minutiae found embedded in any of the variations should help to reveal any preromantic episodes that might be found in the narrative. More importantly, the examination will help to form a sturdy basis for future studies along these lines.

18

The Characters and Their Roles

The story of Tristan, as seen consistently in all of the romances, contains a number of characters. There is Tristan, the hero. Mark is at the crux of the romance, as the brother of the woman who bears Tristan, the king who adores him, and the husband of Tristan's beloved Isolt. Isolt is niece to the giant Morholt, lady to Brengain, and daughter of the king of Ireland. Husdent, the hound that Tristan trained, and Gorvenal or Dinas de Lidan, Tristan's seneschal, are secondary but regular characters as well. Rivallon, Tristan's father, and Blancheflour, his mother, are the main characters in the first part of the romances, in most versions. For the most part, only Tristan's nemeses at Mark's court change from story to story. Likely, they were not present or were not strong enough characters in the original version to have been retained as the story transitioned onto the continent. Alternatively, their original roles might have been lost or so far degraded in the process as to be irrecoverable.[1]

Tristan, Welsh Drystan and Pictish Drust, is not to be found in any Welsh or Cornish king lists or genealogies. He is listed in the triads as a great warrior, but no details of his British associations are given.[2] In the native poetry, among which he is more popular, Tristan is exclusively connected to Essyllt. These three facts suggest that Tristan was not associated with any independent northern British, Welsh, or Cornish kingdom by the time the Welsh materials were being written down.

Drust is, however, a fairly common name in Pictish history. It was borne by ten kings, among them a prehistorical ruler named Drust son of Erp and an eighth-century ruler named Drust VIII, son of Talorcan. The literary Drust's earliest patronymic, as reliably found in every Welsh source that names him, is Tallwch. The resemblance between Drust VIII and literary Drust strongly suggests a connection between the two.[3] In whatever form the story of Tristan/Drystan/Drust first took, it probably took that form in Scotland.[4]

18. The Characters and Their Roles

Rulers named March or Mark are to be found throughout Welsh, Cornish, and Breton literature. They are present in several Welsh genealogies, and the signature of one is present as a witness in the *Book of Llandaff*. It is possible, though by no means necessary, that all Welsh references relate to a single individual.[5] The *vita* of Paul Aurelian (ninth century) and several less reliable sources place a prominent king by that name in Glamorgan during the early sixth century.

Hints of a placement of the story in southern Wales can be found throughout the romances as well. As Rachel Bromwich pointed out, Isolt's judgment by ordeal takes place in Caerleon according to Gottfried.[6] By implication, Caerleon would be in Mark's kingdom. The rest of the passage bears out that assumption with its consistency. In *Chevrefoil*, Tristan's home is clearly stated as being in southern Wales as well.[7] If there was only one Mark, he came from that region.

Additional references place him in a number of different locations, and these alternative points of origin must be addressed as well. In his own researches, Joseph Loth made a connection between two sites named in Béroul's rendition and the geography of Cornwall, *Lancïen/Lencïen* and *Church of St. Sanson*. Both are mentioned during Tristan's heroic escape from his execution at the chapel.[8] These are, respectively, the former manor of Lantyne and a nearby church dedicated to St. Samson.[9] Lantyne is attested to from 1086 in the *Domesday Book*, while the church is not named until about 1280 but is most likely the religious house that Samson founded before his departure for Brittany. Loth then added several other less reputable connections that have been widely discounted.[10] In a much better received article, Oliver Padel confirmed the two Loth sites and added two more likely connections.[11] The remainder of his paper relayed several instances that conveyed Béroul's depth of knowledge regarding contemporary Cornwall. He also noted that Béroul was also the only Tristan writer to locate Mark broadly in Cornwall during the first incarnation of the continental Tristan legend.

Apart from Béroul, all the Tristan romances place Mark specifically in Tintagel, but it has been seen that several of his activities are localized in Wales. As the earliest sources locate an historical king by that name in southern Wales, the inclination is normally to assume that Mark was from that region. However, here the consistency of the romances works to the disadvantage of the scholar. It is widely accepted that the known dynasties and names of kings are greatly outweighed by the unknown in the British-speaking kingdoms of this era. It is possible that the romances have retained in this story the name of a significant Cornish king nowhere else recorded.

It must be remembered, though, that such is only a possibility. During the remainder of his paper, Padel made the important point that Béroul's familiarity with Cornwall did not necessarily mean that the story he was writing about came from that region. He might well have found the information he used from a more contemporary source that had nothing to do with Tristan. It is possible he visited the area himself. This is important to keep in mind when examining the balance of the Tristan literature. In fact, if several generations of scholars are correct and a common original for all known continental Tristan variations stems from a common source, it is important to keep that thought in the front of one's mind when looking at the relevant literature.

Also of interest is Pictland. William Skene's map of ancient Scotland has a region named "Kornaouioi" modernized to Cornouaille or Cornwall and a second called "Damnonioi" or Damnonia/Dumnonia. These two regions are to be found in what would become Caithness and Strathclyde, respectively. The author has no idea at this time what to make of such a coincidence, but it is intriguing in view of the fact that parts of Cornwall were called both names in medieval Britain, that Mark is associated with Cornwall, and that Tristan has been firmly connected to Lothian.[12] It is certainly possible that Mark was originally a king of or in one of these regions and that a memory of that link was retained during the story's stay in Wales. However, without more evidence and given the diversity and depth of evidence placing Mark in southern Wales, it must remain the most likely option.

The Mark character has one additional issue. In Welsh, his name also meant "horse" in Welsh during the medieval period. When poets use the word "march," they cannot be assumed to be speaking of the famed king unless the context of the rest of the work makes that clear. The two Tristan *awdlau* that are extant in Welsh do not make that distinction, adding another layer of understanding to overcome. It must be considered within the realm of possibility that the original Tristan story involved the hero, his rescued princess, a trusty hound, and a stalwart horse. It is feasible that a series of misunderstandings might have brought the "march" from loyal steed to a local king to the husband of the princess. Such an unlikely possibility will not be pursued here, however. There is no evidence for the possibility beyond the name.

Essyllt, the third member of the love triangle, seems to have no history. This is not surprising, as women are rarely if ever found in the genealogies and are inconsistently named in the *vitae*. Essyllt is mentioned as a part of Arthur's court in *Culhwch ac Olwen*, but is named at the very end of the list of people in Arthur's court. It is noteworthy that she is given no patronymics, either. Her placement at the end of the list, her absence in the rest of the story, and the absence of any connections to any dynasty are all strong indications that her name was added well after the story had taken its present form, and likely under the influence of continental romances.[13]

However, the name Essyllt is not entirely unknown in Welsh studies outside of her association with Tristan. In the poetry, Essyllt was the daughter and sole heir of Gwynedd's Cynan Tindaethwy. Cynan (798–816) is the last known legitimate ruler of his dynasty.[14] He was followed by his "brother" Hywel, who reigned immediately before Rhodri Mawr introduced a new ruling house into the kingdom at 825.

Essyllt's connection to him was either as his wife or mother, depending on the source. It did not matter in Medieval Wales. As the single link between the legendary Guenodotian lineage of Maelgwn and Rhun and the powerful family of Rhodri Mawr, Essyllt was long remembered in poetry. She would come to represent everything that the extinguished dynasty was, even as she came to symbolize the legitimacy of the new dynasty.

Naturally, one of the aspects that would be associated with her would be beauty, and therein lies the problem. As the woman in one of the most famous romances of the Middle Ages, Drystan's lover inevitably became a measure of beauty herself. Separating the figure of romance from the historical figure is a regular problem that modern scholars are confronted with in studying the extant Welsh poetry. It is because of this dilemma that the possibility the daughter of Cynan Tindaethwy was the inspiration for the name of Essyllt/Isolt in the romances exists.[15]

The theory is supported by the politics of the time as well. The *Historia Brittonum*, written in the early ninth century, was designed in part to show the ascendancy of Gwynedd over the southern Welsh kingdoms.[16] When Dyfed revamped it a century later, details were changed to reverse that viewpoint.[17] The same northern theme can be seen in the Twrch Trwyth episode, polarized in the triad of Coll and the sow Henwen.

Noteworthy, too, is that from the tenth century, Essyllt in the form Eselt is part of a place name in Cornwall.[18] As the name of a woman surviving in traditional British stories is unusual, so naming a location after any woman is more so. That the name Essyllt is only known in two contexts makes the place name all the more significant here. Over the past few decades, the fact that Essyllt's name is present in a Cornish appellation has been used as evidence that the fame of Drystan's lover was already in Cornwall by this time. However, there is no corresponding Drystan place name in all of Cornwall. Another possibility exists. The name could have come about due to the fame of the Gwynedd heiress and have nothing to do with the Tristan legend. After all, British place names are notoriously unhistorical. Arthur is to be found all over England, Wales, and Scotland. The Bed of Diarmid and Grainne is a common motif found in all the British Isles. Essyllt daughter of Cynan would have represented power, authority, and tradition.

Morholt, the first and most intimidating of Tristan's antagonists, seems to be integral to the plot as well. It is his ultimatum that forces Tristan into a duel at the beginning of his career and his poisoned weapon that forces Tristan to seek out Isolt, his niece in Ireland. And yet Morholt's name looks in no way Celtic.

However, from his first introduction he is called specifically *Le Morholt*, and not simply Morholt. In other words, he is not addressed as a person but as an animal or beast. It is a curiosity that should not have escaped Thomas of Britain's attention and could not have been missed by the thousands of people who heard the story he told; yet it remained there. Their take on the name was followed early on in Tristan scholarship. Early scholars beginning with Gertrude Schoepperle were certain the name had no significance.[19] Eventually however, Bromwich and others remarked that the name vaguely resembles the Celtic sea beasts named *Fomori*.[20] The Fomori are generally associated with the Irish Sea around Scotland and are properly referred to as "the." Their claim, as uncertain as she was in making it, has seemed to hold up well. It does remind eyes of Morholt. They are from the proper area as well.

The Fomori are also otherwise associated with Drust. Probably the most widely known story involving these uniquely northern Celtic creatures is to be found in *Tochmarc Emer*, a story about the wooing of Emer by Cú Chulainn that has been touched upon previously. In the anecdote, the hero fights three of them in protecting a local princess who had been marked for death by sacrifice. The entire account falls into a universal myth known as the dragon-slaying myth. In it, the hero slays the monster and rescues the princess/sacrifice. The intriguing detail here, though, is that in this particular tale a Drust mac Seirb is named as one of Cú Chulainn's men and as specifically taking part in the battle against the monsters. He is mentioned nowhere else in *Tochmarc Emer* and, in fact, is present in no other literature. Because of his unique presence here, it has been generally acknowledged that this Drust was the original dragon slayer in the *Tochmarc Emer* episode and that the Cú Chulainn saga pulled it into its orbit.[21]

If the Cú Chulainn version is any indication, the myth originally involved Drust winning the hand of a princess by saving her from a beast. This sounds something like Tristan's second great fight, in which he kills a dragon to rescue her from marriage to the seneschal and save her kingdom. Both the Morholt and the dragon episodes have parts of the original version, identifying them as doublets of a single original in which Drust killed a monster and won a princess.

Brengain, Welsh *Branwen* and Old Welsh written intermediary *Branguen*,[22] is the name of Essyllt's loyal servant in all versions of the story. The present author has a limited knowledge of the development of the Welsh language, but the first syllable of the name, *bran*, translates directly as "crow."

In the symbolism of Welsh poetry, however, it could come to mean "battle-scavenger" or even "bringer of death." The second syllable, *wen*, is normally translated as "white." White crow is the equivalent of black sheep in the English language.

The name is traditional, and her function is constant as well. She is responsible for causing Tristan and Isolt to fall in love; she intercedes her body between Mark and Essyllt on their wedding night, and helps the couple throughout their lives as they struggle with their romance and keeping their affair hidden. Her personality, her role, and her culpability in the predicament of the young lovers are unswerving throughout all of Tristan literature.

It should be noted that only one other story has a lady with a named handmaiden so early in the literature: *Yvain/Owain*. That tale has a common thread with Tristan in that both have dealt with the kingship cupbearer and its adaptation to the continent. As the author will show in a future publication, the *Owain* tale was originally a kingship ritual, meaning that the hero's eventual wife was also the cupbearer in the early stages of the story. As continental culture had no context for the association of queen to cupbearer, a second personification of the queen assumed that role on the continent — she became the servant who could bear the cup. The invented character, the servant, linguistically had the same name in both the French and Welsh versions.

A doublet was not the solution employed in the Tristan stories, however. The names of Essyllt and Branwen/Branguen are in no way similar, nor do their root words have the same meaning. On the other hand, there seems to be some evidence that Essyllt might well have been added to the Tristan story at some time after his transmission to southern Wales. Because of this, it is possible that Branwen/Branguen could have been the original queen.

Branwen stands in contrast to the characters of Medb or even Gwenhwyfar in that the theory finds little evidence in her name, which translates as "White Crow" or in English speech "Black Sheep." Still, the character shares her name with the Branwen of the *Mabinogi*. That character was the sister of a queen and married a king. Beyond that, little can be determined at this time.

Hu(s)dent is the name of Tristan's hound in Béroul. It is specially trained to hunt without barking. Husdent is a Welsh name, translating to "of the good teeth." He appears in all four of the earliest romances, everywhere in the role of Tristan's pet and partner in the hunt. His uniform presence is odd in view of the fact that he seems to have no particular incident associated specifically with him, however.[23] The hound's lack of purpose suggests that his original role has been erased from the tales, but his presence has managed to linger on without it. If he was a part of an earlier adaptation, it would make good sense that he was involved in the killing of the Fomori; there his hunting skills would have been of greatest use. When the Fomori combat was altered to defeating a knight at the beginning of his career and in a courtly setting, Husdent was no longer welcome in that part of the story. In Eilhart von Oberge, his training in the forest is omitted entirely, though he does suddenly appear later in the story.

Tristan's seneschal and tutor in most of the romances is Guvernal, a Breton name of the twelfth century. Because of its provenance, it seems most likely that the he was inserted into the plot with the legend's transference to the continent and therefore has little value in the current study.

Béroul is of more interest here; he calls the same character Dinas de Lidan. Dinas de Lidan appears to be a misunderstanding of Welsh *Dinas Lidan* with the preposition added to make the name sound French. It translates as "broad fortress."[24] Dinas Lidan appears only once in British history, as a fortress in southern Wales. Though it has often been said that Béroul seems to have an overwhelming amount of local information relating to Cornwall, this place name embedded in his version is proof that his source's information was not confined to that region. Again, it indicates that the Tristan story was at one point relocated to Cornwall from Wales.

Morgan is mentioned or alluded to in all of the earliest romances. He is unanimously connected to the death of Tristan's father and is called either a neighbor or lord of Tristan's kingdom in several interpretations of the legend. It is tempting to look through the genealogies and connect him to the infamous one-time ally of Urien who may have been responsible for his death, or his grandfather. These men are both associated with a Lothian dynasty, the same region from which Tristan came. However, a Morgan son of Owain also appears to have been an influential figure of the tenth century. He was from southeastern Wales, the same region where Dinas Lidan was located. It is impossible to tell where Morgan might have been added to the story, whether at its point of origin or while it was in southern Wales. There is simply not enough information at this time.

The figure of Arthur should also be mentioned in this list of characters, as he is consistently present in all the earliest romances. Reading through them, however, his role grows more significant with time. In Thomas, he is nothing more than part of a vague and distant past. In Béroul, he is a faraway king, while Eilhart allows his hero to join his court for a short time. By the *Prose Tristan*, Arthur is a prominent part of the story, and his knights actively take part in Tristan's life and adventures. It is safe to say that Tristan was slowly drawn into Arthur's orbit as the Arthurian tales became more and more popular. Working backwards, it seems unlikely that Arthur was present in the story when it was transferred to the continent.

Finally we come to Tristan's parents, in three of the four earliest versions

18. The Characters and Their Roles

they are named Rivallon and Blancheflour. This is noteworthy, as it has been seen that Drystan/Drust is normally given the patronymic of Tallwch in British sources.[25] The inconsistency presents a problem and clearly not one of transmissional translation.

Fortunately, it is a problem easily solved. As de la Borderie long ago realized, Pierre le Baud recorded a Tristan son of Rivalen who was the Lord of Vitré between 1030 and 1045.[26] This man lived in Brittany, the same region that was at that time translating Welsh materials into French through both formal and informal means.[27] He also had several noteworthy disputes with his overlord. Loomis believed it was this Breton Tristan who patronized the story of the British Tristan, and in honor of him the hero's patronymic was changed to that of the Vitré lord's father in order to draw a closer parallel to him.[28] After initially believing the Tristan son of Rivalen to be "too insignificant a figure, too late, and in the wrong part of Brittany," Bromwich eventually came to see that significance, floruit, and location need not have been factors in whether the Lord of Vitré had access to the right information and the right poet to influence the development of the legend.[29]

What she left unsaid (the present author cannot believe she might not have considered this) is that acknowledging the suggestion of how the patronymic was changed provides a great deal of insight into the probable development of the Tristan legend. Directly, it tells us that the name had been successfully transferred to the continent by 1045, the year Tristan son of Rivalen died.[30] Realizing when and how the patronymic was changed also reveals that whatever native legend might have been attached to Tristan originally, by the eleventh-century, the names of his parents were being altered. This means that other and less rigid aspects of his story may well have been quite flexible by that time as well.

More broadly, the fact that all the earliest Tristan storytellers, from Thomas to Eilhart, followed that anonymous artist and gave the hero the identical father's name is further confirmation that the continental story was consistent as early as the eleventh century. When the first extant authors began to write about him, they were drawing on sources that extended only to that point.

A study of the more important characters in the Tristan legend has revealed some intriguing results. A Pictish hero is associated with a king of southern Wales and a specific site in the same area. He finds a love interest in what is possibly a famous woman of ninth-century Gwynedd. The only demonstrably precontinental adventure associated with Welsh Drust involves the slaying of at least one *Fomóire*. There is also Tristan's dog, named Husdent, who most likely would have aided him in that battle. The continental stories consistently include a woman named Brangein who acts as Isolt's handmaiden.

Her name might possibly signify her as a cupbearer in her own right. Brangein's presence may imply a second early episode or connection involving kingship. The above is a stimulating combination of names and places revolving around Tristan; the reader will do well to keep them in mind as the author continues to unravel aspects of his legend.

19

Thomas of Britain

That the saga of Tristan spent time in an oral and French environment seems certain. As has been seen with *La Charrette* and *Le Conte*, the transference of Arthurian materials might have involved manuscripts, but much of the information that eventually found its way into the extant French romances transferred to the continent by word of mouth as well. Tristan's romance, as part of the same body of literature, was prey to those same forces of transmission. And as with the two Arthurian stories studied previously, we know little about the exact particulars of its transference.

When and where the story of Tristan was first written down cannot be competently conjectured upon because of the lack of relevant information on the subject. Thomas is only the first known author of the Tristan romance of the continent. His extant redaction consists of six manuscripts and ten fragments, three of which were destroyed in a fire in 1870.[1] The ten combined have been calculated as comprising no more than one-sixth of the poem as he must have created it.

Thomas wrote at some time around 1165, though his most accomplished translator, Arthur Hatto, postulated a year anterior to 1160,[2] and it is known that he quoted about thirty lines directly from the *Brut*,[3] a work firmly established at 1155. For relative dating, Frederick Whitehead noted that Thomas' writing technique is based on Wace and the romance writers of antiquity, especially *Enéas* (1150). Following the analogy, Thomas likely predates *Cligès*, where the more advanced poetic form that would be employed from that point forward in Arthurian romances was first put in practice.[4] Unfortunately, it is only certain that Chrétien's poem was written around 1175. The rather large and inexact interval of 1155 to roughly 1175 is all that can be managed at this time.

Of Thomas of Britain's life and education, nothing is known. Only Gottfried mentions him of all later writers. No study of his literary influences, classical and *medieval*, has ever been conducted either. Because of the general lack of scholarly interest in him, there is no way of knowing how much he might have taken from contemporary authors and events and how much relied on the story he was handed. His anonymity also means there can be no indicators of where a passage has been specifically altered to expunge some undesirable Celtic details, a luxury often taken advantage of with Chrétien de Troyes. All that can be done when reading through Thomas is conjecture. In Arthurian studies, conjecture is generally not that useful.

Of the setting in which Thomas produced his work more can be learned, and a more focused set of dates may be assigned as a result. Bedier said that he wrote in the French of the Angevin courts, though with a trace of Anglo-Norman.[5] Arthur Hatto noted two references to London and suggested that Tristan's first armor may have borne the Angevin arms of the twelfth century.[6] Tristan is bluntly placed in Brittany on several occasions, and the Angevins were of Breton descent. Separately, they are all innocuous facts. Put together, they suggest that Thomas had an affinity with the English dynasty just coming into power as he wrote, that of Henry II.[7]

Henry II, known also as the Count of Anjou, began his career as a vassal to King Louis VII of France. He was also a potential heir to the English throne and as such did not think solely as a vassal. When in 1152 his lord divorced Eleanor of Aquitaine, the richest heiress in Europe, Henry stepped in immediately and wooed her. The two were married within a few months and fast enough to suggest that they had simply waited for a minimum time before marrying.

Henry may well have wed her for love, as the love courts they hosted seemed to indicate, but his marriage had political consequences well beyond embarrassing Louis. The French king's matrimony with Eleanor and his resulting land gain had bolstered France into perhaps the most powerful kingdom in Europe, while Henry's territory had been nothing more than one vassalage within it. Gaining Aquitaine as his lord lost direct control over it put them on a roughly equal footing. In time, the change in power would lead to the Hundred Years' War. For her part, Eleanor must have recognized the political ramifications as well, but she never seemed to have regretted her decision. She thought nothing of Louis as a political figure and had only disgust for him as a husband.

Henry and Eleanor's marriage was a happy one for nearly two decades. The couple was rarely apart from each other and seemed to have been traveling constantly. Their passion and their wandering would set the tone for romance and romance literature over an entire generation. Looking back over the Tristan story, it is not far to see the connection of Louis/Mark, Henry/Tristan, and Isolt/Eleanor. The new lovers traveled constantly, enjoying each other's company intensely. And like the literary triangle, the historical original had

19. Thomas of Britain

a woman loved by one man whom she loved, while a second man had claims on her and a feudal obligation from her lover. It is quite feasible, perhaps even likely, that the romantic triangle was an idea of Thomas' time, first put in writing by Thomas himself.

The characters in Thomas's writing seem to reflect the reality of the day. Though Mark is renowned for his chivalry and power, he is the sedentary king that the influential Louis VII was. Tristan is the valiant knight. He is heir to Mark's throne and a king in his own right much as Henry was a respected knight who would become King of England and later make claims to the French throne. Isolt is married to one man by arrangement, but finds love with another. Her life was a perfect reflection of Eleanor's.

All that was different was the legality of their relationship, and one can see that the differences might have been created to enhance the drama. Though allowing Isolt to divorce Mark and marry Tristan might have precisely paralleled the activities of Eleanor, Louis, and Henry, Thomas must have had more of an eye for the potential of the story than to simply allow art to imitate life so closely. In real life, Louis had no choice but to allow it, and the couple never had any issues with him.

For the sake of a good story, it was much more romantic for the couple to have an active husband to flee from. Hiding for their lives and having only their love to sustain them created passion and a better plot. Thomas could well have imagined Henry and Eleanor wishing they could run away and live only with each other but being unable to do so because of their responsibilities.

Between Henry and Eleanor, most likely Eleanor was the patron for the story. In Thomas' romance, Isolt has the stronger personality of the pair. She is always the partner finding ways to elude her husband and continue their forbidden trysts. She is intelligent, resourceful, and most of all pragmatic. It is she who eventually goes back to Mark so that her lover can finally be free of Mark's vengeance. And unlike the next great female character in Arthurian romance, Guinevere, Isolt's motivations are clear and her character is consistent. She is the best developed character in all the early Arthurian romances. She is very much like the historical figure Eleanor of Aquitaine, whom she emulated.

20

The Literary Source Material

It bears repeating that the story of Tristan derives from a limited number of sources. The Welsh mention him in three venues before the thirteenth century: in two partial and obscure poems found in the *Black Book of Carmarthen*, in several triads of the *Trioedd Ynys Prydein*, and in scattered allusions by the Welsh poets.

The *Black Book* entries are found within a group of five *ymddiddanion*, or dialogue poems. The *awdlau*, or odes, are widely held to have once belonged to a larger narrative.[1] The original editor of the poems, Joseph Loth, believed that they dated to the first half of the twelfth century.[2] However, Rachel Bromwich noted several archaic features that are paralleled in the other dialogue poems of the group. She proposed a date of before 1100 instead.[3] This conclusion seems to have held up over the decades.[4]

One of the relevant fragments mentions Tristan and the other a March, while a certain Cyheig is named in both pieces. The former two characters comprise the traditional male elements on the continent and are therefore to be expected. The poems are considered of use to "Tristan studies" only because Drystan and March are specifically named. The names of the speakers are not given, nor is there enough specific information to be certain of whom they might be or at what point in the Tristan saga the dialogues might take place.[5]

This third figure, Cyheig is the only other tying feature between the two poems. His continental counterpart, if he has one, is unknown. His relationship with the speakers and the other named individuals is left obscure, providing few clues as to the content of the proposed narrative that was intended to surround it. The only direction to be found is that both awdlau involve some form of repentance over Cyheig's death.[6] However, the nature of that event or action has never been satisfactorily explained.

Trioedd Ynys Prydein, the second native body of literature containing Tristan, offers very little information on the hero either. While Tristan (here

Drystan) is named three times in the earliest stratum of triads, two of the instances refer broadly to his prowess; he is an enemy-subduer and a battle-diademed warrior. Only in the third triad are his activities even alluded to. It is in Triad 26 that he, along with Pryderi and Coll mab Collfrewy, are named as swineherders. They have been honored because each of them was once attacked by a famous thief while safeguarding pigs. Drystan's opponent was Arthur. The extended triad explains that Tristan had temporarily taken over swineherder duties so that another person could make contact with Drystan's lover. While he was gone, Arthur and his band had attempted to take the pigs.

One might hope that the episode was a memory of some historical incident; an insight into some aspect of the Tristan legend that a scholar might be able to find hints of in the continental literature. From there, it might even be possible to understand the entire legend from a new perspective. It is unfortunate that optimism would not serve a Tristan lover well here.

As Rachel Bromwich has correctly pointed out, there is something distinctly out of place in putting the heroes Drystan and Pryderi into the role of pig keepers. In *Y Gododdin*, the Taliesin poems, and the odd stanzas and narratives from the earliest period of British poetry, warriors and chieftains are given epithets that refer to them as cattle protectors, pillars for men, wolves on the battlefield, and mead earners. Nowhere is there any mention of a worthy warrior being a pig herder. Beyond the stereotype of pigs being dirty, Celtic society did not hold them valuable; three of them were the equal of one cow. Pigs simply weren't important enough to worry about keeping from raiders. They weren't important enough to make a raid for.

Dr. Bromwich suggested instead that the entire triad was created for a more political purpose. The third listed man, Coll mab Collfrewy, does not appear to have been as much of an influential presence in Welsh literature as the other two; this triad is the only occasion in which the name appears, in fact. His inclusion in the pneumonic only takes place in the expanded version, which is a second good clue to give the passage careful scrutiny. A brief summary of his episode is in order.

In contrast to the first two examples of prime pig keeping, Coll was forced to follow his charge, Henwen, as it bolted. The sow ran all over Wales before finally being pinned down and returned home. In looking over the account as it is laid out, it has almost nothing to do with Coll, and certainly allowing his charge to escape was not a good example of pig keeping. Instead, the significance lies in the swine and the path it takes. The boar takes roughly the same route as the Twrch Trwyth only backwards. And, while the Twrch Trwyth seems to produce pleasant items in the North and more negative objects in southern Wales, Coll's boar takes an opposing there as well. In short, the triad is a parody and a counter to the Twrch Trwyth boar chase in *Culhwch ac Olwen*. Belittling the entire story and by extension Gwynedd is likely the whole point of the entire triad.[7] What this means for the current study is that Tristan's exploits are only laid out once in all of the extant Welsh literature. That singular instance is nothing more than a creation designed to fill out a triad specifically created for the express purpose of insulting Gwynedd.[8] In developing a better understanding of the Tristan story, the British give us nothing. However, the remaining chapters of this book will go a long way in giving some meaning to their lack of interest in him.

As the previous chapter has demonstrated, Thomas came next and is the first continental writer whose version of the Tristan legend has survived. Two simple facts bear that out. The first is that the circumstances of his patronage strongly suggest that the plot he wrote was determined by it. Second is that all other Tristan authors followed his characters and motivations with remarkable uniformity.

Béroul was likely the next extant author. His version survives in only one copy;[9] and that is flawed. The manuscript is filled with duplicate lines and is missing several individual rows and couplets. The poet wrote in the latter half of the twelfth century, possibly before 1191.[10] He composed in a Norman dialect, and it is possible that he had lived in England at one point. Little is known of him personally or of the area or patrons with which he was involved. However, it seems likely that he had some direct access to a British source. As has been seen, he alone uses the Welsh forms of *Husdent* and *Dinas de Lidan* for Tristan's hound and tutor. In 1953, le Gentil made a strong argument that he had gone against the archetype as set out by Thomas,[11] and those two examples as well as his accurate Cornish knowledge (above) support such a conclusion more poignantly than anything that illustrious scholar pointed out. However, Béroul seems to have followed Thomas where it suited him as well. He and all those who followed him duplicated the Eleanor/Louis/Henry love triangle in drawing his characters.

Béroul also introduced one very curious detail to the story; it is with him that the love potion gains the quality of having a limited potency; after three years it is no longer as potent. Chapter 20 will explain the roots of the love potion and provide further evidence that Thomas was the progenitor of the Tristan tale as we now have it.

The next source for Tristan materials is probably the German author Eilhart von Oberge. That is the generally acknowledged name of the author, mainly because an Eilhardus de Oberch is found in the Welsh charters between 1189 and 1209/27.[12] However, it is also possible that Eilhart is only the name of a thirteenth-century redactor of the story. His name is only found in manuscripts no earlier than the fifteenth century. As nothing is known of either the charter signer or the hypothetical redactor, the distinction makes no difference to the present study. Eilhart's work has survived in two complete manuscripts, which are from the fifteenth century and contain modernized words. They vary greatly from each other. An additional four fragments extend back to the late twelfth and into the thirteenth century.

Speculation as to when and where the original author might have composed the work varies widely and those conjectures have shaped the nature and direction of each scholar's studies on the subject for decades. While Frederick Whitehead judged the narration to date from 1150 or 1160,[13] Kurt Wagner suggested about 1170 in his translation and was followed by several recent scholars.[14] Jan van Dam believed it was written by 1176,[15] while dates of c. 1190 and c. 1208 have been proposed.[16] As it has already been seen that the romantic triangle was most likely created by Thomas, however, and the dates for his writing can be firmly set after the publication of the *Brut* in 1155, it is safe to say that roughly 1155 is the earliest possible year for the German romance. That is all that can be said with any certainty about the dating of this version at the moment.

Eilhart's interpretation was written in either the lower Rhine or at the Brunswick court. Both were areas of heavy literary activity and patronage during the latter half of the twelfth century.[17] The former location was naturally suited for early cultural contacts with France, while the latter could claim the residence of Matilda, daughter of the Henry II whom we have already met as the husband of Eleanor and therefore a logical possessor of Tristan information.

Gertrude Schoerpperle believed that Eilhart's version most closely resembled the original in its handling of the materials.[18] However, a point by point evaluation of her evidence reveals that most of her positions have been reversed by more thoroughly educated scholars in the century since she proposed them, while the rest have been rendered otherwise irrelevant. As an example, she cites the limiting time frame of the love potion as an indicator of its earlier date. Again that is not the case. However, giving it a limited period of maximum effectiveness allowed for the plot of the Tristan story to continue developing in a more satisfying manner than is found in Thomas.

Other instances are immediately apparent as one reads through the other accounts. The healing of Tristan from the sword wound is more complicated with Eilhart. His meeting with Essyllt, his means of returning home from Ireland, and the overall portrayal of Mark are better thought out and generally more complex in Eilhart than in either Thomas or Béroul. His modifications can be seen in simple details as well. Items are added with Eilhart, such as when Tristan is credited with being the first person to fish with a bent hook. They are also taken away in a manner that shows the material was originally there. As has been noted above, Eilhart does not depict Tristan educating his hunting dog. The hound simply appears as a fully trained companion, and it is only after reading Thomas and Béroul that one sees why Eilhart might have felt comfortable simply inserting the animal. All of these particulars mark Eilhart as an author who is reshaping an already completed tale much like what Thomas' version would have looked like. He is trying to improve upon it and has only had mixed results.

Several nonrelated items argue against the conclusion that Eilhart produced a more archaic account as well. While Eilhart might have fashioned less of a romance than either Thomas, Gottfried, or Béroul, the world he created was certainly more chivalric in the medieval sense of the word. In Eilhart's rendition, Tristan becomes a member of Arthur's court for the first time. These knights regularly go out on adventures and fight one another to gain further honor. The villains, especially from the point at which Tristan is banished from Cornwall on, are honest and honorable. All this is different from the attitudes one finds in Thomas, and a far cry from anything a more primitive source might have contained. As has been seen while studying *La Charrette* and *Le Conte*, a life of battles, alcohol, and revelry lent itself to hard men. They were more concerned with fame after death and the pleasures of the moment than with the courtly manners of the twelfth century. The concept of befriending a fighter from another war-band would have been foreign to them. The idea of helping a fellow warrior to have trysts with his queen would have been appalling.

On the contrary, further evidence suggests that Eilhart relied heavily on Thomas. In his *Tristant*, the dwarf hired by the antagonists to incriminate Tristan is named Aquitain,[19] a nod to Thomas' patron, Eleanor. Tristan's opponent during the third act of the narrative is Riole from Nantes.[20] Nantes was a prominent city under Henry of Anjou. Eilhart also seems to be adding on to what Thomas has done in finding humor where his progenitor had seen romance. Where the brother of the second Isolt confronted Tristan about his relationship with his sister, was brought to see the first Isolt, and spent the night with Brengain in Thomas, Eilhart gave the same sequence of events but then raised the stakes by Isolt's brother the lady of his choice. With the reader's expectations high, the poor boy is put to sleep through trickery and left without any companion for the evening.

Thomas was not the only extant source he seems to have used. In one instance, Eilhart apparently had at least part of the same unique source materials as Béroul. As has been seen, Tristan's tutor with the enigmatic Frenchman was Dinas de Lidan, whose name is a devolution of the Welsh place name Dinas Lidan. In Eilhart's work, the name is Tinas of Lîtan; Thomas' Guvernal does not figure into the story at all.

In both cases, Eilhart was clearly the person borrowing and altering materials from the other two authors. What happens to Isolt's brother makes no sense unless the audience already expected him to find favors in Isolt's court. Eilhart's Tinas of Lîtan is further removed from the original of Dinas Lidan than Thomas' Dinas de Lidan because of the retention and translation of French *de*. The reverse makes no sense.

Gottfried von Strassburg was probably the next writer of the Tristan legend. In some ways he is a simple writer to make use of. He was, by his own admission, simply rewriting the story as Thomas told it. Comparison with the Thomas fragments confirms that he remained very close to his source in most respects. Scrutiny of the two sources by literary scholars has shown that he well exceeded Thomas in his writing, however.

The German scholar is believed to have written at some time around or before 1210. Our only clues as to his floruit, however, come from his references to the death of Heinrich von Veldeke and the writings of Wolfram von Eschenbach and several other prominent writers of the period.[21] These are by no means a reliable.[22] Gottfried might well have written much later than the assigned date.

Exactly who he was and what lord he might have worked for have been the subject much debate over the past century. It has been suggested that Gottfried was classically trained[23] because of his broad readings. Evidence of his theological training has also been discussed.[24] This discussion has been based on the fact that later poets referred to him as "meister," which in medieval culture was someone who had undergone a lengthy process of study at a religious center. The way he approaches his materials, his references to previous works, and his style all support this latter theory.[25]

Regardless of his official training, Gottfried von Strassburg was a master of language, both French and German. He was extremely well read with regard to his contemporaries and classical works; he regularly calls on the muses and Apollo for inspiration and does so as if they were familiar friends he knew intimately from his own readings. Further, Gottfried shows himself to be knowledgeable in music, poetry, a combination of the two known as *minnesang*, and hunting. All of these hobbies show up in the romance as he enhances Thomas' story with his own understanding of those subjects. His knowledge and presentation are what marks him as superior to his antecedent.

With the *Prose Tristan* we have familiar characters and scenes that have become in many ways a carbon copy of all previous Tristan stories. Still, Bédier is considered the father of Tristan studies, and he believed that *The Prose Tristan* was the last continental romance with any uniquely British information in it. For that reason alone it belongs in any review of sources with potentially original materials.

A cursory perusal of the introduction shows that a Luce from Gat Castle near Salisbury initiated the work. A closer examination reveals that even what little the original author gave of himself was a lie; Luce is otherwise unknown in the historical records, and the Gat Castle that he claims to be from never existed.[26]

A "Helie de Boron" appears in the epilogue as a second author. Likely he was responsible for finishing the book and is credited with most of its contents.[27] Not surprisingly, there is no indication that Helie was in any way related to the more famous Robert de Boron. It seems likely that this author's name, too, was a nom de plume. "Boron" would have been chosen only because of its connection to the famous writer Robert de Boron in hopes of cashing in on his credibility.[28] This leaves the scholar with no person to connect with the work and, therefore, no external means of gathering information about how or why it might have been put together.

The most recent editor of the Tristan portion of the manuscript has given a date of 1230x1235 for the initial story and has suggested that it was reworked and expanded at some time after 1240.[29] These two time-frames may coincide with the two known authors, but there has been no discussion over that possibility at this time. There are over forty manuscripts extant.

Taking only those sections into consideration that speak of Tristan, the *Prose Tristan* is still twice as large as any previous version. This is because of the assimilation of several characters and themes from the rest of Arthuriana. Merlin is inserted, being present at the birth of Tristan and recurring early on in the story. Tristan has a run-in with a stepmother who tries to kill him and is involved with two other women before he meets Isolt. He interacts with several new knights from Arthur's court in new adventures. The Goblet of Infidelity is also present. However, as to original Celtic materials that indicate access to an unknown source, the present author must side with Vinaver that it was simply a sequel to and an elaboration of the *Vulgate*.[30] Potentially, it made use of a good many other twelfth-century verse romances as it interweaved them into a common story thread, but it is entirely devoid of any original materials.[31]

The Madness of Tristan seems be little more than a means of having the two chief characters of the Tristan legend interact under the nose of Mark. In it the hero feigns insanity as he comes to Mark's court. Once there, Tristan alludes to a number of his adventures with Isolt in order to convince her of his identity. The scene is set at a time after Tristan's voluntary banishment. It was written anonymously, contains nothing of value as it only mentions well-known episodes from the other romances, and has generally been ignored by Tristan scholars. The author agrees that, in this respect, the short work has no usefulness whatsoever.

20. The Literary Source Material

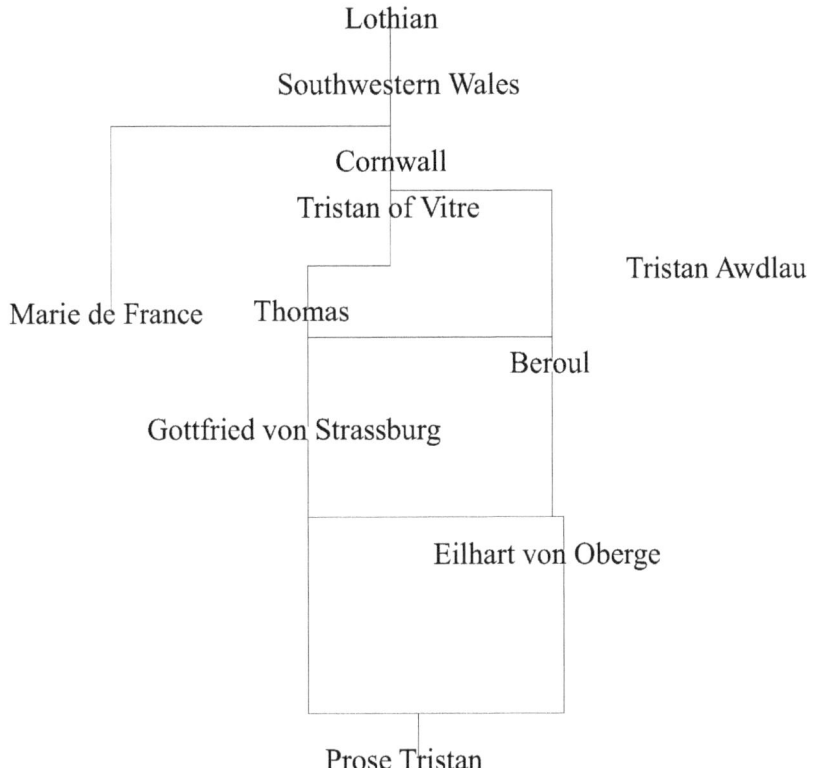

A revised development of the Tristan legend. The traditional separation of archaic and courtly versions is largely absent here, with the influence of Thomas of Britain on all subsequent versions of the story being plainly laid out.

The Welsh poets who spoke of Tristan composed well after the influence of Gwynedd had passed in the ninth century and at a time when Dyfed's reactions to her attempts at unification were long forgotten. They lived in a Wales that was no longer actively struggling for unity and separation; it was one whose lords had accepted English suzerainty for some time. Because of that, many of her heroes had become little more than names, traditional stories attached to them having been forgotten or corrupted. Other protagonists had stories that were so well known that only the briefest of allusions were necessarily, or were used, to touch the audience.

Because of the state of affairs in Wales at that time, it is unsurprising that Drust is associated with nothing more than praises as a paragon of the perfect warrior in their stanzas. Their allusions are too few, too vague, and rely on too much assumed and now-forgotten information to be anything more than tantalizing as things stand. What is more, none of the Welsh writings appear before about 1250, meaning that they date to almost a century after Thomas wrote and well after the explosion of interest in Tristan on the continent. It must be assumed that they were influenced by the story and motifs of Thomas and those who followed him in ways which the modern scholar has no means to measure.

What can be concluded from a study of the sources may be summed up as follows. Drystan was an accepted and traditional hero whose original existence was outside of the Arthurian obit. We know this because as late as Thomas' writing Arthur was not even considered his contemporary.[32] Drystan is nowhere in the earliest sources labeled as a great lover. This most likely means that he was not seen as a romantic character in the earliest British traditions.

As the evidence is sifted, Thomas comes across as being of unique importance to Tristan studies. He appears to have drafted the basic plot from which all later redactors took their cues. The romantic triangle and the cursed lovers likely stemmed from the pen of Thomas, and his inspiration was the royal couple who likely patronized him. He cannot have been writing in 1045 during the time of Tristan son of Rivallon, as his romance can safely be placed at least 115 years later. This means he was not the first continental artist to treat him, or the only inventive one. However, once he had written, all previous attempts at the subject matter were forgotten in favor of his approach. In that respect, he was the father of the Tristan romance.

After Thomas, several authors followed in quick succession. Each writer focused on some aspects of the story that Thomas had created while minimizing others, but essentially they kept the story intact in a way that the grail, the abduction of the queen, and most other Arthurian stories never managed. The question we must ask ourselves is why. The most reasonable answer is because the tale of Tristan and Isolde did not possess the depth and history that the two stories studied above had. There was no wealth of information to be interpreted and recast in light of another look at the British materials. There was no older root from which the story came. There was only Thomas to look to for themes and ideas, without any body of British literature or bardic interpretations from which to draw inspiration on the subject. The story we know as Tristan did not exist before roughly 1160.

21

Motifs and Details: Clues of Celtic Origins

In the previous two tales studied here, this chapter has shown that a great many more details of the Arthurian tales could have been based on the sixth century than can be proven. In each case, an argument was made for their historical validity followed by an acknowledgment of other possibilities. However, in the case of the Tristan legend, such a goal would not be pragmatic. It would seem that here there so many minutiae, motifs, and aspects of the plot came from the continent that there is no way of determining what was covered up. It is therefore more pragmatic to employ this chapter for the express purpose of determining exactly what was and was not British.

Looking through the names alone, it is apparent that the story revolving around Tristan is of British derivation. The names of Drust/Drystan, March, Essyllt, the Fomóire, Brangien, Husdent, and Dinas de Lidan have been generally accepted as Celtic and British. It is only that fact that their origins have been located all over Britain that has led to so many problems in understanding the origins and points of transmission for the story.

Other aspects of the legend seem to be Celtic as well. The first thing that should stand out for the reader is Tristan's extraordinary cultural abilities, which are much more courtly and refined than those of any other Arthurian heroes. Thomas goes to great lengths to show the boy's linguistic abilities, his imitation of birdsongs, his mastery of musical instruments, and his knowledge of the finer points of hunting. Tristan only learns of knighthood and fighting when he comes to live with King Mark at the end of his childhood. His early education, entirely unique among Arthurian heroes, is similar only to that of the heroes in the Fenian cycle. There all of the men living in commune with nature have the same exceptional cultural development, as Ms. Schoepperle long ago saw.[1]

As has been noted above, the dragon story did not come from the continent, either. Nor did Tristan's combat with the champion of Ireland. Both appear to have been variations of the same story used for a different purpose: one in which Drust protected his uncle's kingdom and the other where he defeated the Fomóire and rescued the princess.

The next major point in the story is the voyage home, wherein the fateful ingestion of the love potion occurs. After the two have drunk the mixture, both Tristan and Isolt become unwitting participants in their own romance. The tone and direction of the story change dramatically at that point, making the scene the pivotal one of the story. And yet the way in which the mysterious concoction is treated in the rest of the narrative seems to make little sense. The various writers who treated it had some difficulty in handling its supreme potency. Originally, it remained all consuming, and it was only through the wills of Tristan and Isolt that the pair was able to finally separate at the end of their forest banishment. As the legend developed, the potion was given the quality of weakening with the passage of time because it allowed for the two to separate. However, no matter where in the development of the tale one looks, their ability to live apart and for Tristan to be married are never explained to any satisfaction. As has been seen in Chrétien's works, these are excellent indicators that something Celtic has been poorly interpreted to fit into the thinking of medieval, continental Europe.

Again Schoepperle was able to uncover what was likely the original reason for their behavior in her researches. Whereas love potions are unknown in Ireland, the concept of *geis*, Welsh *tyghet*, was an often-used and widely recognized device in the oral literature of both cultures. Its direct translation was fate, but it was more accurate to call it a curse. It was a personal taboo put on someone, and to break it was to embrace the greatest dishonor. The greatest Irish hero, Cú Chulainn, was killed when all of his geis were exploited to weaken him. Eventually, he was rendered powerless through and was finally killed with relative ease.

Closer to home in the Fenian stories, Diarmid and Grainne's entire story is powered by the concept of *geis*. Grainne is betrothed to an older man of great power and influence named Fionn. Having no wish to marry him, she convinces Diarmid to elope with her. And, when her sexual advances are rejected, she implies she might lay a geis on him unless he takes her as his lover. He obeys her. That one act condemns him and forces them both to hide in the forest like Tristan and Isolt.[2] The concept appears to have been a pan-Celtic one, treated the same in Wales. The taboo imposed on the Welsh character Culhwch of only marrying Olwen is just as powerful for him as it is for Cú Chulainn and Diarmid.

The continent had nothing comparable to the uniquely Celtic notion of the *geis/tyghet*. The Roman and the Germanic traditions had placed men strictly over women in all social contexts. The concept of something as liberal as mutually respectful relationships had only recently been developed in the love courts of Eleanor and Henry II. Even coming from such a liberal perspective, a story where a woman told a man that he had to make love to her on pain of his honor would have been unthinkable.[3] That it came from a princess would have made even less sense, as it would have been considered quite vulgar. By extension, any convention that allowed for such a mode of behavior would have seemed barbaric.

Whichever continental romancer first treated the subject with a non–British audience in mind (and the present author would suggest it was Thomas), he was faced with a double dilemma. There was first of all the utterly foreign concept to deal with, one that made no sense by continental standards and therefore would be extremely difficult to explain to his audience. The second issue was the centrality of that concept to the story. Once it had been introduced, the nature of the account changed from that of a typical hero tale to a true romance. It could not be simply erased from the narrative.

Instead of pulling out the device or trying to explain it away and then finding some other way of getting the pair together, the anonymous literary man substituted it for something that he and his audience could understand: a love potion. And being good at his craft, that person made use of the problem in front of him to make the love story more intense than it had been originally. A mystical concoction served the same function as the *tyghet* in forcing both lovers to remain with each other at all times. However, by having Tristan as well as Isolt ingest the drug, he changed the nature of their love into a two-way devotion. A love potion also allowed the lovers to suffer while together and apart in a way that an enforced promise never could have managed.

Another motif that is demonstrably Celtic and not often repeated in the balance of Arthurian literature is the *Petit Crû*, the spectacular dog that carries a special bell around its neck. That bell has the property that whoever hears it forgets all their sorrows. Bromwich believed it was Thomas' idea,[4] and it does seem to have a touch of continental fabulous in the impossible colors of its coat. However, Schoepperle saw the creature as specifically Celtic, citing animals with similar characteristics in Irish lore. She noted that the bells it carries are found in Cormac's Branch.[5] She also realized that it, and Tristan's hound Husdent, are the only two named dogs in French romance. All forms of animals are named in Celtic myths and legends. These facts argue for a nonmotifal and Celtic origin.

It has already been fairly well established, with comparisons and direct examples, that the story of Tristan and Isolde in many ways parallels the myth of Diarmid and Grainne.[6] In fact, the comparison can be made more broadly than that. Several Irish stories involve lovers going against authority and running off to be with each other. The elopement of young lovers occupies a rather large body of literature in Ireland.

And from this comparison, two points can be made. First, that all the Celtic analogues end in one sudden and dramatic fashion. After successfully evading the would-be husband for some time, a truce is called. When the lovers come to make peace, the male is always killed by the man he has cuckolded.

Second, that not a single Celtic motif is to be found in the Tristan story after Mark accepts Isolt back to his bed and Tristan goes into voluntary exile. In fact, upon their realization of what they have cost each other and caused to occur, the entire story seems to take on an entirely different tone; that tenor is not a Celtic one. The evidence, internal and external, indicates that any Celtic love story involving Tristan had to end with an attempted reconciliation to Mark. For the sake of a king's honor, that attempt could only really end in Tristan's death.

Realizing that, the last portion of the romance, where Tristan goes to another kingdom, saves it, makes friends with its prince, and marries a second Isolt only to die by her actions is nothing more than invention. In light of that revelation, the idea relayed here that the Thomas romance was finished by someone else seems probable.

The story of Tristan, from his emergence at the court of Mark to his disappearance into the forest with Isolt, is infused with things Celtic. However, while studying Lancelot's rescue of Guinevere and Perceval's search for the Holy Grail have revealed consistent stories that belong to an easily placed period, the story of Tristan does not. Instead, it seems to be little more than a hodgepodge of motifs and details taken from a wealth of Celtic sources.

The Celtic motifs laid out in the pages above do constitute a least one distinct episode in what might have been a group of hero tales based around an historically dubious hero Drust. That single episode is the fight against the mythical Fomori and the resulting tyghet placed on Drust by the woman he had won. Beyond that, there seems to be very little of historical value in the story. It has been shown that Tristan's childhood developed on the continent either with the change of patronymics, with the development of the love triangle, or at some point in between. The love triangle was created by Thomas. The idea of Tristan and Isolt's time in the forest is Celtic, but there is nothing in the incidents that can be claimed as unique to the legend of Tristan and Isolt. In short, there seems to be no Celtic tale being retold with major and minor editing, but only a Celtic episode that has been attached to

21. Motifs and Details

a continental plot, with continental values dominating it. The rest of the story has a few scattered Celtic motifs, but they seem to be common in Celtic myth. The components also do not seem to be a part of a greater whole. In this crucial respect, it differs significantly from *La Charrette* and *Le Conte*.

22

The Sixth Century in Tristan

Although the motifs discussed in the previous chapter did not have the same "potentially historical" quality as those examined in *La Charrette* and *Le Conte*, understanding where the story took some of its ideas from has made it more clear as to how an original story might have been interpreted. In the previous two romances, the exercise was of great help in revealing a larger body of details that might well have been Early Medieval in nature and, when added to those elements of the stories that definitely are from the "Arthurian Era," helped to create a more full picture of the original historical actions than the stories remembered. The exercise again proves to be of help here, but in a different manner.

With the Tristan saga, entire episodes have parallels to be found regularly in Irish myth. The duel with Morholt and the fight of the dragon are doublets of a single fight with the Fomori as found in *Tochmarc Emer*. The taking of the love potion is likely a medieval interpretation of the tyghet. The lovers caught sleeping with a sword between them can also be found there, as is their time hiding from Mark in the forest together.

Elements can be found from the same reservoir. Tristan's courtly qualities would have seemed perfectly normal in the Fionn macCumhail's company, as have his birdsongs.

Others are decidedly the creation of the continent. The story and even the name of Tristan's parents change drastically from author to author and are therefore inventions. The romance from their time in the forest on is inconsistent and falls away from the desperate love story of the earlier portion.[1] In all probability this is where Thomas floundered — or perhaps his continuators did.[2]

So much of the story is pure traditional motifs that could in many ways be considered a myth or a simple version of the modern novel. And with all the influences made by contemporary literature and the Fionn cycle, two items seem to stand out as more than motifal. Pictish matrilineal succession and the name of Tristan's kingdom both suggest a connection to something historical.

In Thomas, and followed by every significant writer of the legend, Tristan is the son of a king. Every version studied in this monolith, apart from the *Prose Tristan*, he learns of his paternity as he is nearing adulthood, and that his father is dead. The situation does not require the storyteller to inform us that he is the heir to a kingdom.

At about the same time, depending on the story, Tristan is formally accepted by Mark as his heir apparent. Gottfried and apparently his source, Thomas, have him giving over the governorship of his kingdom to his foster parents. Later writers simply have Tristan move in with his uncle; neither the authors nor any of their characters question his decision. Granted, Tristan is given the same powers as the king himself in his new role, but he, a sovereign king in his own right, accepts the position of a member of another person's court.

In more developed Arthurian tales, this situation would become commonplace. Lesser characters would be beaten by Arthur's knights and would accept membership into Arthur's circle. However, Tristan is no lesser character, Mark is no Arthur, and the Tristan story in its earliest form was written centuries prior to the development of such fineries.

Tristan's relationship with Mark does not explain why the laws of primogeniture are being so blatantly avoided. It makes sense that a young Tristan might want to live with his uncle Mark, but the kingdom of Loenois would be his home and his responsibility. Even more than the morally questionable affair with Isolt, foregoing his duty of birth should be unthinkable to him. For anyone who would question such an assumption, one need only be reminded of the scandal caused when the heir to the British throne married a non-noble divorcee and in so doing rendered himself ineligible for the throne only a few decades ago.

Because it would have been in no way acceptable to a medieval audience, it seems highly unlikely to this author that the notion of giving up one's hereditary right would have been entirely invented. More likely, the continental authors began on the assumption that Tristan had to be the heir and were forced to deal with the incompatible information from the rest of the tale. That is, after all, probably why the issue is well explained at the beginning of the story and then thoroughly forgotten by most of the authors.

That Tristan was never the successor to his father's kingdom becomes clearer as the reader moves through the versions of the saga. When he and his lover are forced to flee from Mark, no extant version has him return to his home kingdom. Instead, they run to and hide in a forest. There they live at near-starvation levels for some time. The devil's advocate might argue that doing so would have lessened the romance, and the great pains the authors all go to in order to explain the pair's sufferings might seem to favor such an argument at first glance. However, the episode is a traditional one. As has been seen in the previous chapter, it is identical to Diarmid and Grainne in the environment, scenes, and danger from the jilted husband. Because of the distinctly Celtic tie, it is clear that it was a part of the yarn long before it traveled to the continent and was molded into a romance and, by default, that Tristan had to run into the forest because he had no patrimony to retreat to.

When the pair is reconciled with Mark, and Tristan is forbidden from returning to Tintagel's court, he again does not go back to his father's kingdom. Nor do his adoptive parents or siblings offer him any aid. Instead, he heads out toward a third kingdom. There he finds new friends, proves himself a superior leader, and marries the king's daughter as the narrative takes an unhappy turn.

On the other hand, several generations of scholars have believed that Tristan's origins are to be found in Pictland. And, as was noted with regard to Lancelot and Gawain in *La Charrette*, the Picts are known for their unusual rites of royal succession. Kings were selected from the female line of the royal family, from the maternal nephews of kings. If Mark, or whatever character he originally replaced, his children could not rule after him, but his sister's sons could. Tristan could inherit his throne. Similarly, Tristan's father could not leave him his kingdom, but he could leave them to his own sisters' sons. If the reader accepts that Tristan was originally a Pictish character, then his maternal uncle might well have announced him as an heir and treated him as such. So, too, Tristan would have had no rights to his native Loenois. In one stroke, an accepted truth of Tristan explains some of the less sensible aspects of the Tristan legend.

Thomas, in fact no writer from the continent, would have been able to grasp that inheritance through the female line was a normal matter of course among the Picts. For that reason, it was necessary to create a special circumstance to explain Mark and Tristan's behavior toward each other.

More importantly for the current study, maternal inheritance suggests that the story must come from no later than the ninth century. It was in 843 that the Picts were permanently put under the kingship of Scotland and patriarchal rule overwhelmed the matrilineal.

The second indicator that the story is considerably older is found in Tristan's home kingdom, Loenois. Typically, the name has been equated with Lothian in southern Scotland.[3] Place name evidence confirms the connection. The *Pictish Chronicles* name it Loonia and the *Anglo-Saxon Chronicle* calls it Loeneis in its 1158 entry.[4]

The Gododdin region, of which the Lothian kingdom was a part, would be conquered by the Northumbrians right around 600, and as with many other geographical points in Britain, its name would be forgotten in common usage within a few generations. This, it has been explained, is likely why the name was so easily altered on its trip to the continent.

Oliver Padel once commented that Lothian was not a Pictish kingdom,[5] and indeed the Welsh genealogies encompass several Gododdin royal families while the Pictish king-lists do not and none of the annals name a man from that area as a Pict. However, very few of the "Men of the North" who were eventually brought down to Wales were Picts, and so an additional transference from a Pictish kingdom to a northern British one is not out of the question. Such a possibility would allow for the literary Tristan to have derived from the historical son of Tallwch of the eighth century. Alternatively, Drust might simply have been a Pictish name that the Lothian House adopted. Possibly, Drust had a Pictish mother and a Lothian father, as the romances claim. He could have been raised in Lothian, or might have had the mindset that his father's homeland was his point of origin. As Lothian was a very short distance over Antonine's Wall to Pictish Fortriu, or across the Firth of Forth to Pictish Fib, it seems plausible. The Damnonioi mentioned earlier encompassed Strathclyde as well as southwestern Pictland, allowing for the possibility that his maternal uncle could have been Pictish as well.

Not much in the Tristan story clearly belongs to a period anterior to 900, but what is there seems to the present author to be incontrovertible. Nowhere else in the Arthurian corpus of literature is a maternal nephew designated as an heir[6] — and yet that very unlikely detail makes perfect sense in the context of preninth century Scottish history. Loenois/Loonis was entirely unrecognizable to the continental elite of the twelfth and thirteenth centuries, and yet it is easily seen to be a linguistic form of Lothian.

What also seems incontrovertible is that the story does not need to be placed in the Arthurian era by this evidence. Lothian and nepotism were around for a good long while before and after 500. In fact, it seems unlikely that he was a figure of the fifth or sixth century. Unlike the two previous tales, there is nothing that necessitates the conclusion. In the earliest romances, Arthur is unmistakably made a figure of a different period. The story is clearly Celtic, possibly historical, but it is extremely unlikely that the Drust/Tristan's career occurred during the "Arthurian" era.

23

Conclusion

Comparatively speaking, searching through the Tristan sources is an exercise in redundancy and futility. The limited number of resources, and the strangely consistent storylines, motifs, and details that five supposedly independent writers have provided, allows for only so much insight into the subject. It might be argued that a similar number of variations on the abduction of Gwenhwyfar are employed. The difference with the Tristan saga is considerably fewer parallels to make use of in better understanding certain aspects of the Tristan story. There is *Tochmarc Emer* for seeing the original doublet and purpose of the Morholt/dragon combats. The myth of Diarmid and Grainne provides a solid instruction on the hero and the nature of the pair's escape into the forest. That is, essentially, all the materials that are useful outside of the Tristan literature. Even that much has been a stretch of the resources available. The two myths used are not true parallels as neither are external to the development of the Tristan legend. Both have been either implicated in the development of the story or used the Tristan materials as part of their sources. And yet something materializes with the paucity of resources at hand. It would appear that the name and basic traits of Tristan, possibly along with the native story, were transferred to the continent at some point before 1045. It was at this time or before that his patronymic was changed to ingratiate a poet with his or her patron. Tristan's name at least was kept active in the oral literature for a century. Around 1160, and under the influence of Eleanor and Henry of Anjou, Thomas of Britain appears to have learned and reshaped the story of Tristan. It is unfortunate that there are not enough native materials to reconstruct what he might have had to begin with. Nor did those who followed him add anything truly Celtic to the story. Their lack of additional British materials has suggested that Thomas may well have been their only source of information.

This leaves the prehistory of the Tristan legend very much an unknown. However, certain information has emerged in the course of this study which, when properly understood and applied to previous studies, offers some tantalizing suggestions. At its core, what has been handed down to posterity is a simple hero-kills-monster-to-win-his-bride myth. The champion has his trusty dog to aid him in his task. The intriguing perspective of the story, however, is much more complex. It is seen most clearly in the history of the legend's transmission in Britain.

It has been over half a century now since Nora Chadwick suggested that the interests of the Gwynedd kings were being played out in the *Historia Brittonum*, several genealogies, and similar literature in the period, at the expense of southern Wales.[1] A hundred years later, the *Historia Brittonum* was revised under the auspices of the Dyfed king, Hywel Dda, as David Dumville rightly concluded only a quarter century ago.[2] The alterations were intended to lower the status of Powys and thereby the Gwynedd line that was partially derived from it. Geneaologies further forwarded the agenda of Dyfed.

It has long been held that the boar hunt scene in *Culhwch ac Olwen*, where the Twrch Trwyth runs all over Wales, was designed as propaganda against Dyfed. Rachel Bromwich realized that the sow "Henwen" in Triad 26 (the triad where Drust is a pigkeeper) was intended to be a retort or a farcical take on Twrch Trwyth's path in the way the pig brought forth a grain of wheat and a bee, and a grain of barley and a second bee in southern Wales. In northern Wales she produced the much more negative wolf cub, eagle, and Palug's Cat.[3]

The author would like to theorize that the Tristan legend was a part of the political literature of the time as well. In the earliest references, Drystan is already a southern Welsh figure,[4] while Essyllt was well known to medieval poets as the daughter of Cynan Tindaethwy and the heiress to Gwynedd.[5] Mention has been made of the fact that references to her are not always separable from allusions to Drystan's lover. It is also known that women were not considered to be of much consequence in heroic societies, and so the name of the lady the Welsh Drust had rescued from the dragon might well have been forgotten or superseded. As suggested above, *Brengain* is the most likely character to have been the original damsel in distress for the tale.

Conversely, it has seemed likely that the name of Essyllt was loaned into the Tristan cycle from the ninth-century princess and that her newly created character pushed the original personality into a lesser role. Considering these examples, it seems feasible that this was done for propagandistic reasons or simply as a burlesque to once again belittle Gwynedd. Perhaps the original popularity and extensive development of the story in Wales was due to its usefulness in that regard.

Apparently, however, Tristan in Wales was only an intermediary step in the development of the story. What has been seen in the literature is that Mark is consistently attached to Cornwall, and a vast majority of the story takes place there. The previous pages have demonstrated that a significant change in the continental version, a watershed, took place in Vitré under another Tristan. The kingdom of this known historical ruler was a part of Cornouailles, and the kings of Cornouailles likely claimed Mark and other famous figures as a part of their lineage. It was at this point that Mark likely transitioned from being a southern Welsh figure to a figure of Cornwall and particularly Tintagel.

Future authors would continue to relocate Tristan at their own discretion. Though Mark would remain in the known region of Cornwall, the extant authors would place the hero in England and all over Brittany.

The development of the legend of Tristan may be of interest for literary reasons, however the Tristan story is in no way a window on the sixth century or any aspect of the Arthurian era. It has no historical value whatsoever, except perhaps in confirming the kingship traditions of the Picts and giving further place name evidence for Lothian. In fact, there is no way of knowing exactly when the Tristan in question actually lived. The son of Talorcan was a figure of the eighth century. The patronymic of the Drust in *Tochmarc Emer* was Seirb. It is possible that the name is equivalent to Erb, and an individual with that father is listed as a Pictish king. He ruled at some point in the first half of the fifth century. It is every bit as possible that Drust was an historical figure from a kingdom or subkingdom of which there are no recorded kings. Drust could simply be an invented figure as old as the Picts in Scotland. The truth may never be known.

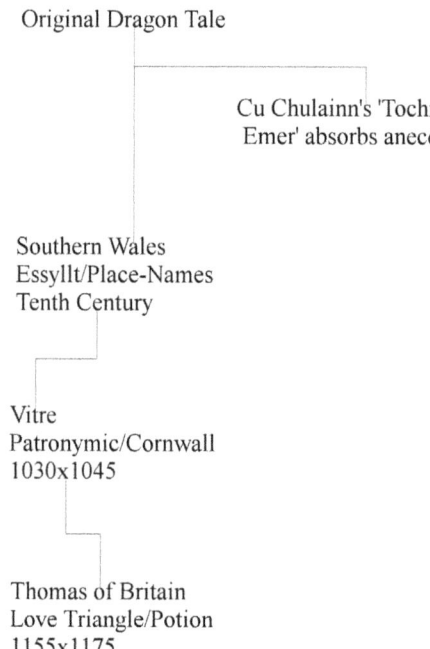

The development of the Tristan plot. Making use of common episodes and basic place-name evidence, the plot of the story is laid out. The story need not be very old, may involve a plot much older than the post–Roman period, and may not have been associated with Arthur until late in its development.

Appendix
Additional Thoughts

Lancelot's Cart

The ceremonial chariot or war cart found on the Meigle stone was not made from an Irish or pre–Roman model for two major reasons. First, it has open sides with two pole shafts to serve as railings. The reconstruction of Irish heroic-age chariots by David Greene has two closed side boards.[1] The carving shows three people — a driver and two passengers side by side, unlike Greene's construct. Also, the wheels have twelve spokes, presumably stronger than the standard eight from Ireland.[2]

Second, there is no archaeological evidence for awnings or chariots designed for more than two people in pre–Roman Britain,[3] nor is there Irish archaeological or literary evidence. This means that the carving is probably not representative of pre–Roman British culture.

The Bed Scene

Chrétien's "bed" scene, like the sword bridge and the infamous "cart," has no parallel in Celtic culture, nor has any French expert ever found an inspiration in contemporary or classical literature. This implies one of two possibilities: either Chrétien has invented the scene or he has misinterpreted something that was Celtic. The bed of Diarmid and Grainne offers a potential reason why it may have appeared in Chrétien's poem. In medieval Ireland, any unusual stone monuments were known as the "Bed of Diarmid and Grainne." That is, Irish legend had it that these were the places where the two famous lovers slept together as they were fleeing from Fionn MacCumhail. The other option, that Chrétien invented the material, is most definitely possible but unlikely in view of his tendency to borrow from other sources.

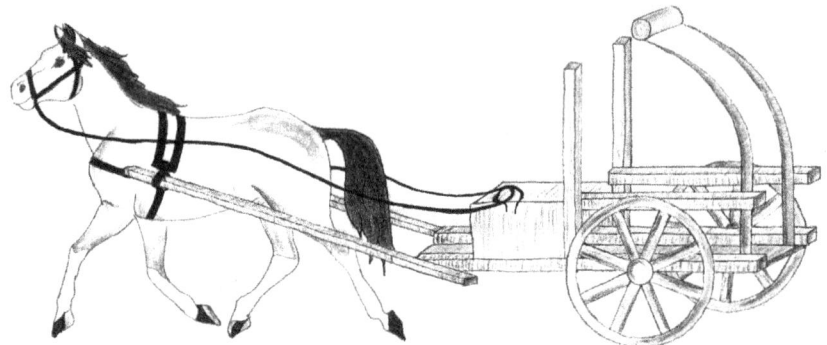

The Meigle Chariot

The Sovereignty Ritual

As a whole, the sovereignty ritual would appear to have been as follows. The best candidate for a vacant kingship would sit on a magical stone such as Lia Fail or the Stone of Scone. If he was to be the next king, the stone would give out a piercing scream. If not, the man would be swallowed by the stone, struck down by lightning, or otherwise punished for his transgression. There followed a ceremony where the successful candidate was symbolically wedded to his kingdom, in the form of a woman. The symbol of that joining was the cup of kingship. The woman herself would begin the ceremony as a hag, reflecting the land laid waste without her proper leader. Upon the conclusion, she would return to a state of beauty, much as the land would be bountiful under the rightful king.

The Possible Identity of Chrétien de Troyes

In going through the three stories, the author has noticed a few curious details and overlaps in the biographies, tendencies, and styles of Chrétien de Troyes and Thomas of Britain, which seem to lead in new directions. The following is an exploration of those directions. How much faith can be put in the ideas put forth and how useful that information might be, the author will leave to others. The present scholar has little knowledge in the relevant styles of poetry of the twelfth century and therefore finds himself ill-equipped to understand its nuances as well as the likely patterns of development and exploration. What the following paragraphs amount to are, in consequence, no more than organized notes.

As has been seen, Thomas was patronized by someone in the Angevin court, possibly the pair of Edward of Anjou and Eleanor of Aquitaine, and of the two Eleanor is the more likely choice. This is important because Eleanor had first been married to Louis VII, the king of France, whom she had despised as a king and a husband. Remarrying with the eventual heir to the English throne might have changed the balance of power in Western Europe and inevitably pushed events to the Hundred Years War, but Eleanor does not appear to have been affected by politics. All indications are that she only married Henry immediately after leaving Louis because of a genuine affection she felt toward him. She, more than nearly any woman of her time, was with the man she chose to be with.

What this means to the study of the Tristan legend is that the plot of the first extant romance may well have been altered to match her life much as *Le Conte* was modified to reflect Philip of Flanders' career. The reader has already been introduced to an author with the ability to make such drastic changes to a received story while maintaining an entertaining narrative that contains much of the original continent. Chrétien de Troyes did just that in all of his Arthurian poems. As has been seen in the pages above, Thomas wrote at some point between 1155 and 1175 whereas Chrétien's career began in around 1175 and extended to 1192. It seems at least possible that the two poets were in actuality only one man.

Chrétien was a brilliant poet for his age, masterful at what he did and emulated for centuries over dozens of kingdoms. Though the five Arthurian works associated with him did little more than retell ancient legends, his genius is undeniable in his talent for giving them an original presentation. His aptitude for drawing together such widespread sources as the Greek and Celtic myths, medieval philosophies, his patron's unusual directions, and British legends into a coherent whole is, perhaps, unmatched in the medieval world.

A more personal connection is found in the poetry of the two men, if only one. On the question of dating the Thomas poem, a well-done wordplay in Thomas' work is used around the words *l'amer* as love, *l'amer* as bitterness, and *la mer* as the sea. This wordplay is attempted again in *Cligés*,[4] with less success. The similarity has not helped to pin down the dating of either poem, but it does show an intimate knowledge of both romances by the person or persons who created them.

Less obvious, but no less significant, is that Eleanor was the mother of Marie de Champagne, patroness of Chrétien de Troyes at her own courts of love. There she emulated her parents, adding an emphasis toward empowering women. To accomplish her goal, she borrowed from many of the themes and philosophies prominent in Eleanor's court and modified them to her own purposes. As has been seen, she commissioned a number of individuals to write poetry and books on the subject of love and romance. To forward her goals, it only makes sense that she might have hired a promising author from her mother's court to help her create the ambience she was looking for. In the strength of *Tristan*'s Isolt, in the willingness to put royalty down, and in the beauty of his writing, she would have seen great potential in Thomas.

More importantly, the story he had written took place in another world, one that already had a small cast of characters and that was full of the fantastic. It was also entirely unexplored. She would have recognized that it was a place where she could form the grandiose image of feminist love she wanted. Thomas would not only have written his story well enough to have her attention, but he would have introduced her to that world.

Other facets of Chrétien's life were seen in Chapter 2, such as his Ovidian translations. They were most likely conducted during the early portion of his career; Frappier once called them his apprenticeship.[5] It is unfortunate under the present circumstances that the chronology of his training is entirely unknown.

Thomas was also familiar with Ovid. As Whitehead once pointed out, his writing technique is based on Wace and the romances of antiquity, especially the Ovidian translation Enéas (1150).[6] His knowledge base could be a result of chance, but it would make better sense if he had conducted translations earlier in his career and had developed his style based on his personal reading experiences. As has been seen earlier in this monolith, Chrétien would quote the Roman poet during the pinnacle of his writing prowess with great fluency. He considered the ancient Roman an expert on the subject of love and seems to have not only referenced him, but in many ways sought to emulate him.

It is also known that Chrétien wrote a Tristan, he says as much in his second extant Arthurian poem *Erec*. And if that is accepted, then it would make sense that he wrote his first extant romance, the anti-Tristan poem *Cligès*, after his Tristan as well. Naturally, as Chrétien's initial Arthurian attempt, it would have been his least developed romance as well. More broadly, by his own words we know that it would have been one of his first attempts at writing any original material; compared to his later efforts it would have been quite flawed. Following Frappier, he likely began his career with the Ovidian materials (which would have fallen in line with Eleanor's thinking and would have appealed to Marie).

Even with the circumstantial evidence presented here, the idea that Chrétien might have been Thomas' pen name seems unlikely. However, it has been widely speculated that Chrétien might have taken on the pseudonym of Paien de Maisieres on at least two occasions. The pair of known pen names, Chrétien/Christian and Paien/Pagan mutually suggesting that neither were the name he went by in day-to-day life.

There is also the negative evidence. Little is actually known about Chrétien's life outside of his writings. His birth year and time of death are unknown.[7] Where he was born and the nature of his childhood are mentioned nowhere, either. As with many of the early continental writers of Arthuriana, he simply appears with the writing of his five Arthurian poems right around 1170 and had disappeared before 1191. His known life begins and ends with his writings. As a mercenary, they were his only contributions to society.

Thomas of Britain was similarly treated. He was an excellent author, as his imitator Gottfried contends. But like Chrétien, his known life centers around his literature. As has been seen, he disappears from history at about the same time Chrétien appears.

Chrétien claims to have written on Tristan, and he was one of the most popular writers of the High Middle Ages. A large body of manuscripts is associated with each of his other romances. It has seemed unlikely to anyone who has studied his work that his Tristan would not have survived, somewhere. However, if Thomas was Chrétien's given name, things would begin to fall into place. Perhaps, though his natural talents showed through in Tristan, the skills that would later come to fruition were still to emerge at that point in his career. Perhaps, by the time his writings were worthy of Marie de Champagne's attention, he had taken on a pen name to separate himself from the work. It might also be that Marie de Champagne chose the name for him.

If Chrétien is merely a *nom de plume* for Thomas of Britain, it would allow for a much more revealing study of Tristan. Several of the author's alterations to the story could be seen by drawing comparisons to Béroul and possibly Marie de France. In time, our awareness of his habits as well as the accumulated knowledge about his patronage to Eleanor and her predilections would point us in a more accurate direction as to what the original materials might have looked like.

From *Erec* to *Le Conte*, a better understanding of how Chrétien first developed his Arthurian style would be of great help in understanding how he worked and what background he came from. Perhaps just as important, it would help modern literary scholars to better recognize the limits of his talents and the depths of his creativity.

The Development of the *Fomori* in the Tristan Saga

In studying the hero's struggle with the *Fomori*, the present author realized that no scholar has yet put forth any suggestions as to exactly how one ancient and universal incident was split into two distinct episodes, nor how a monster was not only personified by but also connected to an aspect a tale with which it originally had no association. Without a plausible explanation of both these alterations, any assumption of so much modification to the core story is entirely unsupportable.

The changes likely began with the transition from a British-speaking audience to a continental one. A kingship succession through the female line would not have been grasped in France or anywhere outside of the Celtic culture of the British Isles. Even if it had been understood, it would not have been accepted. Therefore, a means of explaining why Tristan would be given the right of succession over his uncle's kingdom had to be generated.

Thomas, or whoever realized this issue, was careful to explain that Mark had no children, nor are any of his male relatives present in the story. This precaution eliminated the need to rationalize why there was no designated heir before Tristan. The author also went to great lengths to show Mark's overwhelming admiration of Tristan's knowledge and courtly manners.

The author showed good foresight in not giving Mark any heirs. However, the stroke of brilliance came with the *Fomori*. In the typical plot, the hero has to go to a foreign kingdom in order to rescue a princess from the monster. This episode was already in place before it came to the continent and was necessary to the development of the plot. However the vaguely described Fomori would not have been recognized by a medieval audience. Therefore, the *Fomori* was changed to a more familiar antagonist in a dragon.

That left an unused name and an episode wherein Tristan proved himself invaluable to Cornwall without a villain. Fomori are occasionally described as giants, and Thomas might well have heard that particular description. From there he could have taken the name, altered greatly by the transference to the continent into something like Morholt, and made him a large warrior. Only the "Le" that is consistently prefixed to his name in Thomas lingers to suggest that he was originally something other than a person.

It is unknown how Drust responded to being offered the hand of the woman he had saved before the story was transferred to the continent. The *Tochmarc Emer* incorporated the Fomori episode into an existing story, and his response had to be adapted to it. Cú Chulainn's adventure is initiated in trying to woo Emer so that the episode had to conclude with the hero still free to do so. In the Tristan romances there was a similar need to keep Tristan from marrying her.[8] The means by which the pair is led to their first encounter has already been altered so much as to render it almost impossible to determine if Tristan originally married her. However, as the *Fomori* chapter appears to have been formed on the same model as the Perseus myth, it seems likely that in the original version Drust married the woman he rescued there.

Chapter Notes

Introduction

1. This process may well have taken place and been completed before the twelfth century. Arthur is an extremely popular figure in Welsh legend and most probably had already attracted a number of originally independent figures to his court in the literature.

2. Piggott, "The Sources of Geoffrey of Monmouth I: The Pre Roman King List," *A* 15 (Gloucester, 1941), 269–286.

3. See the bibliography for references to Professor Dumville's most important works on the subject.

4. Hughes, "The Welsh Latin Chronicles: Annales Cambriae and related texts," *PBA* 59 (London, 1975), 234–5.

5. Ibid., 242.

6. *The Gododdin: The Oldest Scottish Poem*, ed. Kenneth H. Jackson (Edinburgh, 1969); *Aneirin: Y Gododdin, Britain's Oldest Poem*, ed. Alfred O. H. Jarman (Llandysul, 1990); Dumville, "Early Welsh Poetry: Problems of Historicity," ed. Brynley F. Roberts, *Early Welsh Poetry: Studies in the Book of Aneirin* (Aberystwyth, 1988), 1–16.

7. Sims-Williams, "The Early Welsh Arthurian Poems," *The Arthur of the Welsh*, eds. Rachel Bromwich, Brynley F. Roberts, and Alfred O. H. Jarman (Cardiff, 1991), 35–6.

8. According to the *Oxford Dictionary*, "saga" is "a narrative having the [real or supposed characteristics of the Icelandic sagas]; a story of heroic achievement or marvellous adventure." James A. H. Murray et al., eds., *The Oxford English Dictionary*, vol. 1 (Oxford, 1961), 364.

9. It is the present author's belief that these would originally have been heroic age legends on their way to developing into epics as outlined in Ker, *Epic and Romance: Essays on Medieval Literature* (Dover, 1957), 13–15.

10. The author does not pretend to be able to fully or partially reconstruct British society in this period. Again, I am making full use of the resources at hand with the understanding that any theory derived from these composite sources may be invalid. The reconstructions are no more than the most reasonable based on the limited information on the period.

11. Apart from Arthur, each of the chief figures in both stories were given at least three names, one by the Welsh, French, and German authors. As the personalities of each character seem to have changed upon transference to the continent, the author has in the pages below chosen to retain the Welsh and French names in order to differentiate those changes. For simplicity and because they will not be used as much, however, the German has been dropped. Thus Cei/Keu, Gwalchmai/Gauvain, Owain/Yvain, Peredur/Perceval, and Gwenhwyfar/Guinièvre each have been assigned two names.

Chapter 1

1. Rhys, *Studies in the Arthurian Legend* (Oxford, 1891); Rhys, "Notes on the Hunting of the Twrch Trwyth," *THSC* (London, 1894–5), 1–34, 146–148.

2. Loomis, "Tristram and the House of Anjou," *MLR* 17 (Cambridge, 1922), 24–30; Loomis, "The Origin of Rivallon in the Tristan Legend," *MLN* 39 (Baltimore, 1924), 319–328; Roger S. Loomis, *Celtic Myth and Arthurian Romance* (New York, 1927a); *Medieval Studies in Memory of Gertrude Schoepperle Loomis*, ed. Roger S. Loomis (New York, 1927b); Loomis, "Discussions: Cause or Coincidence, a Reply to Monsieur Ferdinand Lot," *R* 54 (Paris, 1928a), 515–526; "Calogrenanz and Crestien's Originality," *MLN* 43 (Baltimore, 1928b), 215–222; Loomis, "By What Route did the Romantic Tradition of Arthur Reach the French," *MP* 33.3 (Chicago, 1936), 225–238; Loomis, "'The Spoils

Notes — Chapter 1

of Annwfn': An Early Arthurian Poem," *PMLA* 56 (Menasha, 1941), 887–936; Loomis, *Arthurian Tradition and Chrétien* (New York, 1949); Loomis, "Edward I, Arthurian Admirer," *S* 28 (Cambridge, 1953), 114–127; Loomis, *Wales and the Arthurian Legend* (Cardiff, 1956); *Arthurian Literature in the Middle Ages*, ed. Roger S. Loomis (Oxford, 1959b); Loomis, "The Origins of the Grail Legends," *Arthurian Literature in the Middle Ages*, ed. Roger S. Loomis (Oxford, 1959b), 274–294; Loomis, "A Survey of Tristan Scholarship after 1911," *Tristan and Isolt: A Study of the Sources of the Romance* (New York, rev. 1960); Loomis, *The Grail: From Celtic Myth to Christian Symbol* (Cardiff, 1963).

3. Loomis attempted to forge a closer relationship to the theoretical Irish sources by forwarding meager linguistic evidence that connected Gauvain, Lancelot, Lot, Gareth, and Arthur to various Celtic gods. It was probably to the overall benefit of Celtic studies that he later, and often, discounted his earlier arguments.

4. O'Rahilly, *Ireland and Wales: Their Historical and Literary Traditions* (New York, 1924); Mac Cana, "Aspects of the Theme of the King and Goddess," *EC* 6 (Paris, 1955), 356–413; MacCana, *Celtic Mythology* (Hamlyn, 1970); *The Mabinogi*, eds. Proinsias Mac Cana, Meic Stephens, and R. Brinley Jones (Cardiff, 1992). Bromwich, "Celtic Dynastic Themes and Breton Lays," *ÉC* 9 (Paris, 1961), 439–74; Bromwich, "Concepts of Arthur," *SC* 10/11 (Cardiff, 1976), 163–181; Bromwich, "Celtic Elements in Arthurian Romance: A General Survey," *The Legend of Arthur in the Middle Ages*, ed. P. B. Grout (Cambridge, 1983), 41–55; Bromwich, "First Transmission from England to France," *The Arthur of the Welsh*, eds. Rachel Bromwich, Brynley F. Roberts, and Alfred O. H. Jarman (Cardiff, 1991b), 273–298.

5. The lore was most definitely transmitted by word of mouth, at least in part.

6. Dr. Bromwich provides a neat summary in "First Transmission from England to France," *The Arthur of the Welsh*, eds. Rachel Bromwich, Brynley F. Roberts, and Alfred O. H. Jarman (Cardiff, 1991b), 273–298.

7. I exclude here Professor Jackson, Professor Jones, Professor Alcock, Professor Barber, Dr. Bromwich, and Dr. Kirby, who have all supported his historicity, and Professor Dumville and Dr. Padel, who have denied it.

8. It would be foolish to attempt a comprehensive reference here, but see the bibliography for a list of the relevant texts. In addition, Hughes, *The Church in Early Irish Society* (Cambridge, 1966); *Celtic Britain in the Early Middle Ages: Studies in Welsh and Scottish Sources*, (Cambridge, 1980); and *Church and Society in Ireland, A.D. 400–1200* (Cambridge, 1987). Also, Dumville's *The Anglo-Saxon Chronicle: A Collaborative Edition* (Cambridge, 1983); *Ireland in Early Mediaeval Europe Studies in Memory of Kathleen Hughes* (Cambridge, 1982); and *St. Patrick, A.D. 493–1993* (Cambridge, 1993) are all fundamental texts on the subject.

9. In particular *The Heroic Age* (Cambridge, 1912) and *The Development of Oral Literature* (Cambridge, 1932–40).

10. *Y Gododdin*, trans. Sir Ifor Williams (Cardiff, 1930); "Marwnad Cynddylan," ed. Sir Ifor Williams, *BBCS* 6 (Oxford, 1933), 134–40; *Taliesin, Canu Taliesin: gyda Rhagymadrodd a Nodiadau*, ed. Sir Ifor Williams (Cardiff, 1960); *Aneirin. The Gododdin: The Oldest Scottish Poem*, ed. Kenneth H. Jackson (Edinburgh, 1969); *Culhwch ac Olwen: An Edition and Study of the Earliest Arthurian Tale*, eds. Rachel Bromwich and D. Simon Evans (Cardiff, 1992); "Tristan Poem," trans. Rachel Bromwich, "The 'Tristan' Poem in the Black Book of Carmarthen," *SC* 14/15 (Cardiff, 1979–1980), 57–8; *The Welsh Triads (Trioedd ynys Prydein)*, ed. and trans. Rachel Bromwich (Cardiff, rev. 1978); "'Preiddeu Annwn' and the Figure of Taliesin," ed. and trans. Marged Haycock, *SC* 14/15 (Cardiff, 1984), 52–77.

11. Chadwick, "Pictish and Celtic Marriage in Early Literary Tradition," *Scottish Gaelic Studies* 8 (Edinburgh, 1958a). Though the arguments are at times nearly opaque, more recent work on the topic has only found ways in which to confirm her views.

12. *Críth Gablach*, ed. David A. Binchy (Oxford, 1970); Binchy, "Celtic and Anglo-Saxon Kingship," *O'Donnell Lectures Publications* (Oxford, 1970); Kelly, *A Guide to Early Irish Law, Vol. 3 of Early Irish Law Series*, (Dublin, 1988).

13. Bromwich, "Celtic Dynastic Themes and Breton Lays," *ÉC* 9 (Paris, 1961), 439–74; Bromwich, "Concepts of Arthur," *SC* 10/11 (Cardiff, 1976), 163–181; Chadwick, "Pictish and Celtic Marriage in Early Literary Tradition," Scottish Gaelic Studies 8 (Edinburgh, 1958a), 56–115; Chadwick, "Early Culture and Learning in North Wales," *Studies in the Early British Church*, ed. Nora K. Chadwick (Cambridge, 1958b), 29–120; ed. Nora K. Chadwick, *Studies in Early British History* (Cambridge, 1954); ed. Nora K. Chadwick, *Studies in the Early British Church* (Cambridge, 1958); *The Iron Age in the Irish Sea Province*, ed. Charles Thomas, (London, 1972); Thomas, *Christianity in Roman Britain to 500 A.D.* (London, 1981).

14. Webster, *The Pagan Celts and Their Gods under Rome* (London, 1986); Murray, *The God of the Witches* (London, 1931); Stancliffe, *St. Martin and His Hagiographer: History and Miracle in Sulpicius Severus: History and Miracle in Sulpicius Severus* (Oxford, 1983).

15. Goetinck, *Peredur: A Study of Welsh Tradition in the Grail Legends* (Cardiff, 1975).
16. These are only the most prominent scholars. The grail question is such an intriguing topic that it has invited a rather large number of publications. For a large base of ideas on the subject see the bibliography and the above authors.
17. *Le Roman de Tristan par Thomas, poème du XIII siècle*, ed. and trans. Joseph Bedier, 2 vols. (Paris, 1902–1905).
18. Schoepperle, *Tristan and Isolt: A Study of the Sources of the Romance* (New York, rev. 1960); Owen and Kelly, "Arthurian Romance in the Twelfth and Thirteenth Centuries," *The Arthur of the Germans*, eds. W. H. Jackson and Sylvia A. Ranawake (Cardiff, 2000), 393–460; Newstead, "The Origin and Growth of the Tristan Legend," *Arthurian Literature in the Middle Ages*, ed. Roger S. Loomis (Chicago, 1959), 122–133; Newstead, *Brân the Blessed in Arthurian Romance* (New York, 1966); Bromwich, "Some Remarks on the Celtic Sources of 'Tristan,'" *THSC* (London, 1953), 32–60; Bromwich, "The 'Tristan' Poem in the Black Book of Carmarthen," *SC* 14/15 (Cardiff, 1979–1980), 54–65; Bromwich, "The Tristan of the Welsh," *The Arthur of the Welsh*, eds. Rachel Bromwich, Brynley F. Roberts, and Alfred O. H. Jarman (Cardiff, 1991a), 209–228.
19. Meyer, "The Oldest Version of the Tochmarc Emire," *RC* 11 (Paris, 1890), 434–67; Zimmer, "Keltische Beitrage. I. Germanen, germanische Lehnwdrter und germanische Sagenelemente in der altesten Überlieferung der irischen Heldensage," *ZDA* 32 (Berlin, 1888), 196–334; Zimmer, "Keltische Beitrage. III. Weitere nordgermanische Einflüsse in der Altesten Ueberlieferung der irischen Heldensage," *ZDA* 35 (Berlin, 1891), 1–176.
20. Jackson, "Gottfried von Strassburg," *Arthurian Literature in the Middle Ages*, ed. Roger S. Loomis (Chicago, 1959), 145–156; Vinaver, *Études sur le Tristan en prose: les sources, les manucrits, bibliographie critique* (Paris, 1925); "The Prose Tristan," *Arthurian Literature in the Middle Ages*, ed. Roger S. Loomis (Chicago, 1959), 339–347; "The Significance of Thomas' Tristan," *RMS* 7 (London, 1981), 41–61; Bromiley and Hunt, "The Tristan Legend in Old French Verse," *The Arthur of the French*, eds. Glyn S. Burgess and Karen Pratt (Cardiff, 2000), 112–134; Owen and Kelly, "Arthurian Romance in the Twelfth and Thirteenth Centuries," *The Arthur of the Germans*, eds. W. H. Jackson and Sylvia A. Ranawake (Cardiff, 2000), 393–460.
21. Loth, *Contributions à l'étude des romans de la Table ronde* (Paris, 1912); Padel, "The Cornish Background of the Tristan Stories," *CMCS* 1 (Cambridge, 1981), 53–82; Padel, "Some South-Western Sites with Arthurian Associations," *The Arthur of the Welsh*, eds. Rachel Bromwich et al. (Cardiff, 1991), 229–248.
22. Dark, *From Civitas to Kingdom: British Political Continuity 300–800* (Leicester, 1994).
23. Bromwich, "First Transmission to England and France," *The Arthur of the Welsh*, eds. Rachel Bromwich, Brynley F. Roberts, and Alfred O. H. Jarman (Cardiff, 1991b), 277.
24. Welsh *Lladmerydd*, trans.; the contribution by Dr. Bullock-Davies (*Professional Interpreters and the Matter of Britain*, (Cardiff, 1966), 5) that there was a professional group of poets in the Marches of Wales has added weight to his statement.
25. A reflection most cogently argued by Sir John Rhys in *Studies in the Arthurian Legend* (Oxford, 1891).
26. Williams, *Lectures on Old Welsh Poetry* (Dublin, 1944).
27. Rhys, *Studies in the Arthurian Legend* (Oxford, 1891), 4.
28. For the purposes of this paper I will take the conservative stance that the first most prolific British heroic age was finished before 650 and the second stretched from roughly 1100–1300. Having said that, it must be stressed that the latter heroic age lacks many of the characteristics typical of the heroic age, and is not and would not be an heroic age in the sense of the societies portrayed in *Iliad*, *Mahabharata*, and *Volsungasaga*. Professor Ker took the interesting view that an heroic age's ideals are ended only when romance takes the place of epic (*Epic and Romance: Essays on Medieval Literature* [Dover, 1957], 6). However, this does not mean that a heroic age ends only when this occurs. As he himself says:

> The form of society in an heroic age is aristocratic and magnificent. At the same time, this aristocracy differs from that of later and more specialized forms of civilisation. It does not take an insuperable difference between gentle and simple. There is not the extreme division of labour that produces the contempt of the lord for the villein. The nobles have not yet discovered for themselves any form of occupation or mode of thought in virtue of which they are widely severed from the commons.... (Ker, *Epic and Romance: Essays on Medieval Literature* [Dover, 1957], 7).

According to this thought, the British and Germanic heroic ages would have ended when feudalism began. This is also feasible and would eliminate the period 1100–1300 from the discussion altogether.
29. In later references, this will be named as the Castle of the Four Axemen.
30. This knight is associated with a bull. The mysterious appearance here of a bull will be explained in conjunction with the *Belatacudros*

cult in the author's discussion of the characters in *Le Conte du Graal.*

31. *The Vulgate Version of the Arthurian Romances* says that the tomb is that of his grandfather.

32. The name Bademagus has many hypothetical precursors and even more variations in the extant literature. The form here presented is simply the most recognizable.

33. Lancelot's nurse is known as Jandrée in other romances, and from this point on in the paper.

Chapter 2

1. The tradition was continued no doubt because the most efficient way to educate oneself in this period was through the monasteries. Therefore, those who were writing fictitious poems, such as Chrétien, were most probably the product of religious instruction.

2. This is an often addressed aspect of medieval writing. It is most apparent in the case of Christian writers who lived well before Christianity had been carefully defined. Medieval scholars can be seen taking great pains to reduce and eliminate conflicting statements and philosophies.

3. Nitze, "*Sens* and *Matière* dans les Oeuvres de Chrétien de Troyes," *Romania* 44 (1915–1917), 30; Warren, "On the Latin Sources of *Thèbes* and *Énéas*," *PMLA* 16 (Menasha, 1901), 384; Faral, "Ovide et qualques autres *Roman d'Énéas*," *Romania* 40 (Paris, 1911), 185, 187.

4. Nitze, "*Sens* and *Matière* dans les Oeuvres de Chrétien de Troyes," *Romania* 44 (1915–1917), 28; Hunt, (1971), 327–8. In the case of Chrétien, it has been argued that this aspect of the prologue was a way of telling the reader one of the influences on his *sens*, and thus of excusing himself for a part of its content; Rychner, "Le Prologue du *Chevalier de la Charrette*," *Vox Romanica* 26 (Paris, 1967), 1–23.

5. Bromwich, "First Transmission to England and France," *The Arthur of the Welsh*, eds. Rachel Bromwich, Brynley F. Roberts, and Alfred O. H. Jarman (Cardiff, 1991b), 281.

6. Bromwich, "Concepts of Arthur," *SC* 10/11 (Cardiff, 1976), 175–6.

7. The body of poetry that generated around the Battle of Catraeth may be found in *Y Gododdin*, while some of Urien's praise poetry survives in the collection of Taliesin. A similar set of circumstances may be predicted for Arthur.

8. Jackson, *Language and History in Early Britain: A Chronological Survey of the Brittonic Languages 1st to 12th c. A.D.* (Edinburgh, 1953), 4–6, 9; Jackson, "The British Language during the English Settlement," *Studies in Early British History*, ed. Nora K. Chadwick (Cambridge, 1954), 77.

9. The bards had a penchant for contemporizing nonessential elements, which is why their poems are not considered strictly historical sources.

10. The last date at which Old Cumbric was practiced in the North is, of course, impossible to determine precisely. There is almost nothing known about the kingdoms of Strathclyde and Cumbria between the seventh and tenth centuries. Professor Jackson's best guess about the last use was right around 1092; Jackson, *Language and History in Early Britain: A Chronological Survey of the Brittonic Languages 1st to 12th c. A.D.* (Edinburgh, 1953), 9.

11. Indeed, *TYP* and *Culhwch ac Olwen* are treasure troves of such names, though identification of them has often eluded scholars.

12. For *Preiddeu Annwn* see "'Preiddeu Annwn' and the figure of Taliesin," ed. and trans. Marged Haycock, *SC* 14/15 (Cardiff, 1984), 57; for *Culhwch ac Olwen* see *Culhwch ac Olwen: An Edition and Study of the Earliest Arthurian Tale*, eds. Rachel Bromwich and D. Simon Evans (Cardiff, 1992), lxxxii. Professor Sims-Williams will only give the dates 1100–1160 for "Pa gur?" which, though probably before Chrétien, is not necessarily before him. Sims-Williams, "The Early Welsh Arthurian Poems," *The Arthur of the Welsh*, eds. Rachel Bromwich, Brynley F. Roberts, and Alfred O. H. Jarman (Cardiff, 1991), 39.

13. Loomis, "'The Spoils of Annwfn': An Early Arthurian Poem," *PMLA* 56 (Menasha, 1941), 376. The best examples of this phenomenon were Gonemans, Bron, Palamedes, and Arioel.

14. Padel, "The Nature of Arthur," *CMCS* 27 (Cambridge, 1994), 4–12.

15. Padel, "The Cornish Background of the Tristan Stories," *CMCS* 1 (Cambridge, 1982), 53–82; Bromwich, "First Transmission to England and France," *The Arthur of the Welsh*, eds. Rachel Bromwich, Brynley F. Roberts, and Alfred O.H. Jarman (Cardiff, 1991b), 220–1.

16. Loomis, "By What Route Did the Romantic Tradition of Arthur Reach the French," *MP* 33.3 [Chicago, 1936], 207–8). The extant names were first recorded in 1083, pre-1083, and in the range 1099x1106, respectively.

17. *The Anglo-Saxon Chronicle* assigns the year 547 to the capture of Bamborough.

18. Lewis, "The Historical Background of Early Welsh Verse," *A Guide to Early Welsh Literature*, vol. 1, eds. Alfred O. H. Jarman and Gwillym R. Jones (Cardiff, 1976), 31, 34, 35, 40, 44. Taliesin is believed to have begun his career in Powys but the majority, and the more mature poems, are in praise of the Men of the North. Therefore he, too, may be considered a northern figure.

19. Thurneysen, "Zimmer, Nennius vindicatus," *ZDP* 28 (Halle, 1896), 85, 87; Bruce, *The Evolution of Arthurian Romance, from the Beginnings Down to the Year 1300* (Gottingen, 1923), 9; Jackson, "The Arthur of History," *Arthurian Literature in the Middle Ages*, ed. Roger S. Loomis (Oxford, 1959), 6; Hughes, "The Welsh Latin Chronicles: Annales Cambriae and related texts," *PBA* 59 (London, 1975), 237–9; Bromwich, "Concepts of Arthur," *SC* 10/11 (Cardiff, 1976), 175–6; Dumville, "The Anglian Collection of Royal Genealogies and Regnal Lists," *ASE* 5 (Cambridge, 1976b), 23–50; Charles-Edwards, "The Authenticity of the Gododdin: An Historian's View," *Astudiaethau ar yr Hengerdd*, eds. Rachel Bromwich and R. Brinley Jones (Cardiff, 1978), 63.

20. The graphic is a composite of several author's efforts but follows Professor Dumville in the main.

21. Jackson, "The Sources for the Life of St. Kentigern," *Studies in the Early British Church*, ed. Nora K. Chadwick (Cambridge, 1958), 273–358.

22. MacQueen, "Yvain, Ewen, and Owein ap Urien," *TDGNAHS*, 3rd series 33 (Dumfries, 1956), 107-131; MacQueen, "A Reply to Professor Jackson," *TDGNAHS*, 3rd series 36 (Dumfries, 1959), 175–83; Carney, *Studies in Irish Literature and History* (Dublin, 1955), 79; *The Gododdin of Aneirin*, ed. and trans. John T. Koch (Cardiff, 1995), lxxvii-lxxviii. These rationale dwell upon the fact that the hero's birth and childhood are spent in Lothian (in Germanic hands as of the early seventh century). The place-names are definitely Celtic, implying the source was in circulation before the conquest of Lothian.

23. Chadwick, "Early Culture and Learning in North Wales," *Studies in the Early British Church*, ed. Nora K. Chadwick (Cambridge, 1958b), 70.

24. Ibid., 71.

25. *The Gododdin of Aneirin*, ed. and trans. John T. Koch (Cardiff, 1995), cxxv.

26. Chadwick, "Early Culture and Learning in North Wales," *Studies in the Early British Church*, (Cambridge, 1958b), 91–2. Dr. Chadwick suggested specifically that *Historia Brittonum* was written in Bangor Mawr on the basis that the Elfoddw named in the preface was from there, and because of that monastery's proximity to the Gwynedd court.

27. Chadwick, "Early Culture and Learning in North Wales," *Studies in the Early British Church*, (Cambridge, 1958b), 66–72. Dr. Chadwick believed the document would have been kept in Cumberland (most probably Hoddom) because the saga hero Rhydderch Hael's death is not recorded in it. *Historia Brittonum* gives the Strathclyde king the epithet "Hen," or old, and because Urbgen is here killed by treachery, as opposed to his death in battle as remembered throughout the Llywarch elegy.

28. Jackson, "On the Northern British Section in Nennius," *Celt and Saxon: Studies in the Early British Border*, ed. Nora K. Chadwick (Cambridge, 1963), 6; Hughes, "The Welsh Latin Chronicles: Annales Cambriae and related texts," *PBA* 59 (London, 1975), 237–9; Bromwich, "Concepts of Arthur," *SC* 10/11 (Cardiff, 1976), 175–6; Dumville, "The Anglian Collection of Royal Genealogies and Regnal Lists," *ASE* 5 (Cambridge, 1976b), 23–50.

29. Thurneysen, "Zimmer, Nennius vindicatus," *ZDP* 28 (Halle, 1896), 85, 87; Bruce, *The Evolution of Arthurian Romance, from the Beginnings Down to the Year 1300* (Gottingen, 1923), 9. Jackson opposed the inclusion of this text in the *Northern History* on the basis of Beulon's request that the Anglo-Saxon genaeologies (meaning also the *Northern History*) be omitted from his copy. This was done to his satisfaction, though *Arthuriana* was left intact. Therefore, so the reasoning goes, *Arthuriana* is not a part of the *Northern History*. The author believes it more accurate to say that Beulon did not **believe** that *Arthuriana* was a part of the *Northern History*. His opinion carries no more weight than that of a modern historian. Most probably, he had access to less information about it.

30. Loomis, *Arthurian Tradition and Chrétien* (New York, 1949).

31. Bromwich, "Celtic Elements in Arthurian Romance: A General Survey," *The Legend of Arthur in the Middle Ages*, ed. P. B. Grout (Cambridge, 1983), 44.

32. However, names that have obviously been learned orally do not imply that the material in which they are now found was oral as well.

33. Bullock-Davies, *Professional Interpreters and the Matter of Britain* (Cardiff, 1966), 19; Williams, *Lectures on Old Welsh Poetry* (Dublin, 1944), xl-xli.

34. Bullock-Davies, *Professional Interpreters and the Matter of Britain* (Cardiff, 1966), 20.

35. Lejeune, "The Troubadours" *Arthurian Literature in the Middle Ages*, ed. Roger S. Loomis (Chicago, 1959), 396.

36. Ibid., 398.

37. Nutt, *Studies on the Legend of the Holy Grail* (London, 1888), 235.

38. Anglade, *Anthologie des Troubadours* (Paris, 1929); Lejeune, "The Troubadours," *Arthurian Literature in the Middle Ages*, ed. Roger S. Loomis (Chicago, 1959), 393–399.

39. Paris, "Études sur les Romans de la Table Ronde: Lancelot du Lac," *R* 19 (Paris, 1883), 459–534.

40. The discussion is hardly settled, nor is there any agreement. As recently as 1976 Eugene

reinterpreted the grail ceremony. This time it was based on the Jewish religion, thus making Chrétien a Jew or at least a sympathizer; Frappier, "Chrétien de Troyes," *Arthurian Literature in the Middle Ages*, ed. Roger S. Loomis (Chicago, 1959), 158; Vigneras, "Chrétien de Troyes rediscovered," *MP* 32 (Paris, 1934–5), 341–2 and sources cited therein.

41. Guyer, *Dissertation: The Influence of Ovid on Chréstien de Troyes* (Chicago, 1921), 217–18.
42. *Cligès*, ll. 2–5.
43. Ibid., ll. 475–523
44. *Le Chevalier de la Charrette*, ll. 4177–4262.
45. The main characters, Cligès and his lover, are Ovidian, but Cligès' parents, Alexander and Soredamors, represent traditional love and are married.
46. Krueger agrees with the tongue in cheek treatment in *Women Readers and the Ideology of Gender in Old French Romance* (Cambridge, 1993), 54–66.
47. *La Charrette*, ll. 113–114.
48. Capellanus, *De Amore: Libri Tres*, ed. E. Trojel (Munich, 1972), 310–11.
49. Capellanus, *The Art of Courtly Love*. ed. John J. Parry (New York, 1959), 184–6.
50. Rules no. 184 and 186, respectively.
51. *Erec*, l. 83.
52. Owen, *The Evolution of the Grail Legend* (Edinburgh, 1968), 507; Pelan, *L' influence du Brut de Wace sur les romanciers français de son temps* (Geneva, 1931 rep. 1974).
53. *La Chanson de Roland*, ll. 2635–7.
54. Ibid., l. 793.
55. *Cligès*, l. 1289; *La Chanson de Roland*, l. 794. The term "epic pair" is to be found in many epics and foundation myths. It signifies brothers whose names mean roughly the same thing, e.g., Hengest and Horsa both mean horse. At least one of an epic pair is usually invention.
56. *Cligès*, ll. 1704–12; *La Chanson de Roland*, l. 2456.
57. Known from, respectively, *Erec* (l. 5779) and *Yvain* (l. 597).
58. *Cligès*, l. 468.
59. *Roman d'Eneas*, ll. 5337, 5891.
60. Ibid., l. 5891.
61. *Erec*, ll. 1655–69; *Aeneid*, 4.138–9.
62. Vergil, *Aeneid*, 4.19.
63. *Elegiae*, 33–6, 79.
64. *Cligès*, l. 635; *De Rerum Natura*, 3, l. 1056; Laurie, *Two Studies in Chrétien de Troyes*, (Geneva, 1972), 78.
65. *Erec*, l. 23.
66. Lucan, 8.156–7.
67. *Erec*, l. 6738.
68. *Cligès*, ll. 547–51.
69. *Erec*, ll. 2021–3.
70. Ibid., 63.
71. Augustine, *Confessions*, 11, 1.1

72. Ibid., 4, 12.18
73. Ibid., 7, 17.23; Laurie, *Two Studies in Chrétien de Troyes* (Geneva, 1972), 63, 68, 81.
74. Laurie, *Two Studies in Chrétien de Troyes* (Geneva, 1972), 106–7.
75. Owen, *The Evolution of the Grail Legend* (Edinburgh, 1968), 516.
76. *La Charrette*, ll. 1841–3937.
77. *Erec*, ll. 404 and 424, respectively.
78. Kelly, *Eleanore of Aquitaine and the Four Kings* (Cambridge, 1950), 157–67.
79. Helinand de Froidmont, *Les Vers de la Mort*, trans. Michael Boyer and Monique Santucci (Paris, 1983), 19.349. However, one wonders if this is a note of sympathy, or whether the "frailty of the female sex" (2–3) he speaks of is an intentional irony with regard to Marie's feminism; McCash, "Marie de Champagne's 'Cuer d'ome et cors de Fame': Aspects of Feminism and Misogyny in the Twelfth Century," *The Spirit of the Court*, eds. Glyn S. Burgess and Robert A. Taylor (Toronto, 1985), 244–5.
80. *The Chronicler of Tours* and the contributor to the *Annales of Rouen*.
81. Thus "A" was the first, apparently Marie critiqued it, and "B" and "C" are either further drafts or one of them is the final version.
82. Henderson, "A Critical Edition of Evrat's *Genesis: Creation to the Flood*," unpublished Ph.D. thesis (Toronto, 1977), 69.
83. McCash, "Marie de Champagne's 'Cuer d'ome et cors de Fame': Aspects of Feminism and Misogyny in the Twelfth Century," *The Spirit of the Court*, eds. Glyn S. Burgess and Robert A. Taylor (Toronto, 1985), 243.
84. Owen, "Chrétien and the *Roland*," *An Arthurian Tapestry: Essays in Memory of Lewis Thorpe*, ed. Kenneth Varty (Glasgow, 1981), 140.
85. The exceptions here are Marie de Champagne and Andreas Capellanus, whose consistent influence stems from Marie's patronage of Chrétien and her insistence that he follow Andreas Capellanus' rules of courtly love.
86. The regularity with which Keu, Ginover, Arthur, Gauvain, and Meleagant appear in the abduction, in similar roles, argues strongly for a common original source or at least a common tradition. This will be thoroughly demonstrated in the following chapter.

Chapter 3

1. The author has here assumed some knowledge of other abduction romances on the part of the reader in order to maintain the fluidity of the argument. A more detailed discussion of each of the more pertinent romances will be forthcoming in the next chapter.
2. Gauvain's presence in *Le Chevalier de la*

Charrette will be fully discussed in the following chapter.

3. Melwas occurs in both British and continental versions. Therefore, his name was known on the continent and in Wales. The Valerin/Urien character is not found in this role in Britain.

4. The only instances where Guinièvre is made the victim of two kidnappings are *The Vulgate Versions of the Arthurian Romances* and Mallory's *Le Morte d'Arthur*, both late and conglomerative works. It is safe to assume tradition only assigned her one abduction.

5. Several instances of transplanted heroes come to mind. Theodoric the Great and the Burgundian kings at Attila's court in *Nibelungenlied* and William the Conqueror at Arthur's court in *Culhwch ac Olwen* are the most notable. The drawing of lesser individuals into a more popular figure's orbit is a common feature of heroic age tales.

6. Sims-Williams, "The Early Welsh Arthurian Poems," *The Arthur of the Welsh*, eds. Rachel Bromwich, Brynley F. Roberts, and Alfred O. H. Jarman (Cardiff, 1991), 59.

7. *TYP*, 382. This theory is based on the Maheloas of *Erec* (l. 1947). An interesting aside here is that that the enemy of the isles whom Arthur has confrontations with in *Historia Regum Britanniae* is Gillomarus (or a derivative thereof). The element *Gilla* or *Gil* translates also from Irish to English as young man or servant.

8. This is so in most heroic age literatures, among them those of Ireland, the Germanic peoples, and India.

9. Gwenhwyfar is given three fathers in *TYP*, suggesting confusion, not information. Romances would be equally unhelpful in that regard.

10. Theoretically, if all versions name her as the abductee, and the versions have clearly developed different plot twists, the base story must have included her and been old enough to allow such diversity to develop before it made its way to the continent.

11. This would clearly place the abduction tale outside the realm of a literary source for Arthur. However, it does remain a source for the fifth and sixth centuries.

12. Tatlock, *The Legendary History of Britain* (Berkeley, 1950), 154. This would make the character's English popularity particularly ironic. Professor Tatlock believed Geoffrey created this character to make fun of Angus of Moray, a Scottish rebel killed in 1130.

13. Loomis, *Arthurian Tradition and Chrétien* (New York, 1949), 92.

14. Loomis, *Wales and the Arthurian Legend* (Cardiff, 1956), 161–2.

15. *TYP*, 415.

16. Jones, "Some Arthurian Material in Keltic," *Aberyswyth Studies* 14 (Aberystwyth, 1936), 37. He also compares the figures Morgan Hud/Morgan le Fay, Banw/Ban of Berwick, and Melwas/Meliagraunce.

17. Loomis, *Celtic Myth and Arthurian Romance* (New York, 1927a), 190–5.

18. These are Lluch Llenlleawc the Irishman, Llyauynauc, Lludd Llurugawc, and Llyr Lluyddawc, respectively.

19. Loomis, "The Spoils of Annwfn: An Early Arthurian Poem," *PMLA* 56 (Menasha, 1941), 929–30.

20. *TYP*, 420.

21. Particularly hazardous in Arthurian research, with the sketchy and diverse patterns of transference and varying points of origin for both personal names and plots.

22. The *Os* prefix stems from Aesir, the gods of the Norse pantheon.

23. *TYP*, 544.

24. Villemarqué, *Les Romans de la Table Ronde et les Contes des anciens Bretons* (Paris, 1842), 50.

25. Pope, *From Latin to Modern French with Especial Consideration of Anglo-Norman* (Manchester, 1934 rev. 1952), 147.

26. Goodrich, *King Arthur* (London, 1986), 172.

27. Dr. Thomas Clancy, personal interview, 1996.

28. Anderson, *Kings and Kingship in Early Scotland* (Edinburgh, 1973), 88.

29. Lloyd-Morgan, "Lancelot in Wales," *Shifts and Transpositions in Medieval Literature*, ed. Karen Pratt (Cambridge, 1994), 169–179. Her argument is based on the fact that there is no existing Welsh version of the Lancelot rescue, or of Lancelot, except in translations where Lancelot is prominent and his presence is therefore necessary.

30. Lloyd-Morgan, "Lancelot in Wales," *Shifts and Transpositions in Medieval Literature*, ed. Karen Pratt (Cambridge, 1994), 178.

31. *Cligès*, l. 1694; *Erec*, l. 1694.

32. Zatzikhoven, *Lanzelet*, ed. Roger S. Loomis, trans. Kenneth G.T. Webster (New York, 1951), 27; Hector and Nora Chadwick, *The Development of Oral Literature*, vol. 3 (Cambridge, 1940), 763–4. The hero being raised in the company of fairies is a stock feature in oral tales.

33. Hector Chadwick, *The Heroic Age* (Cambridge, 1912), 334.

34. Hector and Nora Chadwick, *The Development of Oral Literature*, vol. 3 (Cambridge, 1940), 201.

35. O'Rahilly based his history of early Ireland on the myths and legends of the Irish; *Early Irish History and Mythology*, (Dublin, 1946a), v.

36. Zatzikhoven, *Lanzelet*, ed. Roger S.

Loomis, trans. Kenneth G.T. Webster, (New York, 1951), 11.

37. Based on the material summarized here, it may well be that Kei was the original hero.

38. Bromwich, "Celtic Dynatic Themes and Breton Lays," *ÉC* 9 (Paris, 1961), 439–74; "Celtic Elements in Arthurian Romance: A General Survey," *The Legend of Arthur in the Middle Ages*, ed. P.B. Grout (Cambridge, 1983), 41–44; "First Transmission to England and France," *The Arthur of the Welsh*, eds. Rachel Bromwich, Brynley F. Roberts, and Alfred O. H. Jarman (Cardiff, 1991b), 276–81.

39. The simplest reason for this is that Celtic bards had a habit of transposing characters and themes, so that the consistency demonstrated with *La Charrette* can hardly be thought to have occurred in an oral environment.

Chapter 4

1. *Two Lives of Gildas*, trans. Williams, (Llanerch, 1890, rep. 1988), 102.

2. Rider, "Arthur and the Saints," *King Arthur through the Ages* (London, 1990), 6.

3. The author could hardly do the topic of Glastonbury's claims justice and stay within the theme of this book. A good beginning would be *The Archaeology and History of Glastonbury Abbey. Essays in Honour of the Ninetieth Birthday of C.A. Ralegh Radford*, eds. Leslie Abrams and James P. Carley (Woodbridge, 1991); Davies, "Property Rights and Property Claims in Welsh 'Vitae' of the Eleventh Century," *Hagiographie, cultures, et sociétés ive-xiie siécles*, ed. P. Riché (Paris, 1981), 515–33; Loomis, "Edward I, Arthurian Admirer," *S* 28 (Cambridge, 1953), 114–127; *Didot Perceval*, ed. and trans. William A. Nitze (Chicago, 1932–7).

4. Foot, "Glastonbury's Early Abbots," *The Archaeology and History of Glastonbury Abbey*, eds. Leslie Abrams and James P. Carley (Woodbridge, 1991), 167, 169; Finberg, "St. Patrick and Glastonbury," *Irish Ecclesiastical Record* 107 (Dublin, 1967), 346.

5. Roberts, "*Culhwch ac Olwen, The Triads*, and Saints' Lives," *The Arthur of the Welsh*, eds. Rachel Bromwich, Brynley F. Roberts, and Alfred O. H. Jarman (Cardiff, 1991), 82.

6. Cross, *Lancelot and Guinevere: A Study on the Origins of Courtly Love* (New York, 1970). Abductions are known under the title of *aitheda*, or elopements.

7. The saints in the *vitae* rarely have confrontations with anyone but kings. This is so that when the antagonist admits he is less powerful, the saint gains a maximum amount of prestige from the confrontation. On the other hand, it seems the earliest abductions (more specifically those named as *aitheda*) always have the king and an army in pursuit of the wife; Cross, *Lancelot and Guinevere: A Study on the Origins of Courtly Love* (New York, 1970), 52.

8. For a full discussion of the Modena relief, see Loomis, *Medieval Studies in Memory of Gertrude Schoepperle Loomis*, ed. Roger S. Loomis (New York, 1927b).

9. Version A, l. 10. Hereafter the two versions will be referred to simply as "A" and "B."

10. Arthur's absence is a point of dispute; "An Early Ritual Poem in Welsh," ed. and trans. Williams, *S* 13 (Cambridge, 1938), 38–51.

11. l. A.2. It would seem the Glastonbury monks created the connection to their own monastery between the otherworld "Isle of Glass" and Glastonbury.

12. Exception possibly being made for the atypical account in *Historia Regum Britanniae* that Modred is Arthur's nephew and he is Arthur's heir. It may well, though, be merely another reflection of contemporary events. Tatlock noted that in 1135 Stephen refused to accept his uncle's daughter Matilda as a sovereign. Similarly, Modred refuses to accept the rule of his aunt over him and claims the kingship himself; Tatlock, *The Legendary History of Britain* (Berkeley, 1950), 426–7.

13. Thomson, "Owain: Chwedl Iarlles y Ffynnon, *The Arthur of the Welsh*, eds. Rachel Bromwich, Brynley F. Roberts, and Alfred O. H. Jarman (Cardiff, 1991), 166.

14. This is a well-recorded feature of heroic age battles, e.g., *Mahabharata, Nibelungenlied*, the elegy of Owain son of Urien, and the cycles of Ulster, Gilgamesh, and the bogatyri. However, it does not sound out of place considering the prominence of such a small number of knights in medieval battles.

15. Bromwich authoritatively states there is no linguistic relationship between Medrawt and Melwas in her edited version of TYP (384), further evidence for the unreliability of *Historia Regum Britanniae*.

16. The only available translation is by Webster, edited by Roger S. Loomis.

17. Webster and Loomis both translated this as "French." However, this is not a linguistically agreeable approximation and in light of its celticity it should be rethought. The author does not deny that some elements do derive from Chrétien, but the vast differences in *ethos* and plot between the two argue for a more ancient source for Zatzikhoven's book.

18. Zatzikhoven, *Lanzelet*, ed. Roger S. Loomis, trans. Kenneth G. T. Webster (New York, 1951), 151.

19. Ibid., 5.

20. Without exception each is in a section with traditional material (Webster, "Welsches Buoch," *Harvard Studies and Notes in Philology and Literature* 16 [Harvard, 1934], 22 fl.).

21. Contra Ranawake, "The Emergence of German Arthurian Romance: Hartmann von Aue and Ulrich von Zatzikhoven," *The Arthur of the Germans*, eds. W.H. Jackson and Sylvia A. Ranawake (Cardiff, 2000), 48.

22. Zatzikhoven, *Lanzelet*, ed. Roger S. Loomis, trans. Kenneth G. T. Webster (New York, 1951), 42, 55, and 100.

23. Though the fact that *Lanzelet* includes the fostering of the hero by a fay, and Lancelot in *La Charrette* (ll. 2347–62) has a ring from a fay, would lend itself to theory that they both derive from a common oral source.

24. Spaarnay, "Hartmann von Aue and his Successors," *Arthurian Literature in the Middle Ages*, ed. Roger S. Loomis (Chicago, 1959), 439.

25. ll. 16862–17092.

26. l. 22221.

27. ll. 1521–45.

28. see Chapter 3 above; Gowans, *Cei and the Arthurian Legend* (Cambridge, 1988), 16–17.

29. ll. 12957–8, 13386, 16713, and 17762–72.

30. ll. 8423, 8659, and 13181.

31. Spaarnay, "Hartmann von Aue and His Successors," *Arthurian Literature in the Middle Ages*, ed. Roger S. Loomis (Chicago, 1959), 442.

32. Ranawake, "The Emergence of German Arthurian Romance: Hartmann von Aue and Ulrich von Zatzikhoven," *The Arthur of the Germans*, eds. W. H. Jackson and Sylvia A. Ranawake (Cardiff, 2000), 39.

33. *Iwein*, ll. 15–17, 267.

34. The names of both the abducted and abductor are linguistically compatible in all versions. In addition, many of the elements culturally belong to a period before 1100 and probably before 900. It is most economical to believe that there was only one such source.

35. Caradoc of Llancarfan and Geoffrey of Monmouth both wrote in the 1130s. The abductor and rescuer are both different, as are their settings. It is safe to assume that such diversity in a story that is essentially the same would have taken something more than thirty years.

Chapter 5

1. Chrétien tends to go to extremes in his descriptions, e.g., those of the maidens and the dwarf who drives the cart that Lancelot comes into town in. He is also very positive in his descriptions of noble-oriented ceremonies and structures. Apparently this added to the perfect ambience of the Arthurian world. This makes the heroes' stay in a dining hall even more noteworthy.

2. l. 1292.

3. Kenyon, *Medieval Fortifications* (Leicester, 1990), 126–30. This is with the exception of servants.

4. As understood at the current level of archaeological development.

5. *Hrolf Kraki's Saga*, trans. Anderson (New York, 1988), 31. In both cases, a hypothetical prototype would date to the fifth or sixth centuries through two of the characters, Hugleik and Hengest.

6. *Beowulf*, trans. Crossley-Holland (Oxford, 1982), 35.

7. Alexander Curle was adamant in his paper on the Mote of Mark that there was no ale-hall of any sort there or elsewhere; "Report on the Excavation, in September 1913, of a Vitrified Fort at Rockcliffe, Dalbeattie, Known as the Mote of Mark, *PSAS* 12, 4th series (Edinburgh, 1914), 125–69. And though his paper was written almost a century ago, the party which agreed with him is no less certain now.

8. Alcock, *Dinas Powys* (Cardiff, 1963), 62. Though Alcock does have reservations about Alt Clut: "Reconnaissance on Early Historic Fortifications and Other Royal Sites in Scotland," 1974–84, 4: "Excavations at Alt Clut, Clyde Rock, Strathclyde," 1974–5, *PSAS* 120 (Edinburgh, 1990), 95–149. Early on he admitted that there were no other structures like those he proposed at site 1B of Dinas Powys; *Dinas Powys* (Cardiff, 1963), 68.

9. Dark, *Civitas to Kingdom* (Leicester, 1994), 178–81.

10. Laing, "Timber Halls in Dark Age Britain—Some Problems," *TDGNAHS*, 3rd series 46 (Dumfries, 1969), 110–27.

11. *La Charrette*, l. 5034.

12. Though it should be noted that Professor Hector and Dr. Nora Chadwick's summary of all heroic age societies concluded that this custom was not consistent, except in respect to the Celtic peoples; *The Development of Oral Literature*, vol. 1 (Cambridge, 1932), 94.

13. *The Histories*, 4.64.

14. *Ab Urbe Condita*, 23, 24.11–12.

15. Ibid., 10, 26.11

16. *Taín Bó Cuailgne*, trans. Thomas Kinsella (Oxford, 1969), 124, 126, etc.

17. *Mabinogion*, trans. Gwyn Jones and Thomas Jones (London, 1974), 192 and 226.

18. "The Saga Englynion about Urien's Head," trans. John T. Koch and John Carey, *The Celtic Heroic Age*, eds. John T. Koch and John Carey (Malden, 1994), 344–5.

19. Dr. Anne Ross devoted an entire chapter to the subject of the Celtic head cult; *The Pagan Celts* (London, 1967), 61–126.

20. Later sagas seem to include beheading for a trophy on occasion, but *Beowulf*, the *Poetic Edda*, and the *Prose Edda*, contain no such instance.

21. Herodotus, *The Histories*, 1. 216.
22. Caesar, *De Bello Gallico*, 14.1.
23. Strabo, *The Geography*, 4.5.4.
24. Dio Cassius, *Dio's Roman History*, 77.12.
25. *Mabinogion*, trans. Gwyn Jones and Thomas Jones (London, 1974), 98.
26. A traditional compert story is defined by its hero being the product of divine conception, which would be the only Christian manner of explaining the marriage practices of a bygone era.
27. *Críth Gablach*, ed. David A. Binchy (Oxford, 1970), 70.
28. Ibid., 70–1.
29. *The Laws of Hywel Dda*, ed. and trans. Dafydd Jenkins (Llandyul, 1986), 50.
30. A woman who has lived with one man for seven years or more was considered to be a *gwriag briod*.
31. *The Laws of Hywel Dda*, ed. and trans. Dafydd Jenkins (Llandysul, 1986), 48. The term "fondle" is Middle Welsh *gofysio*. Alternatively *dodi byseth ynddi*, "putting fingers into." *The Laws of Hywel Dda*, ed. and trans. Dafydd Jenkins (Llandysul, 1986), 241.
32. *La Charrette*, ll. 544–8.
33. *Arthurian Romances*, trans. Douglas D. R. Owen (London, 1989), 192.
34. *La Charrette*, ll. 931–60.
35. *Arthurian Romances*, trans. Douglas D. R. Owen (London, 1989), 197.
36. *La Charrette*, l. 959.
37. Ibid., ll. 5500–15.
38. I use the term as defined in H. M. Chadwick's *The Heroic Age* (Cambridge, 1912), in which he carefully shows that the period of heroic culture in Indian, Greek, Irish, Norse, and British history all contained the same basic values and motivations. This system is a combination of chivalry to compatriots and opposing warriors and brutality to defeated foes.
39. *La Charrette*, ll. 1583–92.
40. *Arthurian Romances*, trans. Douglas D. R. Owen (London, 1989), 206.
41. *Taín Bó Cuailgne*, ed. and trans. Thomas Kinsella (Oxford, 1969), 114–25.
42. The duels are the only way the mighty, lone Cú Chulainn can be kept from killing thirty of Medb's army every night. The salvation of the army is provided by Medb and Aillil, who summon the best of their warriors, get them drunk, and promise them their daughter as a reward for killing their sole enemy. Refused, they accuse each of their warriors of cowardice. The proud warriors have no other choice but to fight, and die, after that.
43. Especially *Bhagavad Gita*, which occupies Book 4.
44. See in particular the duels in Books 3, 7, and 21.
45. *The Gododdin: The Oldest Scottish Poem*, ed. Kenneth H. Jackson (Edinburgh, 1969), 116. A1, l. 22.
46. Ibid., 116. A1, ll. 28–29.
47. Ibid., 128. A28, ll. 33–4. These two stanzas are considered ancient by both Jackson and Charles-Edwards. On the basis of his linguistic reconstruction of the poem, Professor Koch dates the first to between 655 and 700 and the second before 638. However his opinions, as well as his reconstruction of the poem, are still under a great deal of debate. Charles-Edwards, "The Authenticity of the Gododdin: An Historian's View," *Astudiaethau ar yr Hengerdd*, eds. Rachel Bromwich and R. Brinley Jones (Cardiff, 1978), 78; *The Gododdin of Aneirin*, ed. and trans. John T. Koch (Cardiff, 1995), 201.
48. *Canu Taliesin: gyda Rhagymadrodd a Nodiadau*, ed. Sir Ifor Williams (Oxford, 1960), 23–6.
49. "Uryen Erechwyð; Urien of Erechwyð," trans. Koch, *The Celtic Heroic Age*, eds. John T. Koch and John Carey (Malden, 1994), 340.
50. *Taín Bó Cuailgne*, trans. Thomas Kinsella (Oxford, 1969), 91–2.
51. Mesca Ulaid; The Intoxication of the Munstermen," trans. J. Carmichael Watson, *The Celtic Heroic Age*, eds. John T. Koch and John Carey (Malden, 1994), 117.
52. The dual nature of the Celtic warriors is not mentioned by the classical authors. Instead their ferocity is dwelled upon. Both the Romans and the Greeks had no means of learning how their enemies lived outside of war, nor did they have an interest in learning about their mythology and legends. Given that information, it is doubtful whether either culture would have been able to grasp that the tribes that they held to be so barbaric were capable of modesty and respect for women.
53. *Críth Gablach*, ed. David A. Binchy (Oxford, 1970), 76.
54. Ibid., 77.
55. Ibid., 79.
56. The etymology of Bademagus' name is not understood, and its history may well remain hidden forever. However, with characteristic ingenuity, Loomis saw him as another representation of Brân in Arthurian literature; Loomis, *Arthurian Tradition and Chrétien* (New York, 1949), 240–50.
57. *La Charrette*, ll. 3375–87.
58. trans. Douglas D. R. Owen (London, 1989), 230.
59. There appears to be no antecedent in Celtic myth or legend, nor is there any hints of it to be found in the history of the period or in Christian texts that the author is aware of after extensive searching. Given Chrétien's penchant for modifying instead of creating, however, it is most likely he has simply altered something beyond anyone's ability to see the original.

60. Meleagant abducts Lancelot while he is still on his father's lands, which means that he cannot harm him.
61. Diodorus Siculus, *The Bibliotheca Historia of Diodorus Siculus*, trans. John Skelton, eds. F. M. Salter and H. L. K. Edward, (1968–71), 5.30
62. "The Boyhood Deeds of Finn," trans. John Carey, *The Celtic Heroic Age*, eds. John T. Koch and John Carey (Maldon, 1994), 190.
63. "Togail Bruidne Dá Derga; The Destruction of Dá Derga's Hostel," trans. Whitley Stokes, *The Celtic Heroic Age*, eds. John T. Koch and John Carey (Maldon, 1994), 167.
64. *The Laws of Hywel Dda*, trans. Dafydd Jenkins (Llandysul, 1986), 46.
65. *La Charrette*, ll. 1020 et al.
66. *Le Conte*, ll. 1549 et al.
67. The author will refrain here from theorizing about the original version of the "Bed Scene," as there are too many options to help forward the argument presented in the pages below. For a review of the various possibilities and an extremely tentative conclusion see the second appendix titled "The Bed Scene."
68. Gorre is not actually called an island, but the implications are that the only way to get to it is to cross over or under water.
69. Dr. Brusegan has made the argument against Gorre being an otherworld by alternative means; Brusegan, "L'autre monde et *Le Chevalier de la Charrette*," *Lancelot-Lanzelet: Hier et Aujourdhui*, eds. Danielle Buschinger and Michael Zink (Reineke, 1995), 77–85.
70. L. Loomis, "The Sword Bridge of Chrétien de Troyes and its Celtic Original," *PMLA* 4 (Columbia, 1913), 170.
71. Ibid., 185–6.
72. "Bricriu's Feast," trans. George Henderson, *The Celtic Heroic Age*, eds. John T. Koch and John Carey (Maldon, 1995), 109.
73. *Mabinogion*, trans. Gwyn Jones and Thomas Jones (London, 1974), 108.
74. *Diu Crône* allows Gauvain passage to the island without mishap. The other versions with Gauvain as the hero do as well.
75. In fact there are only three versions in which he does not appear. These are the portions of the scene in *Ymddiddan Gwenhwyfar ac Arthur* that is extant, the corrupted and biased *Vitae Gildae*, and the composite known as *Le Morte d'Arthur*. In the last of these, the second hero is, curiously, named Lavaine.
76. In *Iwein*, one of the characters briefly describes the abduction and recovery of the queen, using only Gauvain's name as the rescuer.
77. The absolute dearth of suggestions from Celtic experts is most telling. Loomis could only suggest it represented a crannog.
78. Eschenbach, *Parzival*, 6.297; ed. and trans. Arthur T. Hatto (Baltimore, 1980), 155.

79. "Pa Gur?," trans. Roberts, *Culhwch ac Olwen*, eds. Rachel Bromwich and D. Simon Evans (Cardiff, 1992), ll. 31 and 35.
80. Ibid., ll. 70–1.
81. In fact the mutually exclusive properties suggest these qualities were borrowed *ad hoc* from Irish myth.
82. ll. 381–3; trans. Gwyn Jones and Thomas Jones (London, 1974), 107.
83. Ibid., 128.
84. Gowans, *Cei and the Arthurian Legend* (Cambridge, 1988), 22. The reference is to a trick played on Arthur by a saint, who humiliates him.
85. Cross and Nitze, *Motif-Index of Early Irish Literature* (Chicago, 1952), 91. See Tom Peete Cross for a more exhaustive list; Cross, *Lancelot and Guinevere: A Study on the Origins of Courtly Love* (New York, 1970), 52.
86. Cross, *Lancelot and Guinevere: A Study on the Origins of Courtly Love* (New York, 1970), 61; Cross and Nitze, *Motif-Index of Early Irish Literature* (Chicago, 1952), 466–9, R151–151.1, R161-R161.1, F322.2.
87. Cross, *Lancelot and Guinevere: A Study on the Origins of Courtly Love* (New York, 1970), 52.
88. It is very possible that Lancelot was drawn from *Cligès* or an earlier work and replaced Gauvain in the role of hero. Perhaps Kei predated them both. However, there is no evidence of Arthur ever having been the hero of the tale.
89. Such is the case in the most famed abduction myth, "Echtra Chorbmaic uí Chuínn" or "The Adventure of Cormac [son of Art and] grandson of Conn."
90. With this statement, however, one must acknowledge the very real prestige of Arthur and his ability to reduce other characters—even magicians—into minor role-players. It does not seem that this would be the case here, though. A similar prominence did not keep the great kings of Irish myth from dealing with gods and powerful magicians.
91. Bromwich, "Celtic Dynastic Themes and Breton Lays," *ÉC* 9 (Paris, 1961), 441.
92. Geoffrey of Vinsauf, *Documentum de modo et arte dictandi et versificandi*, trans. Robert P. Parr (Milwaukee, 1968), 132.
93. The standard works on Celtic influences in the continental romances are by Dr. Bromwich; Bromwich, "Celtic Dynastic Themes and Breton Lays," *ÉC* 9 (Paris, 1961), 439–74; Bromwich, "First Transmission from England and France," *The Arthur of the Welsh*, eds. Rachel Bromwich, Brynley Roberts, and Alfred O. H. Jarman (Cardiff, 1991b), 273–89.

Chapter 6

1. Kelly, "Chrétien de Troyes," *The Arthur of the French: The Arthurian Legend in Medieval*

French and Occitan Literature, ed. Glyn Burgess and Karen Pratt, 154 (Cardiff, 2006), 159–160.
2. Rhys, Studies in the Arthurian Legend (Oxford, 1891), 142.
3. La Charrette, l. 322; trans. Douglas D. R. Owen (London, 1989), 189.
4. La Charrette, l. 325–6; trans. Douglas D. R. Owen (London, 1989), 189.
5. ed. Henry O. Sommer (Washington, 1909–16), 162.
6. James A. H. Murray et al., eds., Oxford English Dictionary (Oxford, 1961), 35.
7. Greene, "The Chariot as Described in Irish Literature," The Iron Age in the Irish Sea Province, ed. Charles Thomas (London, 1972), 59–73, with picture.
8. Caesar, De Bello Gallica, trans. S. A. Handford (Baltimore, 1951), 5.15–17, 5.19.
9. Tacitus, Agricola, trans. H. Mattingly, rev. S. A. Handford (Middlesex, 1970), 12.
10. Tacitus, Agricola, trans. H. Mattingly, rev. S. A. Handford (Middlesex, 1970), 35–6.
11. No. 4.
12. Now a part of the Edinburgh museum.
13. No. 10 in the registry of Pictish stones.
14. The drawing above is based on that of David Longley in Dr. Laing's article and seems compatible with the Edinburgh find. Laing, "Archaeological Notes on some Scottish Early Christian Stones," PSAS 114 (Darking, 1985), 279.
15. A majority of scholars have argued for a date nearer the ninth century, though Dr. Laing has shown evidence for a fifth- or sixth-century creation of this type of stone in "Archaeological Notes on Some Scottish Early Christian Stones," PSAS 114 (Darking, 1985), 277–87.
16. See the first appendix, "Lancelot's Cart."
17. Vita Columbae, 2.44
18. From the "Prose Lancelot" section of The Vulgate Version of the Arthurian Romances one learns that he also removes the sarcophagus from the cemetery; Vulgate, trans. Henry O. Sommer (1909–16), 175.
19. It could be argued that the delay is a typical romantic strategem of postponing pleasure to intensify it. However, Guinièvre is unaware of the postponement, thereby effectively halving the effect. It also gives Gauvain a more than even chance of saving the queen first. One must question Chrétien's intentions with regard to the tomb episode.
20. Erec, ll. 5547–6007.
21. Zatzikhoven, Lanzelet, ed. Roger S. Loomis, trans. Kenneth G. T. Webster (New York, 1951), 234.
22. La Charrette, ll. 1357–60.
23. trans. Douglas D. R. Owen (London, 1989), 203.
24. Glyn S. Burgess and Keith Busby, Lanval (London, 1986), l. 634. Lanval leaps upon it before becoming consort to the Queen of Avalon.
25. Zatzikhoven, Lanzelet, ed. Roger S. Loomis, trans. Kenneth G. T. Webster (New York, 1951), 96.
26. Wirnt von Grafenurg, Wigalois, trans. John W. Thomas (London, 1977), 120.
27. Heinrich von dem Türlin, Diu Crône, trans. John W. Thomas (London, 1989), ll. 17331–51.
28. Mabinogion, trans. Gwyn Jones and Thomas Jones (London, 1974), 140.
29. Wirnt von Grafenburg, Wigalois, trans. John W. Thomas (London, 1977), 120.
30. La Morte d'Arthur, 15–16; The Vulgate Version of the Arthurian Romances, trans. Sommer (1909–16), 6.11.2.
31. "Co(i)mpert Conchobuir [Maic Nessa]; The Conception of Conchobar son of Nes," trans. John Carey, The Heroic Age, eds. John T. Koch and John Carey (Maldon, 1994), 49.
32. Byrne, Irish Kings and high-Kings (London, 1973), 27.

Chapter 7

1. Owen, The Evolution of the Grail Legend (Edinburgh, 1968), 106.
2. These scholars have argued for a written Northern Memoranda composed possibly of strictly historical data, but quite probably also of saga material and poetry like that which remains of Urien, Eledd, and Llywarch Hen. It is also known that Y Gododdin and some of the Taliesin poems were probably first composed by two of the bards whom the Historia Brittoum names.

Chapter 8

1. This is significant because the poems Le Chevalier de la Charrette and Le Conte du Graal are the only two in which he claims his patron has given him his source.
2. The four major theories focus on the Celtic, Christian, Jewish, and archetypal universal elements of the ceremony.

Chapter 9

1. The main criticisms of this important figure over the past sixty years has been by Helen Adolph and Armel Diverres. There seems to have been exceptionally few disagreements between the two on the relevant information; Adolph, "A Historical Background to Chrétien's Perceval," PMLA 58, (Menasha, 1943), 597–620; Diverres "The Grail and the Third Crusade: Thoughts on Le Conte du Graal by Chrétien de

Troyes," *Arthurian Literature X* (Cambridge, 1990), 13–109.
2. *Le Conte*, l. 13.
3. Adolph, "A Historical Background to Chrétien's *Perceval*," *PMLA* 58 (Menasha, 1943), 601.
4. Ibid., 602.
5. Diverres, "The Grail and the Third Crusade: Thoughts on *Le Conte du Graal* by Chrétien de Troyes," *Arthurian Literature* 10 (Cambridge, 1990), 28.
6. Krey, "William of Tyre," *S* 16 (Cambridge, 1941), 155.
7. The precise date is disputed. Conceivably, he could at some point have become bored with the project or simply found he had painted himself into a corner. Alternatively, he may have ceased writing when his patron died and there was no further cash flow. There is also the possibility Chrétien's death cut the poem short; his obit is unknown.
8. Adolph, "A Historical Background to Chrétien's *Perceval*," *PMLA* 58 (Menasha, 1943), 597–620.
9. Ibid., 598.
10. Diverres, "The Grail and the Third Crusade: Thoughts on *Le Conte du Graal* by Chrétien de Troyes," *Arthurian Literature* 10 (Cambridge, 1990), 32–42.
11. For instance, the weeping cousin who berates Perceval and the damsel who humiliates him at Arthur's court are analogous to the cousins whom he had dealings with in Jerusalem.
12. Alan Rufus was an ally of William the Conqueror and a member of a junior branch of the Breton ducal family. He was made Count of Richmond by William the Conqueror; Stenton, *The First Century of English Feudalism 1066–1166* (London, 1932), 24–5; Mason, "The 'Honour of Richmond' in 1086," *EHR* 78 (London, 1963), 703–4.
13. *Le Conte*, l. 3675; Ritchie, *Chrétien de Troyes and Scotland* (Oxford, 1952), 8; Bromwich, "First Transmission to England and France," *The Arthur of the Welsh*, eds. Rachel Bromwich, Brynley Roberts, and Alfred O. H. Jackson (Cardiff, 1991b), 277. *Escoce Watre* and *Cotouatre* are not direct translations of Scot's Water. However, the three terms are visually similar, and Scot's Water is the best translation in context with the episode it comes from. In Arthurian onomastics that is all that may reasonably be hoped for.
14. Ritchie, *The Normans in Scotland* (Edinburgh, 1954), 352.
15. *Le Conte*, ll. 8341–45.
16. trans. Douglas D. R. Owen, (London, 1989), 461.
17. Newell, "Arthurian Notes," *MLN* 17 (Baltimore, 1902), 277–8.
18. William of Malmesbury, *De Rebus Gestis Regum Anglorum*, ed. William Stubbs (London, 1889), 287, 342.
19. *Le Conte*, ll. 336 and 839.
20. *The Anglo-Saxon Chronicle*, E-1092; Ritchie, *Chrétien de Troyes and Scotland* (Oxford, 1952), 9–10.
21. Ritchie, *The Normans in Scotland* (Edinburgh, 1954), 16–17.

Chapter 10

1. *Le Conte*, ll. 3156–97.
2. *Le Conte*, trans. Douglas D. R. Owen (London, 1989), 416–7.
3. The chief object of the ceremony, be it a chalice, platter, or even a rock in the case of *Parzival*.
4. The main intention will be to explain the nature of the grail though an analysis of potential sources of information for the romances.
5. The dominant reading material for English speakers has been and will remain Sir Thomas Malory's *Le Morte d'Arthur*, written in 1485. It is a rather late version. In it the grail legend has developed to such an extent that only those who are perfect Christians may see it.
6. The last prominent scholar to adhere to this theory was Professor James Bruce in his *The Evolution of Arthurian Romance from the Beginnings to the Year 1300* (Gottingen, 1923).
7. Phrases such as "Dex vos angart; May God keep you," "se Dex m'amant; So help me God," "Cui Dex donroit si boen eür; If God grants him good fortune," "Dex vos saut; May God protect you," and "Por deu; in the name of God" recur throughout the poem, as do set phrases for conversations such as "Par foi; By my faith." It reminds the reader of the centrality Christianity plays in the lives of the heroes. References to saints, such as St. Peter (ll. 2175, 4215), St. Paul (l. 49), St. Martin (l. 7252), St. David (l. 4100), and St. Richter (l. 1879) serve to reinforce this connection. However, they are elements that are unnecessary to the pre-Chrétien plot (witness *Vita Gildae* and *Ymddiddan*) and could easily be imposed on an already existing story.
8. William of Malmesbury, *De Antiquitate Glastonie Ecclesie*, ed. and trans. John Scott (Woodbridge, 1981), Books 1 and 2.
9. *Le Conte*, ll. 706–10.
10. It is true that Chrétien never explicitly states that the grail is Christian, but his hero is firmly so. One can hardly imagine a poet of Western Europe writing a romance for one of the most prestigious Roman Catholic families and allowing his main hero to participate in pagan rites. Those who followed Chrétien unanimously made the grail a Christian object.

11. *Le Conte*, l. 1627.
12. *Le Conte*, ll. 113–16.
13. *Le Conte*, trans. Douglas D. R. Owen (London, 1989), 375.
14. Bruce, *The Evolution of Arthurian Romance, from the Beginnings Down to the Year 1300* (Gottingen, 1923), 258–9.
15. Bruce, *The Evolution of Arthurian Romance, from the Beginnings Down to the Year 1300* (Gottingen, 1923), 257. The lance of Chrétien's poem has no special meaning, but his First Continuator gives it a Christian quality.
16. *Matthew*, 4.19.
17. The author finds Bruce's limited examples of contrary instances in the East unsatisfying. They only serve to strengthen the position that the traditional ceremony called for a temple in the Orthodox church; *The Evolution of Arthurian Romance from the Beginnings Down to the Year 1300* (Gottingen, 1923), 259
18. Peebles, *Legend of Longinus in Ecclesiastical Tradition and in English Literature* (Baltimore, 1911), 209–13.
19. Professor Loomis' theory that the lance was based on the Spear of Luin and owned by Lug is unconvincing. He based it on one early but spurious text, the *First Continuation*, and three extremely late grail versions, *Huth Merlin*, Malory, and *Demanda del Sancto Grial*, to prove the correlation. These are all less than reliable pieces of evidence. Moreover, Loomis evidenced only one parallel to the ceremony's objects in all of Celtic mythology, and that comparison is weak. Summarized, the spear of Luin and the spear of Chrétien both boil blood to a point when held, and both are held point downwards. These may be unusual details, but put together they hardly qualify for the water tight link Loomis believed it was. Nutt also made that comparison, though he did not give details; Loomis, *Arthurian Tradition and Chrétien* (New York, 1949), 379–82; Nutt, *Studies on the Legend of the Holy Grail* (London, 1888), 184.
20. *Didot Perceval*, ed. and trans. William A. Nitze (Chicago, 1932–7), 150–1.
21. Weston, *The Quest of the Holy Grail* (London, 1913), 64.
22. Loomis, *The Grail: From Celtic Myth to Christian Symbol* (Cardiff, 1963), 62.
23. These claims are so consistent and valid from a territorial standpoint that Dr. Kenneth Dark has proven it is possible to mark off the boundaries of fifth- and sixth-century Wales using dedications to minor saints from this period; Dark, *Civitas to Kingdom* (Leicester, 1994).
24. Remy, "Graal," *The Catholic Encyclopedia*, eds. Charles G. Herbermann et al. (London, 1907), 6.7211.
25. It can only be a possibility that Chrétien, which means "Christian," had Jewish training. It may be that he was Jewish and wrote for Christian nobles, or that he was born a Jew and converted; this would explain his name. He may have been Christian but had accessed and been influenced by the Jewish religion through the various traders.
26. Weinraub, *Chrétien's Jewish Grail* (Chapel Hill, 1976), 81.
27. *Le Conte*, l. 623.
28. *Le Conte*, ll. 2985–3023.
29. *Le Conte*, l. 6239.
30. *Le Conte*, l. 3050–67.
31. Weinraub, *Chrétien's Jewish Grail* (Chapel Hill, 1976), 52.
32. Ibid., 70.
33. Ibid., 76.
34. One may recall that Jerusalem and Philip's stay there were the inspiration for the grail castle.
35. Weinraub, *Chrétien's Jewish Grail* (Chapel Hill, 1976), 66–7.
36. Ibid., 56.
37. The Montpellier manuscript of *Le Conte du Graal* does state that the grail bearer was a descendent of Israel, a Jew.
38. Weinraub, *Chrétien's Jewish Grail* (Chapel Hill, 1976), 68.
39. Ibid., 55.
40. Weston, *The Quest of the Holy Grail* (London, 1913), 98–139.
41. Ibid., 79.
42. As Weston put it, the ceremony usually involves a mourning period of three to seven days for the Old Year, followed by a rebirth in a new year; Weston, *The Quest of the Holy Grail* (London, 1913), 78.
43. The concept survives in such archaic phrases as "life-blood."
44. It is necessary for Weston's argument that the grail king and the host served by the grail be two people — one the person who answers the question, the other the symbolic personification of nature. The current belief about the relationship of the grail-king and the man served by the grail is that there is evidence the two were separated at one point but that they were originally one character.
45. Weston, *The Quest of the Holy Grail* (London, 1913), 82; *From Ritual to Romance* (London, 1920), 47.
46. Loomis, *Celtic Myth and Arthurian Romance* (New York, 1927a), 282.
47. These are all most clearly seen in the *Vulgate Version of the Arthurian Romances* and *Le Morte d'Arthur*. When Gauvain goes to the castle and is partially successful, he sees the grail. When Lancelot is cured from his madness and later when he arrives at the grail castle, he is told he is perfect in all but one regard and sees the object in its second form. Only Perceval, Galahad, and Bors see the grail in its final form.

48. Weston, *The Quest of the Holy Grail* (London, 1913), 94.
49. Ibid., 83.
50. Jackson, *The International Popular Tale and Early Welsh Tradition* (Cardiff, 1961), 40–1.
51. Loomis, *Arthurian Tradition and Chrétien* (New York, 1949), ix; *Wales and the Arthurian Legend* (Cardiff, 1956), 51.
52. Villemarqué, *Les Romans de la Table Ronde et les Contes des anciens Bretons* (Paris, 1842). It could be argued that the idea of Irish churchmen spreading pagan Celtic rites across Europe seems unlikely, but this is exactly what happens with the *Beowulf* author. Much of what remains of pre–Christian European culture was preserved in a similar manner.
53. As was discussed in Chapters 1 and 2, the general feeling is now more that there was a pan-Celtic background for the grail and other stories.
54. The Norman world included Great Britain, for the most part, and also Normandy and a good share of the rest of France.
55. *Culhwch ac Olwen*, l. 221; Roberts, "The Treatment of Personal Names in the Early Welsh Versions of *Historia Regum Britanniae*," B 25 (Cardiff, 1973), 278.
56. TYP, 416, 555; Lloyd-Morgan, "Breuddwyd Rhonabwy and Later Arthurian Literature," *The Arthur of the Welsh*, eds. Rachel Bromwich, Brynley Roberts, and Alfred O. H. Jarman (Cardiff, 1991), 197; Sims-Williams, "The Early Welsh Arthurian Poems," *The Arthur of the Welsh*, eds. Rachel Bromwich, Brynley Roberts, and Alfred O. H. Jarman (Cardiff, 1991), 44.
57. Loomis, *Arthurian Tradition and Chrétien* (New York, 1949), 347–55.
58. Lejeune, "The Troubadours" *Arthurian Literature in the Middle Ages*, ed. Roger S. Loomis (Chicago, 1959), 396; TYP, 490.
59. Nutt, *Studies on the Legend of the Holy Grail* (London, 1888), 231–4 and 158–9, respectively.
60. Loomis believed the grail king was Brân, therefore his nephew Pryderi must be Perceval. They both brought devastation onto a kingdom by sitting in a perilous seat. The flaw in the theory is that Perceval's chair only emerges much later in the grail legend.
61. Campbell, *More West Highland Tales* (Edinburgh, 1840–1860).
62. Hélinand de Froidmont, *Les vers de la Mort*, trans. Michael Boyer and Monique Santucci (Paris, 1983), 11; Loomis, "The Origins of the Grail Legends," *Arthurian Literature in the Middle Ages*, ed. Roger S. Loomis (Oxford, 1959b), 277.
63. Loomis, "The Origins of the Grail Legends," *Arthurian Literature in the Middle Ages*, ed. Roger S. Loomis (Oxford, 1959b), 277.
64. Ibid., 288.
65. Chrétien told his readers that the castle of the grail was called Corbenic, which meant "Saintisme vaissel" or "most holy vessel" in Chaldean. Since "c" and "t" were constantly mistaken for each other in manuscripts, and the Dutch *Lancelot* gives the name of the castle as *Cambenoyt*, and a manuscript of Manassier has *Corlenot*, Loomis suspected that the original form was *Corbenoit*; in other words, the "Castle of the Blessed Horn." He goes on to suggest the original term may also have been *Torbenoit*—the "Castle of the Blessed Bull." Such is a stretch from quite flimsy evidence; Loomis, "The Origins of the Grail Legends," *Arthurian Literature in the Middle Ages*, ed. Roger S. Loomis (Oxford, 1959b), 288.
66. *Le Haut Livre du Graal: Perlesvaus*, ed. William Nitze (Totowa, 1937), l. 9547.
67. The one exception to this rule is *Peredur*, which quite possibly has suffered from a play on the word *per*, Welsh for basin. Peredur then became the "basin-seeker."
68. TYP, 240–2.
69. Cross and Slover, *Ancient Irish Tales* (Dublin, rep. 1969), 199, 328, 353; Loomis, *Celtic Myth and Arthurian Romance* (New York, 1927a), 159–75, 236–41; *Arthurian Tradition and Chrétien* (New York, 1949), 339; *Wales and the Arthurian Legend* (Cardiff, 1956), 156.
70. The strong oral tradition in Wales and Brittany during the eleventh, twelfth, and thirteenth centuries attest to this. For a convenient summary of some evidence for this activity see Loomis, *Arthurian Tradition and Chrétien* (New York, 1949), 12–24.
71. Vendryes, "L'Unité en trois personnes chez les Celtes," *Compterendus de l'Acadamie des Inscriptions et des Belles Lettres* (Paris, 1935), 325; Sjoested, *Gods and Heroes of the Celts*, (trans. Miles Dillon (London, 1949), 17, 31, 43, and passim; Mac Cana, *Celtic Mythology* (Hamlyn, 1970), 48; TYP, 155–6.
72. Bromwich, "Celtic Dynastic Themes and Breton Lays," *EC* 9 (Paris, 1961), 439–41.
73. The direct connection to kingship has not been explored here, but will be in Chapter 13.
74. O'Rahilly, "On the Origin of the Names Érain and Ériu," *Ériu* 35 (Dublin, 1946b), 11–13.
75. Mac Cana, "Aspects of the Theme of the King and Goddess," *EC* 6 (Paris, 1955), 78; Appendix 3.
76. *Le Haut Livre du Graal: Perlesvaus*, ed. William Nitze (Totowa, 1937), ll. 38, 1081, 1646, etc.
77. Zatzhikoven, *Lanzelet*, ed. Roger S. Loomis, trans. G.T. Webster (New York, 1951), 898.
78. Türlin, *The Crown (Diu Crône)*, trans. John Wesley Thomas (Lincoln, 1989), ll. 29532–4.

79. Nutt, *Studies on the Legend of the Holy Grail* (London, 1888), 191.
80. Christians do have legends about such places, but in all cases they have been influenced by local culture.
81. Weston believed the stag hunt was to conclude with the animal changing into a maid. This assumption was based on the late works *Dutch Lancelot, Tyolet,* and *MacPhie's Black Dog*; Weston, *The Legend of Lancelot du Lac* (London, 1901), 30–3. Loomis argued that the tale would naturally have ended with a maiden receiving the stag's head, and also used much later materials; Loomis, *Arthurian Tradition and Chrétien* (New York, 1949), 68–70.
82. Bromwich, "Celtic Dynastic Themes and Breton Lays," *EC* 9 (Paris, 1961), 460–1.
83. Ibid., 462–3.
84. Dr. Roberts article discusses the underlying theme of loss of sovereignty throughout the British world. The subsequent emergence of the sovereignty theme in twelfth-century British tales can be seen as a result of this phenomenon; Roberts, "Geoffrey of Monmouth and Welsh Historical Tradition," *NMS* 20 (Nottingham, 1976), 1–26.
85. Maynadier, *The Wife of Bath's Tale: Its Sources and Analogues* (London, 1901), 25–42; Bugge, "Fertility myth and female sovereignty in the weddynge of Sir Gawen and Dame Ragnell," *CR* 39.2 (University Park, 2004), 198–218.
86. Goetinck, *Peredur: A Study of Welsh Tradition in the Grail Legends* (Cardiff, 1975), 129–55.
87. Roberts, "Geoffrey of Monmouth and Welsh Historical Tradition," *NMS* 20 (Nottingham, 1976), 29–40.
88. Rhys, "Notes on the Hunting of the Twrch Trwyth," *THSC* (London, 1896), 146–148.
89. Loomis had also hypothesized that there was a connection between the question ceremony in *Le Conte* and the other grail romances to myth involving Conn. In it he and his descendants were confirmed in the high-kingship by Lug and his wife, the Sovranty of Érin. The repetition in the scene, and the centrality of Lug, the cup-bearer, and the guest are similar. However, the question, "To whom shall the cup be given?" which belongs to the myth, is nothing like Perceval's question of "Who is the old man being served with the grail?" nor is there any trail showing how the change could have been made, or any explanation why such a change could have occurred or why it would have made the object more Christian for Chrétien's audience.
90. Bruce hit on this fact as the primary reason not to follow the theory; Bruce, *The Evolution of Arthurian Romance, from the Beginnings Down to the Year 1300* (Gottingen, 1923), 275.
91. Brown, *The Origin of the Grail Legend* (New York, 1966), 25. He claimed that every scene but the palace of silver and copper pillars in *Perlesvaus* was merely coincidence or a universal motif.
92. It would be arrogant to assume that someone in the twenty-first century could know all of the intricacies of twelfth-century literature.
93. Alternatively, the Ritual Theory accounts for the grail castle's proximity to water, the Ritual and Celtic theories account for the grail king's castration.

Chapter 11

1. The role of Cei in early Welsh literature has been discussed in Chapter 5. After Geoffrey introduced Arthur to the continent, the Welsh and continental authors used him as little more than a comical device or instructional tool to enhance the hero.
2. Loomis, *Celtic Myth and Arthurian Romance* (New York, 1927a), 178–84; *Arthurian Tradition and Chrétien* (New York, 1949), 347–55; *Wales and the Arthurian Legend* (Cardiff, 1956), 35, 173.
3. Interestingly, *Peredur* is the romance that evidences the most primitive elements and therefore is probably closer to *Dysgyl* than any other story.
4. In Chrétien the grail king is anonymous. However, the presence of the name Pelles slightly later in the extant *Arthuriana* does not necessarily force the conclusion that it was a late arrival to the Arthurian world. Chrétien may well have had stylistic reasons for leaving such a mysterious figure nameless, or simply may not have had the name and worked around it. His solution was to attach a name to him that symbolized Christ, thus adding a further veil of mystery to the legend.
5. *Le Haut Livre du Graal: Perlesvaus,* ed. William Nitze (Totowa, 1937), ll. 38, 1080, 1645, 2928, 3572, 4989, 5198, 6108, 8674, 8669, 9821.
6. For a complete guide to the listings of Pelles in the French poems, see Geoffrey West; West, *An Index of Proper Names in French Arthurian Verse Romances 1150–1300* (Toronto, 1969).
7. Loomis, *Celtic Myth and Arthurian Romance* (New York, 1927a), 145.
8. *Erec*, ll. 1993–2011.
9. Gerald of Wales, *The Journey through Wales. The Description of Wales*, ed. and trans. Lewis Thorpe (London, 1978), 1.3.
10. *Early Welsh Genaeological Tracts,* ed. Peter C. Bartrum (Cardiff, 1966).
11. Irby-Massie, *Military Religion in Roman Britain* (Boston, 1999), 108 (as a god for Roman enlisted men and as a warrior god); Ross, *Pagan*

Celtic Britain (London, 1967), 127; Webster, *The Pagan Celts and Their Gods under Rome* (London, 1986), 146 fn. 37.

12. Webster, *The Pagan Celts and Their Gods under Rome* (London, 1986), 74–5; Irby-Massie, *Military Religion in Roman Britain* (Boston, 1999), 104.

13. Ross, *Pagan Celtic Britain* (London, 1967), 371.

14. *Le Haut Livre du Graal: Perlesvaus*, ed. William Nitze (Totowa, 1937), ll. 5917–65.

15. Loomis, *Arthurian Tradition and Chrétien* (New York, 1949), 347–55.

16. However, knowing that he is more fully integrated into the Arthurian literature, he may well have been the original hero of the tale, later to be displaced by a newer one. See Weston for a more thorough discussion on the subject; Weston, *The Legend of Sir Gawain*, (London, 1897).

17. Busby, *Gauvain in Old French Literature* (Amsterdam, 1980). Busby's evaluation is a masterful examination of Gauvain's role in medieval French literature.

18. As will be seen, several scenes in this work are quite old and lend themselves to believing this version comes from an older source. The author can at this time offer no explanation why this source does not mention Perceval and instead makes Gauvain the grail hero.

19. *Culhwch ac Olwen: An Edition and Study of the Earliest Arthurian Tale*, eds. Rachel Bromwich and D. Simon Evans (Cardiff, 1992), l. 221.

20. Roberts, "The Treatment of Personal Names in the Early Welsh Versions of *Historia Regum Britanniae*," *B* 25 (Cardiff, 1973), 278. As Geoffrey is noted for his creative use of traditional material and characters, however, this presents no serious inconsistency with a Peredur/Gonemans link.

21. West, *An Index of Proper Names in French Arthurian Verse Romances* (Toronto, 1969), 5; West, *An Index of Proper Names in French Arthurian Prose Romances* (Toronto, 1978), 10.

22. Pokorney, "Der cymrische Sagenheld Peredur," *Beiträge zur Namenforsung* 1 (Berlin, 1948), 38.

23. *Culhwch ac Olwen: An Edition and Study of the Earliest Arthurian Tale*, eds. Rachel Bromwich and D. Simon Evans (Cardiff, 1992), ll. 185 and 725. Here he is claimed as a resident of Dyfed.

24. *Culhwch ac Olwen: An Edition and Study of the Earliest Arthurian Tale*, eds. Rachel Bromwich and D. Simon Evans (Cardiff, 1992), l. 216.

25. Pokorney, "Der cymrische Sagenheld Peredur," *Beiträge zur Namenforsung* 1 (Berlin, 1948), 38.

26. H. Chadwick, *The Heroic Age* (Cambridge, 1912), 350–1.

27. In *Parzival* the brother is named Feirfeiz, which is very possibly a garbled form of *Fitz*, or prince.

28. One conspicuous example is St. Garmon. By the ninth century, all of his activities were assigned to St. Germanus of Auxerre.

29. *Gododdin: The Oldest Scottish Poem*, ed. Kenneth H. Jackson (Edinburgh, 1969), A31.

30. *Early Welsh Genaeological Tracts*, ed. Peter C. Bartrum (Cardiff, 1966), 147 and 45, respectively. Bartrum questions the validity of the former entry, however.

Chapter 12

1. The order will be that of Chrétien. *Sir Perceval* has occasionally been used as a source to support whichever position has been argued. The author shall follow the majority of scholars, however, in choosing not to use it. Its obviously lengthy stay in an oral environment has not allowed it to retain a functional understanding of the episodes or the plot.

2. Loomis, *The Grail: From Celtic Myth to Christian Symbol* (Cardiff, 1963), 5; though see Lovecy for specific examples; Lovecy, "Historia Peredur ab Efrawg," *The Arthur of the Welsh*, eds. Rachel Bromwich, Brynley Roberts, and Alfred O. H. Jarman (Cardiff, 1991), 177–8.

3. Goetinck, *Peredur:A Study of Welsh Tradition in the Grail Legends* (Cardiff, 1975), 304–17.

4. The main contenders have been Dr. Williams, Dr. Lovecy, and Dr. Lloyd-Morgan. Professor Thurneysen has also written a landmark paper on the subject, but the only reference the author has found was to an article in *Zeitschrift Celtique Philosophie*. This was a review of Mary Williams' *Essai sur la composition du roman gallois de Peredur* (Paris, 1909); Williams, *Essai sur la composition du roman gallois de Peredur* (Paris, 1909); Lovecy, "The Celtic Sovereignty Theme and the Structure of *Peredur*," *SC* 12/13 (Cardiff, 1978), 133–46; Lloyd-Morgan, "Narrative Structure in *Peredur*, *ZCP* 38 (Berlin, 1981), 187–231.

5. It is known that the versions which are extant are compilations, so that it is very possible that some of those episodes listed before the marriage originally occurred after. Keeping in mind, however, Peredur's tendency to become attached to a woman and suddenly leave, this suggestion is hardly necessary. Peredur is not a hero because of the woman he marries, he is because of his adventures and the women that he attracts to his bed. It makes no sense that a marriage would ever have signified the end of his tale; Goetinck, *Peredur: A Study of Welsh Tradition in the Grail Legends* (Cardiff, 1975), 21; Lovecy, "Historia Peredur ab Efrawg," *The*

Arthur of the Welsh, eds. Rachel Bromwich, Brynley Roberts, Alfred O. H. Jarman (Cardiff, 1991), 177–80; *The Mabinogi*, eds. Proinsias Mac Cana, Meic Stephens, and R. Brinley Jones (Cardiff, 1992), 105–6

6. Lovecy, "Historia Peredur ab Efrawg," *The Arthur of the Welsh*, eds. Rachel Bromwich, Brynley Roberts, and Alfred O. H. Jarman (Cardiff, 1991), 171.

7. *The Mabinogi*, eds. Proinsias Mac Cana, Meic Stephens, and R. Brinley Jones (Cardiff, 1992), 122.

8. For a complete comparison of the two versions, see Goetinck; Goetinck, *Peredur: A Study of Welsh Tradition in the Grail Legends* (Cardiff, 1975), 59–78.

9. Sections 1b and 2 according to Thurneysen; Thurneysen, *ZCP* 8 (Berlin, 1912), 185–9.

10. *Didot Perceval*, ed. William Roach, (Philadelphia, 1941), 119–125. This gives a survey of the main participants in the debate and leans heavily toward the opinions of Dr. Brugger, who agrees with Robert de Boron's authorship.

11. *Didot Perceval*, ed. and trans. William A. Nitze (Chicago, 1932–7), 152; *Didot Perceval*, ed. William Roach (Philadelphia, 1941), 5; le Gentil, "The Work of Robert de Boron and the *Didot Perceval*," *Arthurian Literature in the Middle Ages*, ed. Roger S. Loomis (Chicago, 1959), 258.

12. Pickens, "Robert de Boron (the Estoire dou Graal, Merlin and the Didot-Perceval)," *The Arthur of the French: The Arthurian Legend in Medieval French and Occitan Literature*, eds. Glyn Burgess and Karen Pratt (Cardiff, 2006), 247–248, 257; le Gentil, "The Work of Robert de Boron and the *Didot Perceval*," *Arthurian Literature in the Middle Ages*, ed. Roger S. Loomis (Chicago, 1959), 251–262.

13. *Parzival*, ed. and trans. Arthur T. Hatto, (Baltimore, 1980), 11; Wynn, "Wolfram von Eschenbach," *Dictionary of Literary Biography vol. 38*, eds. James Hardy and Will Hasty, (London, 1994), 185. Springer believed the writing may have continued into 1212; Springer, "Wolfram's *Parzival*," *Arthurian Literature in the Middle Ages*, ed. Roger S. Loomis (Chicago, 1959), 220.

14. Wynn, "Wolfram von Eschenbach," *Dictionary of Literary Biography vol. 38*, eds. James Hardy and Will Hasty (London, 1994), 187.

15. Many of the differences between himself and Chrétien are similar to the differences between his *Willehelm* and its French source; Springer, and Chrétien's instant popularity is well-documented; "Wolfram's *Parzival*," *Arthurian Literature in the Middle Ages*, ed. Roger S. Loomis (Chicago, 1959), 224; Nellmann, "Wolfram und Kyot als 'vindaere wilder maere,' *ZDA* 117 (Wiesbaden,1988), 31–67.

16. See Chapter 5.

17. Loomis, *Arthurian Tradition and Chrétien*, (New York, 1949), 451, 454; Springer, "Wolfram's *Parzival*," *Arthurian Literature in the Middle Ages*, ed. Roger S. Loomis (Chicago, 1959), 239–40.

18. It has been theorized that Gahmuret's life may be based on Richard the Lionheart's life or Book 4 of his own book.

19. *Parzival*. trans. Arthur Thomas Hatto. (Baltimore, 1980), Book 1.44

20. Chadwick, "Pictish and Celtic Marriage in Early Literary Tradition," *Scottish Gaelic Studies* 8 (Edinburgh, 1958b), 109.

21. There were specific criteria to meet for this to occur, but Wolfram would have been in no position to understand them, and so he applied his knowledge of his own culture to a scene in which the details were not fully explained.

22. Bricriu's Feast," trans. George Henderson, *The Celtic Heroic Age*, eds. John T. Koch and John Carey (Maldon, 1995), 89.

23. Nitze, "Perlesvaus," *Arthurian Literature in the Middle Ages*, ed. Roger S. Loomis (Chicago, 1959), 268. The date of publication has been the source of a great deal of debate, with scholars suggesting dates as late as 1250. For a survey of the relevant arguments see Kelly, *Le Haut du Graal: Perlesvaus, A Structural Study*, trans. Thomas Kelly (Geneva, 1974), 9–15.

24. As has been seen, Guinièvre does not appear in the earliest Welsh literature. However, there does seem to have been both a tradition that Arthur's son died before his father, and that Arthur and Cei had a falling out. Neither of these made there way into the later Arthurian legend, but are present here along with her death.

25. *Le Haut Livre du Graal: Perlesvaus*, ed. William Nitze (Totowa, 1937), ll. 6702–6705 and 13,414–13,428; *Perlesvaus Prose English, The High Book of the Grail. A Translation of the Thirteenth Century Romance of Perlesvaus*, trans. Nigel Bryant (Ipswich, 1978), 195 and 387, respectively.

26. *Le Haut Livre du Graal: Perlesvaus*, ed. William Nitze, ll 2064–2066; (Totowa, 1937), *Perlesvaus Prose English, The High Book of the Grail. A Translation of the Thirteenth Century Romance of Perlesvaus*, trans. Nigel Bryant (Ipswich, 1978), 70.

27. *Le Haut Livre du Graal: Perlesvaus*, ed. William Nitze (Totowa, 1937), ll. 5389–5394; *Perlesvaus Prose English, The High Book of the Grail. A Translation of the Thirteenth Century Romance of Perlesvaus*, trans. Nigel Bryant (Ipswich, 1978), 151.

28. Spaarnay, "Hartmann von Aue and his Successors," *Arthurian Literature in the Middle Ages*, ed. Roger S. Loomis (Chicago, 1959), 443. Recently confirmed and expounded upon by Wallbank ("Three Post-Classical Authors: Heinrich von dem Türlin, der Stricker, der Pleier," *The Arthur of the Germans*, eds. W. H. Jackson

and Sylvia A. Ranawake (Cardiff, 2000), 81–89.
29. Türlin, *The Crown (Diu Crône)*, trans. John Wesley Thomas (Lincoln, 1989), ll. 2220–1.
30. Ibid., ll. 1521–45.
31. Ibid., ll. 5767–5807.
32. For opposing commentaries on the continuations see Thompson; Thompson, "The Traditions of Chrétien's *Perceval*," *Arthurian Literature in the Middle Ages*, ed. Roger S. Loomis (Chicago, 1959), 206–217. For *Vulgate* see Frappier; Frappier, "Chrétien de Troyes," *Arthurian Literature in the Middle Ages*, ed. Roger S. Loomis (Chicago, 1959), 295–318; Grimsby, "The Continuations of Chrétien de Troyes," *The New Arthurian Encyclopedia*, ed. Norris J. Lacy (London, 1991), 99–101; Burns, "Vulgate Cycle," *The New Arthurian Encyclopedia*, ed. Norris J. Lacy (London, 1991), 496–9.
33. The interruption is not traditional, either. The entire story is based on a misunderstanding of Caradoc's epithet *vreichvras*—strong arm.
34. Frappier, "Chrétien de Troyes," *Arthurian Literature in the Middle Ages*, ed. Roger S. Loomis (Chicago, 1959), 300.
35. Haycock, "'Preiddeu Annwn' and the figure of Taliesin," *SC* 14/15 (Cardiff, 1984), 62, 69 fn. 14.
36. Pomponius Mela, *Choreographia*, 3.6.48.
37. To the author's knowledge, Professor Koch has been the only scholar to discuss and translate the newly discovered Gaulish writings, so that the following comments are based on his translation and impressions.
38. "Two Gaulish Religious Inscriptions," trans. John T. Koch, *The Celtic Heroic Age*, eds. John T. Koch and John Carey (Maldon, 1994), 1.
39. Haycock, "'Preiddeu Annwn' and the figure of Taliesin," *SC* 14/15 (Cardiff, 1984), 57; Sims-Williams, "The Early Welsh Arthurian Poems," *The Arthur of the Welsh*, eds. Rachel Bromwich, Brynley Roberts, and Alfred O. H. Jarman (Cardiff, 1991), 54.
40. Haycock, "'Preiddeu Annwn' and the Figure of Taliesin," trans. Marged Haycock, *SC* 14/15 (Cardiff, 1984), 75 l. 17.
41. *The Life of Samson of Dol*, trans. Thomas Taylor (Llanerch, rep. 1991), xxxix; Davies, "Property Rights and Property Claims in Welsh 'Vitae' of the Eleventh Century," *Hagiographie, cultures, et sociétés ive-xiie siécles*, ed. P. Riché (Paris, 1981), 515; Diune, "La vie de S. Samson, à propos d'un ouvrage récent," *Annales de Bretagne* 28 (Paris, 1912–13), 332–56.
42. Sims-Williams, *Religion and Literature in Western England, 600–800* (Cambridge, 1990), 80; Poulin, "Hagiographie et Politique. La première de S. Samson de Dol," *Francia* 5 (Paris, 1977), 1–26.
43. For historical reasons Sir Ifor Williams believed 1055–1062. Professor Thurneysen estimated the eleventh century, Mr. Lewis said 1170–90, and Charles-Edwards guessed 1050–1120; Williams, *Pedeir Keinc y Mabinogi* (Cardiff, 1930), xl-xli; Thurneysen, *Dei Irisch Helden-und Königsage bis zum siebzuhnten Jahrhundert* (Halle, 1921), 24–7, 626–7, 668; Lewis, "Branwen" *LlC* 10 (Cardiff, 1968), 230–3; Lewis, "Branwen," *Y Traethodydd* (Cardiff, 1969a), 137–42; Lewis, "Branwen," *Y Traethodydd* (Cardiff, 1969b), 185–92; Lewis, "Branwen," *Ysgrifau Beirniadol* 5 (Cardiff, 1970), 30–43; Charles-Edwards, "The Date of the Four Branches of the *Mabinogi*," *THSC* (London, 1971), 263 fl..
44. TYP, 242.

Chapter 13

1. Lewis, *Temples in Roman Britain* (Cambridge, 1966), 143.
2. Ross, *Pagan Celtic Britain* (London, 1967), maps 5 and 7.
3. Lewis, *Temples in Roman Britain* (Cambridge, 1966), 144; Watts, *Christians and Pagans in Roman Britain* (New York, 1991), 209.
4. St. Albion and other martyrs are traditionally said to have been persecuted as early as the first century, but their floruits are now usually given as mid-third century; Thomas, *Christianity in Roman Britain up to about A.D. 500* (London, 1981), 42–50.
5. *Vita Cadoci* has the saint raise Caw from the dead and convert him, while Uinniau and Columba each converted their local kings. Samson's activities have already been noted, while David, Brioc, Kentigern, and Patrick all had to contend with local pagans.
6. Murray, *The God of the Witches* (London, 1931), 31.
7. They are February 2, May 1, August 1, and November 1.
8. Stancliffe, *St. Martin and his Hagiographer: History and Miracle in Sulpicius Severus* (Oxford, 1983), 71.
9. Stancliffe, Clare. *St. Martin and his Hagiographer: History and Miracle in Sulpicius Severus: History and Miracle in Sulpicius Severus* (Oxford, 1983); *Vitae Martini*, 13.9, 14.1, 14.3–7, 15.1, and 15.4.
10. *Pro Templis*, trans. Warmington (1969), 18. 15–20, 24, 50–51.
11. Augustine, trans. Brian Battershaw and G. R. Lamb (1961), 39–40.
12. Paulinus of Milan, *Vita Sancti Ambrosii, mediolensis episcopi, a paulino eius notario ad beatum Augustinum conscripta*, trans. Mary Simplicia Kaniecka (Washington D.C., 1928), 18.4; Gregory of Tours, trans. Thorpe (New York, 1971), 10.31.

13. The above is only a smattering of instances, for a more complete argument see Matthews, *Western Aristocracies and Imperial Court AD 364–425* (Oxford, 1975), 154–60.
14. *The Mabinogi*, eds. Proinsias Mac Cana, Meic Stephens, and R. Brinley Jones (Cardiff, 1992), 109.
15. Brun is also a devolved form of Brân, who seems intrinsically connected to the grail.

Chapter 14

1. *Le Conte*, ll. 2034–51, 5758–98, and 7855. Other romances assign Perceval, Gauvain, and Lancelot a number of other partners.
2. *Le Conte*, ll. 7776–828; trans. Douglas D. R. Owen (London, 1989), 477.
3. Nutt, *Studies on the Legend of the Holy Grail*, (London, 1888), 191.
4. *Le Conte*, ll. 3049–52; trans. Douglas D. R. Owen (London, 1989), 415.
5. *Le Conte*, ll. 3060–4; trans. Douglas D. R. Owen (London, 1989), 415.
6. *Le Conte*, ll. 3302–9; trans. Douglas D. R. Owen (London, 1989), 418.
7. Radford, "Report on the excavations at Castle Dore," *The Journal of the Royal Institute of Cornwall* (Truro, 1951); Colvin, "The King's Works Before the Norman Conquest," *The History of the King's Works, the Middle Ages*, eds. R.A. Brown and Howard M. Colvin (London, 1963), 2–4.
8. *Le Conte*, ll. 868–77; trans. Douglas D. R. Owen (London, 1989), 386.
9. See the third appendix, "The Sovereignty Ritual."
10. It should be noted that there are several similar myths involving Irish kings, *Ecstasy of the Phantom* is simply the least corrupted.
11. This was O'Rahilly's guess; "On the Origin of the Names Érain and Ériu," *Ériu* 35, (Dublin, 1946b), 17.
12. *Le Conte*, ll. 1059; trans. Douglas D. R. Owen, (London, 1989), 388.
13. Ultimately, some form of bonding with the land is an Indo-European trait, and may well be universal among kingships. However, the form it takes in the grail romances is distinctly Celtic.
14. Chadwick, *The Heroic Age* (Cambridge, 1912), 351.
15. A blood feud would force a warrior to leave his lord, and losing one's king while remaining alive was the worst kind of disgrace. A warrior's only hope was to migrate to a region that had no knowledge of it.
16. Köhler saw this aspect of the Arthurian world as an attempt to reaffirm the crumbling medieval institutions of feudalism and court life. Chrétien nowhere shows such a concern for such things, nor did Marie have any interest in maintaining the male-dominated world in which she lived; Köhler, *Ideal und Wirklichkeit in der Höfischen Epik: Studien zur form der Frühen Artus-und Graldichtung* (Tübingen, 1956).
17. Chadwick, *The Heroic Age* (Cambridge, 1912), 349.
18. *The Mabinogi*, eds. Proinsias Mac Cana, Meic Stephens, and R. Brinley Roberts (Cardiff, 1992), 122.
19. Ibid., 120.

Chapter 15

1. *Le Conte*, ll. 8691–8714; trans. Douglas D. R. Owen (London, 1989), 489. *The Turk and Gowin* and *Sir Gawen and the Grene Knight* make the same associations.
2. Ritchie, *The Normans in Scotland* (Edinburgh, 1954), 153.
3. There is an unofficial and much later document that records the witnesses called; Ritchie, *The Normans in Scotland* (Edinburgh, 1954), 152.
4. This is because of the very early names to be found in the episodes of the two Kentigern *vitae*, which deal with the ancient British kingdom of Gododdin. See Chapter 1.

Chapter 16

1. As a curiosity, Cei would not have made a good Christian hero because of his established personality, Samson because he could not be claimed as a knight, Gwalchmai because even before Chrétien he was famed for his lady-chasing, and Arthur because Geoffrey of Monmouth had already made him the center of an entire genre. Only Perceval suited his needs.
2. Dumville, "Early Welsh Poetry: Problems of Historicity," ed. Brynley F. Roberts, *Early Welsh Poetry: Studies in the Book of Aneirin* (Aberystwyth, 1988), 1.

Chapter 17

1. The landmark work of Rachel Bromwich in *Trioedd Ynys Prydein*, updated in 1978 and more recently, is a wealth of information on how Celtic items have found their way onto the continent. She touched on the phenomenon in more broad strokes in *Arthur of the Welsh*. Bromwich, "First Transmission from England to France," *The Arthur of the Welsh*, eds. Rachel Bromwich, Brynley, Roberts, Alfred O. H. Jarman (Cardiff, 1991), 273–298.
2. Bromwich's Tristan articles, beginning in 1953 and to be found in the bibliography, are

still standard reference material for the subject. As will be seen, Loth brought attention to the connection of the Tristan story to Cornwall, while Zimmer did a great deal of work in understanding the Pictish origins of the story, and Schoepperle showed it to be a variation of Diarmid and Grainne.

3. There is a great deal of contradiction here, suggesting a misunderstanding with the source as to why Tristan goes back to Ireland, or a flawed attempt to render the dragon/Morholt doublet seamless. In the Thomas version Tristan returns from Ireland speaking of Isolt's beauty before the subject of the king having children is brought up. He coincidentally finds some beautiful hair and announces that he will only marry its owner. Oddly, Tristan immediately knows to go to Ireland. Other versions have Mark specifically saying he will only marry Isolt, knowing that she is the daughter of his former lord. This suggests a certain order of development that will be pursued over the next few chapters.

4. Béroul, *The Romance of Tristan*, ed. and trans. Alan S. Fedrick (New York, 1970), 9–32.

5. Bromiley and Hunt, "The Tristan Legend in Old French Verse," *The Arthur of the French*, ed. Glyn S. Burgess and Karen Pratt (Cardiff, 2000), 118.

6. Padel, "The Cornish Background of the Tristan Stories," *CMCS* 1 (Cardiff, 1981), 56. *Tristrams saga*, long thought to be an accurate translation of Thomas of Britain's fragmentary *Tristan*, has been shown conclusively to have strayed from the original; Tómasson, "Hvænger var Tristrams s_gu snúi_?," Gripla 2 (Reykjavik, 1977), 47–8. There are now doubts about Gottfried as well; Haug, "Reinterpreting the Tristan Romances of Thomas and Gotfrid; Implications of a Recent Discovery," *Arthuriana* 7 (West Lafayette, 1997), 47–52.

7. Whitehead, "The Tristan Poems," *Arthurian Literature in the Middle Ages*, ed. Roger S. Loomis (Chicago, 1959), 138–40, 146; Jackson, "Gottfried von Strassburg," *Arthurian Literature in the Middle Ages*, ed. Roger S. Loomis (Chicago, 1959), 150. *The Prose Tristan* seems to have simply added Arthurian themes and made its characters more interconnected to the rest of the Arthurian world in general. The key essentials of the story have, however, remained intact.

Chapter 18

1. As forerunners of the modern novel, the romances developing around Arthur appear to have focused much more on the motives and actions of secondary characters than anything in Irish myth and legend. The likely development is that the lesser antagonists were created by the writers on the continent as they reinterpreted the basic Tristan story. That would explain their inconsistent names and activities.

2. On Triad 27 see below.

3. Zimmer, "Keltische Beitrage. III. Weitere nordgermanische Einflüsse in der Altesten Üeberlieferung der irischen Heldensage," *ZDA* 35 (Berlin, 1891), 1–176; Bruce, *The Evolution of Arthurian Romance, from the Beginnings Down to the Year 1300*, vol. 1 (Gottingen, 1923), 178; Vendryes, "La Lettre Tambée duciel dans les litteratures celtique compte-rendus des séances de trusting l'Académie des Inscriptions et Belles et Belles-Lettres," *ÉC* 5 (Paris, 1949), 346; "The Cornish Background of the Tristan Stories," *CMCS* 1 (Cambridge, 1982), 55.

4. Drustanus does appear on a memorial stone near Dore Castle. However, the patronymic of Cunomorus does not resemble Tallwch, and it is the sole instance of a Drystan South of Scotland outside of the romances and a direct association with Arthur. Padel's argument that Drust is probably Welsh would support more weight if there were a single association with a Welsh locale in the earliest references, or even if he appeared, somewhere, on the dozens of genealogies listing thousands of different royal family members; "The Cornish Background of the Tristan Stories," *CMCS* 1 (Cardiff, 1981), 454–56.

5. Bromwich, "Some Remarks on the Celtic Sources of 'Tristan'" *THSC* (London, 1953), 46–49.

6. Ibid., 49; Béroul, *The Romance of Tristan*, by Béroul, ed. Alfred Ewert (Oxford, 1939), ll. 3757–8; *Die Lais der Marie de France*, ed. Karl Warnke (Berlin, 1925), ll. 15–16.

7. Line 16.

8. Béroul, *The Romance of Tristan, by Béroul*, ed. Alfred Ewert (Oxford, 1939), ll. 1155, 2359, 2394, 2438, 2453, and 2979, 2994, respectively.

9. Loth, *Contributions à l'étude de Romans de la Table Ronde* (Paris, 1912), 270–1; Padel, "The Cornish Background of the Tristan Stories," *CMCS* 1 (Cardiff, 1981), 71–72.

10. Padel, "The Cornish Background of the Tristan Stories," *CMCS* 1 (Cambridge, 1981), 59–63; Bromwich, "Some Remarks on the Celtic Sources of 'Tristan,'" *THSC* (London, 1953), 59–60; Newstead, "The Origin and Growth of the Tristan Legend," *Arthurian Literature in the Middle Ages*, ed. Roger S. Loomis (Chicago, 1959), 125; Brugger, "Loenois as Tristan's Home," *MP* 22 vol. 2 (Chicago, 1924), 159–185.

11. Padel, "The Cornish Background of the Tristan Stories," *CMCS* 1 (Cambridge, 1981), 60–2.

12. See below.

13. *Culhwch ac Olwen: An Edition and Study of the Earliest Arthurian Tale*, eds. Rachel

Bromwich and D. Simon Evans (Cardiff, 1992), 110.

14. *Annales Cambriae* only claims that the next ruler, Hywel, was his brother; there is no mention of his paternity. The Irish give him no legitimacy.

15. This is not to imply that the romance was begun after the ninth century, only that Essyllt was added to it at that time. The story might have been created at some point after 900, or Tristan may have been connected with another, now superseded, figure.

16. Chadwick, "Early Culture and Learning in North Wales," *Studies in the Early British Church*, ed. Nora K. Chadwick (Cambridge, 1958), 29–120.

17. *Vatican Recension of the Historia Brittonum*, ed. David N. Dumville (Cambridge, 1985), 4–8.

18. Padel, "The Cornish Background of the Tristan Stories," *CMCS* 1 (Cambridge, 1981), 66.

19. Schoepperle saw no connection between the beasts and Morholt. In a personal communication to her, Kuno Meyer relayed that the stress in *Fomori* was on the first syllable, whereas the French *Morholt* stressed the second. He believed that on linguistic grounds the two names could not be related either; Kuno Meyer as cited by Schoepperle, *Tristan and Isolt* (New York, rev. 1960), 331.

20. Bromwich, "The Tristan of the Welsh," *The Arthur of the Welsh*, eds. Rachel Bromwich, Brynley Roberts, and Alfred O. H. Jarman (Cardiff, 1991), 221–2; Bromwich, "Some Remarks on the Celtic Sources of 'Tristan,'" *THSC* (London, 1953), 38–41; Loth, *Contributions à l'étude des romans de la Table ronde* (Paris, 1912), 29.

21. Zimmer, "Keltische Beitrage. I. Germanen, germanische Lehnwdrter und germanische Sagenelemente in der altesten Überlieferung der irischen Heldensage," *ZDA* 32 (Berlin, 1888), 196–334; Meyer, "The Oldest Version of the Tochmarc Emire," *RC* 11 (Paris, 1890), 433–8; Newstead, "The Origin and Growth of the Tristan Legend," *Arthurian Literature in the Middle Ages*, ed. Roger S. Loomis (New York, 1959), 122–134; Bromwich was consistent in that regard throughout her career.

22. Bromwich, "Some Remarks on the Celtic Sources of 'Tristan,'" *THSC* (London, 1953), 55; Bromwich, "First transmission from England to France," *The Arthur of the Welsh*, eds. Rachel Bromwich, Brynley Roberts, and Alfred O. H. Jarman (Cardiff, 1991b), 280.

23. He has been associated with the forest episode in the extant romances, but again serves no real function there.

24. Loth, *Contributions à l'étude de Romans de la Table Ronde* (Paris, 1912), 90–2.

25. Padel, "The Cornish Background of the Tristan Stories," *CMCS* 1 (Cambridge, 1982), 55; Bromwich, "The Tristan of the Welsh," *The Arthur of the Welsh*, eds. Rachel Bromwich, Brynley Roberts, and Alfred O. H. Jarman (Cardiff, 1991), 210.

26. de la Borderie, *Revue de Bretagne et de Vendée*, 18 (Nantes, 1865), 436; le Baud, *Histoire de Bretagne* (Paris, 1638), 7–9.

27. There is no record of Tristan's mother's name in Welsh, nor is this unexpected. Histories of the period and in the culture of the fifth and sixth century rarely recorded women's names, except when they were involved in more "masculine" activities.

28. Loomis, "The Origin of Rivallon in the Tristan Legend," *MLN* 39 (Chicago, 1924), 326.

29. Bromwich, "Some Remarks on the Celtic Sources of Tristan," *THSC* (London, 1953), 57; Bromwich, "The Tristan of the Welsh," *The Arthur of the Welsh*, eds. Rachel Bromwich, Brynley Roberts, and Alfred O. H. Jarman (Cardiff, 1991a), 210. Under the influence of Lozac'hmeur's contribution to *Histoire Littéraire culturelle de la Bretagne*, ed. Jean Balcou and Yves le Gallo (Paris, 1987), 149.

30. de Corson, *Grandes Seigneuries de Haute-Bretagne*, vol. 2 (Rennes, 1898), 392.

Chapter 19

1. Bromiley and Hunt, "The Tristan Legend in Old French Verse," *The Arthur of the Germans*, ed. Glyn S. Burgess and Karen Pratt (Cardiff, 2000), 118.

2. Gottfried von Strassburg, *Tristan*, ed. and trans. Arthur T. Hatto (New York, 1960), 356–358.

3. Schoepperle, *Tristan and Isolt* (New York, rev. 1960), 180.

4. Whitehead, "The Tristan Poems," *Arthurian Literature in the Middle Ages*, ed. Roger S. Loomis (New York, 1959), 134–5.

5. *Le Roman de Tristan par Thomas*, ed. and trans. Joseph Bedier, vol. 2 (Paris, 1905), 11–34.

6. Gottfried von Strassburg: *Tristan*, ed. and trans. Hatto (New York, 1960), 356–7; *Les Fragments du roman de Tristan, poème du XIIe siècle*, ed. Bartina H. Wind (Paris, 1960), 16.

7. *Les Fragments du roman de Tristan, poème du XIIe siècle*, ed. Bartina H. Wind (Paris, 1960), 16; Loomis ("Tristram and the House of Anjou," *MLR* 17 (Cambridge, 1922), 24–30 gives a full argument to that end.

Chapter 20

1. Bromwich, "The 'Tristan' Poem in the Black Book of Carmarthen," *SC* 19/20, (1979/1980), 54.

2. Loth, *Contributions à l'étude des romans de la Table ronde* (Paris, 1912), 403–413.
3. Bromwich, "The Tristan of the Welsh," *The Arthur of the Welsh* (Cardiff, 1991a), 209–228.
4. Padel, "The Cornish Background of the Tristan Stories," *CMCS* 1 (Cambridge, 1982), 58; Jones, "The Black Book of Carmarthen 'Stanzas of the Graves,'" PBA 53 (London, 1967), 100. The significance of this specification revolves around Geoffrey of Monmouth, who published his highly influential book in 1136. A dating in the early twelfth century allows for the possibility that it was shaped by him, whereas before 1100 does not.
5. Bromwich's hypothesis seems a strong one, however. In the second poem, she suggests that the speaker might be Brangien referring to having lost her virginity for Isolt's sake. It is unfortunate that more has not been discovered in the words of these two fragments.
6. Because Drystan and March are mentioned by name as well as a Cyheig. As Kehenis/Kaherdin figures prominently and consistently in the Tristan stories, Loth suggested the two might be somehow connected. On linguistic grounds, Bromwich found the theory untenable, while the present scholar would suggest that Cyheig might be one indicator of a very different original story; Loth, *Contributions à l'étude des Romans de la Table Ronde* (Paris, 1912); Bromwich, "Some Remarks on the Celtic Sources of 'Tristan,'" *THSC* (London, 1953), 58.
7. Bromwich, "The Tristan of the Welsh," *The Arthur of the Welsh,* eds. Rachel Bromwich, Brynley Roberts, and Alfred O. H. Jarman (Cardiff, 1991a), 214–215.
8. TYP 51–52; *Culhwch ac Olwen*, ed. Rachel Bromwich and D. Simon Evans (Cardiff, 1992), lxvii. Bromwich alternately offered the suggestion that the "Henwen" triad might have been indicative of a much older story equitable with the hunting of the Twrch Trwyth, but the farcical interpretation makes more sense. As she put it in 1961, the other two pig keepers make no sense in their role, and the third item in such a triad is usually the reason for the triad.
9. MS B.N. frond 2171.
10. Whitehead suggested that the *mal dagres* in line 3849 was supposed to read *mal d'Acre*, and an epidemic occurred in that year in Acre. It was a prominent occurrence at the time. More recent scholarship has tended to lean against the connection. Whitehead, "The Tristan Poems," *Arthurian Literature in the Middle Ages*, ed. Roger S. Loomis (Chicago, 1959), 134–5; Hunt in Bromiley and Hunt, "The Tristan Legend in Old French Verse," *The Arthur of the French*, ed. Glyn S. Burgess and Karen Pratt (Cardiff, 2000), 113.
11. Le Gentil, "La légende de Tristan vue par Béroul et Thomas: Essai d'interprétation," *RP* 7 (Turnhout, 1953), 111–118.
12. Bumke, *Mäzene im Mittelalter. Die Gönner und Auftrageber der höfischen Literatur in Deutschland 1150–1300* (Munich, 1979), 108.
13. Whitehead, "The Tristan Poems," *Arthurian Literature in the Middle Ages*, ed. Roger S. Loomis (Chicago, 1959), 135.
14. Buschinger, "Conjectures sur Eilhart von Oberg," *Figures de l'écrivain au moyen âge. Actes du Colloque du Centre d'Etudes Mediévales de l'Université de Picardie Amiens 18–20 mars 1988*, ed. Danielle Buschinger (Göppingen, 1991), 63–72; Wolff and Schröder, "Eilhart von Oberg," vol. 2 (New York, 1980), 410–418; *Tristant I: Die alten Bruehstücke*, ed. Kurt Wagner (Bonn, 1924), 21.
15. van Dam, *Zü Vorgeschichte des höfischen Epos: Lamprecht, Eilhart, Valdeke* (Bonn, 1923), 121–8.
16. Respectively, Mertens and Hucker; Mertens, "Eilhart, der Herzog und der Truchseß. Der *Tristant* am Welfenhof," *Tristant et Iseut, mythr européen*, ed. Danielle Buschinger (Göppingen, 1987), 262–281; Hucker, "Literatur im Umkreis Kaiser Ottos IV," *Die Welfen und ihr Braunschweiger Hof im hohen Mittelalter*, ed. B. Schneidermüller (Weisbaden, 1995), 382–395.
17. Tervooren Beckers, Helmut Beckers, and Hartmut Beckers (eds.), *Literatur und Sprache im rheinisch-maasländischen Raum Zwischen 1150 und 1450* (Berlin, 1989); B. Schneidmüller (ed.) *Die Welfen und ihr Braunschweiger Hof im hohen Mittelalter* (Weisbaden, 1995).
18. Schoepperle, *Tristan and Isolt* (New York, rev. 1960), 8.
19. Eilhart von Oberge, *Eilhart von Oberge's Tristant*, ed. and trans. J. W. Thomas (Lincoln, 1978), 93.
20. Eilhart von Oberge, *Eilhart von Oberge's Tristant*, ed. and trans. J. W. Thomas (Lincoln, 1978), 110.
21. Gottfried von Strassburg, *Tristan*, ed. and trans. Arthur T. Hatto (New York, 1960), 367–8.
22. Chinca, "Tristan Narratives from the High to the Late Middle Ages," *The Tristan of the Germans*, eds. W. H. Jackson and Sylvia A. Ranawake (Cardiff, 2000), 120.
23. Hoffa, "Antike elemente bei Gottfried von Strassburg," *ZDA* 52 (Berlin, 1910), 339–350.
24. Gottfried von Strassburg, *Tristan*, ed. and trans. Arthur T. Hatto (New York, 1960), 10; Stökle, *Die theologischen Ausdrücke und Wendungen im Tristan Gottfrieds von Strassburg* (Tübingen, 1915).
25. Stevens, "The renewal of the classic: aspects of rhetorical and dialectical composition in Gottfried's *Tristan*," *Gottfried von Strassburg and the Medieval Tristan Legend: Papers from an*

Anglo-North American Colloquium (Cambridge, 1990), 67–89; Glendinning, "Gottfried von Straßburg and the school tradition," *DVJ* 61 (Stuttgart, 1987), 617–638; Christ, *Rhetorik und Roman. Untersuchungen zu Gottfrieds von Straßburg "Tristan* (Meisenheim, 1977).

26. *The Romance of Tristan*, ed. and trans. Renée L. Curtis (New York, 1994), xvii.

27. Baumgartner, "Luce del Gat et Hélie de Boron: le chevalier et l'écriture," *R* 106 (Paris, 1985), 326–40.

28. Ibid., xvii.

29. *The Romance of Tristan*, ed. and trans. Renée L. Curtis (New York, 1994), xvi.

30. Vinaver, "The Prose Tristan," *Arthurian Literature in the Middle Ages*, ed. Roger S. Loomis (Chicago, 1959), 339. It is a position that has been generally taken now; Pratt, "Lancelot with and without the Grail: Lancelot do Lac and the Vulgate Cycle," *The Arthur of the Germans*, ed. Glyn S. Burgess and Karen Pratt (Cardiff, 2000), 318.

31. Vinaver, *Études sur le Tristan en prose: les sources, les manuscrits, bibliographie critique* (Paris, 1925), 5–20; Baumgartner, *Le Tristan en prose: essai d'intrepetation d'un roman medieval* (Geneva, 1975), 101–117.

32. As Hatto has commented, Thomas places him a generation after Arthur.

Chapter 21

1. Schoepperle, *Tristan and Isolt* (London, rev. 1960), 283–6.

2. Ibid., 402–409.

3. It is intriguing that, twenty years later and in a different type of love court, a woman's insistence would be perfectly acceptable for Lancelot to receive just such offers.

4. Bromwich, "Some Remarks on the Celtic Sources of Tristan," *THSC* (London, 1953), 50.

5. Ibid., 50; Schoepperle, *Tristan and Isolt* (New York, rev. 1960), 320–5.

6. Schoepperle, *Tristan and Isolt* (New York, rev. 1960), 391–446 contains a fairly complete list.

Chapter 22

1. *Gottfried von Strassburg*, ed. and trans. Michael S. Batts (New York, 1971), 70; Gottfried von Strassburg: Tristan, ed. and trans Arthur T. Hatto (New York, 1960), 20, 361–2; Bédier, *Le Roman de Tristan*, vol. 2 (Paris, 1905), 77–80.

2. Bouchard, "The Possible Nonexistence of Thomas, Author of 'Tristan and Isolde'" (Chicago, 1981), 66–72.

3. Brugger, "Loenois as Tristan's Home," *MP* 22 vol. 2 (Chicago, 1924), 186–191.

4. Johnston, *Place-Names of Scotland* (London, 1934), 243.

5. "The Cornish Background of the Tristan Stories," *CMCS* 1 (Cambridge, 1981), 238.

6. As a maternal nephew of Arthur, Gawain has often been cast in that role. However, Gawain's relationship with Arthur is a development of Geoffrey pushed along by his prominence in the Welsh tales, his influence is a natural progression from that point, and he is never designated as Arthur's heir even then. Instead, his own son Modred is put in that position and that is what leads to the literary end of his kingdom.

Conclusion

1. Chadwick, "Early Culture and Learning in North Wales," *Studies in the Early British Church*, ed. Nora K. Chadwick (Cambridge, 1958), 29–120.

2. *Vatican Recension of the Historia Brittonum*, ed. David N. Dumville (Cambridge, 1985), 4–8.

3. TYP 51–52; *Culhwch ac Olwen*, eds. Rachel Bromwich and D. Simon Evans (Cardiff, 1992), lxvii. Bromwich alternately offered the suggestion that the "Henwen" triad might have been indicative of a much older story equitable with the hunting of the Twrch Trwyth, but the farcical interpretation makes more sense. As she put it in 1961, the other two pig keepers make no sense in their role, and the third item in such a triad is usually the reason for the triad.

4. Bromwich, "Some Remarks on the Celtic Sources of Tristan," *THSC* (London, 1953), 48–50. In Marie de France's *Chevrefoil* as well (l. 16). Likely also, Dinas de Lidan was meant to be Dinas Lidan in southern Wales.

5. *Geirfa Barddoniaeth Gynnar Gymraeg*, ed. Lloyd George (Cardiff, 1931–1965), 491; TYP 349–350.

Appendices

1. Greene, "The Chariot as described in Irish Literature," *The Iron Age in the Irish Sea Province*, ed. Charles Thomas (London, 1972), 69.

2. Ibid., 65.

3. Laing, "Archaeological Notes on Some Scottish Early Christian Stones," *PSAS* 114 (Darking, 1985), 278.

4. Paris, *Journal des savants* (Paris, 1902), 354–5.

5. Frappier, "Chrétien de Troyes," *Arthurian Literature in the Middle Ages*, ed. Roger S. Loomis (Chicago, 1959), 157.

6. Whitehead, "The Tristan Poems,"

Arthurian Literature in the Middle Ages, ed. Roger S. Loomis (Chicago, 1959), 134–5.

7. Although it has often been suggested that he died before completing *Le Conte* because of the note of a later author, it is also very possible that he simply stopped writing when his patron died.

8. It is very possible that in a previous version of the story Drust killed the *Fomori* and simply married the princess himself as well.

Bibliography

Primary Sources

The Anglo-Saxon Chronicle. Translated by George Norman Garmonsway. London, 1986.

"The Anglo-Saxon Chronicle MS A." Edited by Jane Bately. In *The Anglo-Saxon Chronicle: A Collective Edition*. Edited by David N. Dumville and Simon Keynes. Cambridge, 1986.

Adamnan. *The Life of Columba, Founder of Hy*. Edited and translated by Williams Reeves. Llanerch, 1988.

Andrew of Wyntoun. *The Original Chronicle of Andrew of Wyntoun*. Edited by and François J. Amours, John Thomas Tosbach, and George Neilson. 4 vols. Edinburgh, 1906.

Aneirin. *The Gododdin: The Oldest Scottish Poem*. Edited by Kenneth H. Jackson. Edinburgh, 1969.

———. *Aneirin: Y Gododdin, Britain's Oldest Poem*. Edited by Alfred O. H. Jarman. Llandysul, 1990.

———. *The Gododdin of Aneirin*. Edited and translated by John T. Koch. Cardiff, 1995.

L'atre périlleux. Edited by Brian Woledge. Paris, 1936.

Aue, Hartmann von. *Iwein*. Translated by Patrick M. McConeghy. New York, 1984.

Bede. *A History of the English Church and People*. Translated by Leo Sherley-Price. Revised by Ronald Edward Latham. London, 1978.

Beowulf. Translated by Kevin Crossley-Holland. Oxford, 1982.

Béroul. *The Romance of Tristan, by Béroul*. Alfred Ewert.[AS1] Oxford, 1939.

———. *The Romance of Tristan*. Translated by Alan S. Fedrick. New York, 1978.

"The Boyhood Deeds of Finn." In *The Celtic Heroic Age: Literary Sources for Ancient Celtic Europe and Early Ireland and Wales*, 183–90. Edited by John T. Koch and John Carey. Translated by John Carey. Malden, 1994.

Caesar, Julius Gaius. *The Gallic Wars*. Translated by Stanley Alexander Handford. Baltimore, 1951.

Capellanus, Andreas. *The Art of Courtly Love*. Translated by John Jay Parry. New York, 1959.

———. *De Amore: Libri Tres*. Edited by Emil Trojel. Munich, 1972.

Chrétien de Troyes. *Les chansons courtoises de Chrétien de Troyes*. Edited by Marie Claire Zai. Lang, 1974.

———. *Arthurian Romances*. Translated by Douglas David Roy Owen. London, 1989.

"Co(i)mpert Conchobuir [maic Nessa]: The Conception of Conchobar son of Nes." In *The Celtic Heroic Age: Literary Sources for Ancient Celtic Europe and Early Ireland and Wales*. 48–51. Edited by John T. Koch and John Carey. Translated by John Carey. Malden, 1994.

"Conall Corc and the Corco Luigde."

Translated by Vernam Hull. *PMLA* 62:887–909 Menasha, 1943.
Críth Gablach. Edited by David A. Binchy. Oxford, 1970.
Culhwch ac Olwen: An Edition and Study of the Earliest Arthurian Tale. Edited by Rachel Bromwich and D. Simon Evans. Cardiff, 1992.
"The Death of Diarmait mac Cerbaill." In *The Celtic Heroic Age: Literary Sources for Ancient Celtic Europe and Early Ireland and Wales*, 200–03. Edited by John T. Koch and John Carey. Translated by John Carey. Malden, 1994.
Didot Perceval. Translated by William A. Nitze. Chicago, 1932–7.
The Didot Perceval, according to the Manuscript of Modena and Paris. Translated by William Roach. Philadelphia, 1941.
Dio Cassius. *Dio's Roman History*. 9 vols. Translated by Earnest Cary. London, 1914.
Diodorus Siculus. *The Bibliotheca Historia of Diodorus Siculus*. Edited by Frederick Millet Salter and H. L. K. Skelton Edward. Translated by John Skelton. Oxford, 1968–1971.
Duanaire Finn English and Irish, 3 vols. Vol. 1 edited by Eoin MacNeill. Dublin, 1908.
_____. Vols. 2 and 3 edited by Gerard Murphy. Dublin, 1936–53.
"An Early Ritual Poem in Welsh" ("*Ymddiddan Gwenhwyfar ac Arthur*"). Edited and translated by Mary Williams. S 13: 38–51. Cambridge, 1938.
Early Welsh Genaeological Tracts. Edited by Peter C. Bartrum. Cardiff, 1966.
Eilhart von Oberge. *Tristant I: Die alten Bruehstücke*. Edited and translated by Kurt Wagner. Bonn, 1924.
_____. *Eilhart von Oberge's Tristant*. Edited and translated by John Wesley Thomas. Lincoln, 1978.
Eschenbach, Wolfram von. *Wolfram von Eschenbach: Parzival*. Edited by Gottfried Weber. Darmstadt, 1963.
_____. *Parzival*. Translated by Arthur Thomas Hatto. Baltimore, 1980.
_____. *Parzival*. Translated by Helen M. Mustard and Charles E. Passage. New York, 1961.
Fingal Rónáin, and Other Stories. Edited by David Greene. Dublin, 1955.
"Fled Bricrenn; Bricriu's Feast." *Irish Text Society* vol. 2. Edited and translated by George Henderson. Dublin, 1899, rev. 1994, *The Celtic Heroic Age: Literary Sources for Ancient Celtic Europe and Early Ireland and Wales*. Edited by John T. Koch and John Carey. Malden, 1994, 64–95.
Florence of Worcester. *Chronicle of Florence of Worcester*. Translated by Thomas Forester. London, 1854.
The Four Ancient Books of Wales. Translated by William F. Skene. Edinburgh, 1868.
Freculf, Bishop of Lisieux. *Chronicorum libri Dvo*. Edited by Emil Grunauer. *De Fontibus historiae Freculfi*. [AS2]Winterthur, 1864.
Geoffrey of Monmouth. *The History of the Kings of Britain*. Translated by Lewis G. M. Thorpe. New York, 1966.
_____. *Historia Regum Britanniae of Geoffrey of Monmouth*. Edited by Acton Griscom and Robert Ellis Jones. London, 1929.
Geoffrey of Vinsauf. *Documentum de modo et arte dictandi et versificandi*. Translated by Robert P. Parr. Milwaukee, 1968.
Gildas. *The Ruin of Britain*. Translated by Michael Winterbottom. London, 1978.
Gottfried von Strassburg. *Tristan*. Translated by Arthur Thomas Hatto. New York, 1960.
Gottfried von Strassburg. Edited by and Translated by Michael S. Batts. New York, 1971.
Grafenburg, Wirnt von. *Wigalois*. Translated by John Wesley Thomas. London, 1977.
Gregory of Tours. *The History of the Franks*. Translated by Lewis G. M. Thorpe. Baltimore, 1971.
Le Haut Livre du Graal: Perlesvaus. Edited by William Nitze. Totowa, 1937.
_____. *Perlesvaus Prose English, The High Book of the Grail. A Translation of the*

Thirteenth Century Romance of Perlesvaus. Translated by Nigel Bryant. Ipswich, 1978.
Hélinand de Froidmont. *Les vers de la Mort.* Translated by Michael Boyer and Monique Santucci. Paris, 1983.
Herodotus. *The Historia.* Translated by Aubrey de Sélincourt. London, 1972.
Historia Brittonum. Edited and translated by John Morris. Chichester, 1978. *The Vatican Recension of the 'Historia Brittonum.'* Edited by David N. Dumville. Cambridge, 1985.
Hrolf Kraki's Saga. Translated by Poul Anderson. New York, 1988.
The Law of Hywel Dda. Edited and translated by Dafydd Jenkins. Llandysul, 1986.
"Lebor Gabála Érenn: The Book of Invasions." In *The Celtic Heroic Age: Literary Sources for Ancient Celtic Europe and Early Ireland and Wales,* 213–66. Edited by John T. Koch and John Carey. Translated by John Carey. Malden, 1994.
Libanius. *Selected Orations.* Edited by Eric Herbert Warmington. 2 vols. New York, 1968.
Liber Landavensis: The Book of Llandaf. Edited by Sir John Rhys and J. Gwenogvryn Evans. Oxford, 1883.
The Life of St. David. Translated by Ernest Rhys. Newtown, 1927.
The Life of St. Samson of Dol. Translated by Thomas Taylor. Llanerch, 1991.
Livy. *Ab Urbe condita.* Edited by Carol Flamstead Walters and Robert Seymour Conway. 10 vols. Oxford, 1914–1965.
The Llandaff Charters. Edited by Wendy Davies. Cardiff, 1979.
Mabinogion. Translated by Charlotte Guest. London, 1877.
———. Translated by Gwyn Jones and Thomas Jones. London, 1974.
———. Translated by Sir Ifor Williams. Cardiff, 1930.
Malory, Sir Thomas. *Caxton's Malory.* Edited by James W. Spisak. Berkeley, 1983.
Marie de France. *The Lais of Marie de France.* Translated by Glyn S. Burgess and Keith Busby. London, 1986.

———. *Die Lais der Marie de France.* Edited by Karl Warnke. Berlin, 1925.
"Marwnad Cynddylan." Edited by Sir Ifor Williams. *BBCS* 6: 134–40. Oxford, 1933.
"———." In *The Celtic Heroic Age: Literary Sources for Ancient Celtic Europe and Early Ireland and Wales,* 360–2. Edited by John T. Koch and John Carey. Translated by John T. Koch. Malden, 1994.
"Mesca Ulad: Intoxication of the Ulstermen." In *The Celtic Heroic Age: Literary Sources for Ancient Celtic Europe and Early Ireland and Wales,* 95–117. Edited by John T. Koch and John Carey. Translated by J. Carmichael Watson. Malden, 1994.
A Monk of Rhuys and Caradoc of Llancarfan. *Two Lives of Gildas.* Translated by Hugh Williams. Llanerch, 1990.
"The Oldest Version of the Tochmarc Emire." Translated by Kuno Meyer. *RC* 11: 434–67. Paris, 1890.
"Pa gur?" In *Culhwch ac Olwen: An Edition and Study of the Earliest Arthurian Tale.* Edited by Rachel Bromwich an D. Simon Evans. Translated by Brynley Roberts. Cardiff, 1992, xxxv.
Paulinus of Milan. *Vita Sancti Ambrosii, mediolensis episcopi, a paulino eius notario ad beatum Augustinum conscripta.* Translated by Mary Simplicia Kaniecka. Washington, DC, 1928.
Polybius. *The Histories.* Edited by George Patrick Goold. 6 vols. Cambridge, 1975.
"'Preiddeu Annwn' and the figure of Taliesin." Edited and translated by Marged Haycock. *SC* 14/15: 52–77. Cardiff, 1984.
Robert de Boron. *Robert de Boron: Le Roman de L'Estoire dou Graal.* Translated by William Roach. Paris, 1927.
———. *Robert de Boron: Merlin Roman du XIIIe siécle.* Translated by Alexandre Micha. Geneva, 1974.
Le Roman de Tristan par Thomas, poème du XIII siècle. Edited and translated by Joseph Bedier. 2 vols. Paris, 1902–1905.
The Romance of Tristan. Edited and translated by Renée L. Curtis. New York, 1994.

"The Saga Englynion about Urien's Head." In *The Celtic Heroic Age*, 344–5. Edited and translated by John T. Koch and John Carey. Malden, 1994.

Silius Italicus, Tiberius Cato. *Punica*. 2 vols. Translated by James Duff Duff[AKS3]. Cambridge, 1934.

Sir Perceval of Gales. Edited by John Campion and Ferdinand Hothausen. New York, 1913.

Strabo. *The Geography*. 8 vols. Translated by Horace Leonard Jones. New York, 1923.

Tacitus, Cornelius. *The Agricola and the Germania*. Translated by Harold Mattingly. Rev. ed. by Stanley Alexander Handford. Middlesex, 1970.

Táin Bó Cuailgne. Translated by Thomas Kinsella. Oxford, 1969.

Taliesin. *Canu Taliesin: gyda Rhagymadrodd a Nodiadau*. Edited by Sir Ifor Williams. Cardiff, 1960.

The Tale of Tristan's Madness. Translated by Alan S. Fedrick. New York, 1978.

Thomas of Britain. *Gottfried von Strassburg: Tristan*. Translated by Arthur Thomas Hatto. New York, 1960.

———. *Les Fragments du roman de Tristan, poème du XIIe siècle*. Edited by Bartina H. Wind. Paris, 1960.

"Togail Bruidne Da Derga: The Destruction of Da Derga's Hostel." In *The Celtic Heroic Age*, 155–174. Edited and revised by John T. Koch and John Carey. Translated by Whitley Stokes. Malden, 1994.

Tóruigheacht Dhiarmada agus Ghráinne: The Pursuit of Diarmid and Gráinne. Translated by Ness Ní Shéaghdha. *Irish Text Society* 48, Dublin, 1967.

"Tristan Poem." Translated by Rachel Bromwich. "The 'Tristan' Poem in the Black Book of Carmarthen." *SC* 14/15:57–8. Cardiff, 1979–1980.

The Tripartite Life of Patrick, with Other Documents Relating to that Saint. Translated by Whitley Stokes. London, 1887.

Türlin, Heinrich von dem. *The Crown (Diu Crône)*. Translated by John Wesley Thomas. Lincoln, 1989.

"Two Gaulish Religious Inscriptions." In *The Celtic Heroic Age*, 1–4. Edited by John T. Koch and John Carey. Translated by John T. Koch. Malden, 1994.

The Vulgate Version of the Arthurian Romance: Edited from Manuscripts in the British Museum. 8 vols. Translated by Henry Oskar Sommer. Washington, 1909–1916.

Wauchier de Denain. *Continuations of the Old French Perceval of Chrétien de Troyes: The First Continuation*. Edited and translated by William Roach. Philadelphia, 1949.

The Welsh Triads (Trioedd ynys Prydein). Rev. ed. Edited and translated by Rachel Bromwich. Cardiff, 1978.

The White Book: Welsh Tales and Romance Reproduced from the Peniarth Manuscripts. Edited by J. Gwenogary Evans. Private Press, 1907.

William of Malmesbury. *De Antiquitate Glastonie Ecclesie*. Edited and translated by John Scott. Woodbridge, 1981.

———. *De Rebus Gestis Regum Anglorum*. Edited by William Stubbs. London, 1889.

Zatzikhoven, Ulrich von. *Lanzelet*. Edited by Roger Sherman Loomis. Translated by Kenneth Graham Tremayne Webster. New York, 1951.

Secondary Sources

Abrams, Leslie, and James P. Carley (eds). *The Archaeology and History of Glastonbury Abbey. Essays in Honour of the Ninetieth Birthday of C. A. Ralegh Radford*. Woodbridge, 1991.

Adams, Thomas. "'Pur vostre corsu jo em paine': The Augustinian Subtext of Thomas' Tristan," *MA* 68: 278–91. Cambridge, 1999.

Adolf, Helen. "A Historical Background to Chrétien's *Perceval*." *PMLA* 58: 597–620. Menasha, 1943.

Alcock, Leslie. *Dinas Powys*. Cardiff, 1963.

———. "Was there an Irish Sea Culture-Province in the Dark Ages." In *The Irish Sea Province*, 55–65. Edited by Donald Moore. Cardiff, 1970.

_____. *Arthur's Britain.* New York, 1971.

_____. "Reconnaissance on early historic fortifications and other royal sites in Scotland, 1974–84, 4: Excavations at Alt Clut, Clyde Rock, Strathclyde, 1974–5." *PSAS* 120: 95–149. Edinburgh, 1990.

Anderson, Marjorie, and Alan Orr Anderson. *Kings and Kingship in Early Scotland.* Edinburgh, 1973.

Anglade, Joseph. *Anthologie des Troubadours.* Paris, 1929.

Balcou, Jean, and Yves le Gallo, eds. *Histoire Littéraire culturelle de la Bretagne.* Paris, 1987.

Barley, Maurice Willmore, and Rich Patrick Crosland Hansen, eds. *Christianity in Britain, 300–570.* Leicester, 1968.

Baud, Pierre la. *Histoire de Bretagne.* Paris, 1638.

Baumgartner, Emmanuéle. "Luce del Gat et Hélie de Boron: le chevalier et l'écriture." *R* 106: 326–40. Paris, 1985.

_____. *Le Tristan en prose: essai d'intrepetation d'un roman medieval.* Geneva, 1975.

Binchy, David. "Celtic and Anglo-Saxon Kingship." In *O'Donnell Lectures Publications.* Oxford, 1970.

Borderie, Arthur de la. *Revue de Bretagne et de Vendée.* 18 Nantes, 1865, 436.

Bouchard, Constance. "The Possible Nonexistence of Thomas, Author of 'Tristan and Isolde,' 66–72. Chicago, 1981.

Bromiley, Geoffrey, and Tony Hunt. "The Tristan Legend in Old French Verse," *The Arthur of the French.* Edited by Glyn S. Burgess and Karen Pratt. Cardiff, 2000, 112–34.

Bromwich, Rachel. "Some Remarks on the Celtic Sources of 'Tristan.'" *THSC:* 32–60. London, 1953.

_____. "Celtic Dynastic Themes and Breton Lays." *ÉC* 9: 439–74. Paris, 1961.

_____. "Concepts of Arthur." *SC* 10/11: 163–81. Cardiff, 1976.

_____. "The 'Tristan' Poem in the Black Book of Carmarthen." *SC* 14/15: 54–65. Cardiff, 1979–1980.

_____. "Celtic Elements in Arthurian Romance: A General Survey." In *The Legend of Arthur in the Middle Ages.* Edited by P. B. Grout. Cambridge, 1983, 41–55.

_____. "The Tristan of the Welsh." *The Arthur of the Welsh,* 209–228. Edited by Rachel Bromwich, Brynley F. Roberts, and Alfred O. H. Jarman. Cardiff, 1991a.

_____. "First transmission from England to France." In *The Arthur of the Welsh,* 273–298. Edited by Rachel Bromwich, Brynley F. Roberts, and Alfred O.H. Jarman. Cardiff, 1991b.

Bromwich, Rachel, and R. Brynley Jones, eds. *Astudiaethau ar yr Hengerdd.* Cardiff, 1978.

Bromwich, Rachel, Brynley F. Roberts, and Alfred O. H. Jarman, eds. *The Arthur of the Welsh.* Cardiff, 1991.

Brouland, Marie Thérèse. "Peredur ab Efrawg." In *Perceval-Parzival; Hier et Aujourdhui,* 59–70. Edited by Danielle Buschinger and Wolfgang Spiewok. Reineke, 1994.

_____. "La souveraineté de Gwenhwyfar-Guinièvre." In *Lancelot-Lanzelet; Hier et Aujourdhui,* 53–64. Edited by Danielle Buschinger and Michel Link. Reineke, 1995.

Brown, Arthur C. L. *The Origin of the Grail Legend.* New York, 1966.

Brown, Reginald Allen, and Howard M. Colvin, eds. *The History of the King's Works, the Middle Ages.* London, 1963.

Bruce, James Douglas. *The Evolution of Arthurian Romance, from the Beginnings Down to the Year 1300.* Gottingen, 1923.

Brugger, Ernst. "Loenois as Tristan's Home." *MP* 22 vol. 2: 159–191 Chicago, 1924.

Bugge, Robert. "Fertility myth and female sovereignty in the weddynge of Sir Gawen and Dame Ragnell." *CR* 39.2: 198–218. University Park, 2004.

Bumke, Joachim. *Mäzene im Mittelalter. Die Gönner und Auftrageber der höfischen Literatur in Deutschland 1150–1300.* Munich, 1979.

Brusegan, Rosanna. "L'autre monde et *Le*

Chevalier de la Charrette." In *Lancelot-Lanzelet: Hier et Aujourdhui*, 77–85. Edited by Danielle Buschinger and Michael Zink. Reineke, 1995.

Bullock-Davies, Constance. *Professional Interpreters and the Matter of Britain*. Cardiff, 1966.

Burgess, Glyn, and Karen Pratt, eds. *The Arthur of the French: The Arthurian Legend in Medieval French and Occitan Literature*. Cardiff, 2006.

Burgess, Glyn, and Robert A. Taylor, eds. *The Spirit of the Court*. Toronto, 1985.

Burns, E. Jane. "Vulgate Cycle." In *The New Arthurian Encyclopedia*, 496–9. Edited by Norris J. Lacy. London, 1991.

Busby, Keith. *Gauvain in Old French Literature*. Amsterdam, 1980.

_____ and Norris Lacy, eds. *Medieval Studies in Honor of Douglas Kelly*. Amsterdam, 1994.

Buschinger, Danielle. "Conjectures sur Eilhart von Oberg." In *Figures de l'écrivain au moyen âge. Actes du Colloque du Centre d'Etudes Mediévales de l'Université de Picardie Amiens 18–20 mars 1988*, 63–72. Edited by Danielle Buschinger. Göppingen, 1991.

_____, ed. *Tristant et Iseut, mythr européen*, 262–281. Göppingen, 1987.

Buschinger, Danielle, and Wolfgang Spiewok, eds. *Perceval-Parzival; Hier et Aujourdhui*. Reineke, 1994.

Buschinger, Danielle, and Michael Zink, eds. *Lancelot-Lanzelet: Hier et Aujourdhui*. Reineke, 1995.

Byrne, John Francis. *Irish Kings and High-Kings*. London, 1973.

Campbell, John Francis. *More West Highland Tales*. Edinburgh, 1840–1860.

Carney, James. *Studies in Irish Literature and History*. Dublin, 1955.

Chadwick, Hector. *The Heroic Age*. Cambridge, 1912.

Chadwick, Hector, and Nora Kershaw. *The Development of Oral Literature*. 3 vols. Cambridge, 1932–40.

Chadwick, Nora Kershaw. "Pictish and Celtic Marriage in Early Literary Tradition," *Scottish Gaelic Studies* 8: 56–115. Edinburgh, 1958a.

_____. "Early Culture and Learning in North Wales." In *Studies in the Early British Church*, 29–120. Edited by Nora K. Chadwick. Cambridge, 1958b.

Chadwick, Nora K., ed. *Studies in Early British History*. Cambridge, 1954.

_____. *Studies in the Early British Church*. Cambridge, 1958.

_____. "On the Northern British Section in Nennius." In *Celt and Saxon: Studies in the Early British Border*. Edited by Nora K. Chadwick. Cambridge, 1963.

Chambers, Edmund Kerchever. *Arthur of Britain*. London, 1927.

Charles-Edwards, Thomas. "The Date of the Four Branches of the *Mabinogi*." *THSC*: 263–298. London, 1971.

_____. "The Authenticity of the Gododdin: An Historian's View." In *Astudiaethau ar yr Hengerdd*, 44–71. Edited by Rachel Bromwich and R. Brinley Jones. Cardiff, 1978.

Chinca, Mark. "Tristan Narratives from the High to the Late Middle Ages." In *The Tristan of the Germans*, 117–34. Edited by W. H. Jackson and S. A. Ranawake. Cardiff, 2000.

Christ, Winfried. *Rhetorik und Roman. Untersuchungen zu Gottfrieds von Straßburg "Tristan."* Meisenheim, 1977.

Clancy, Thomas. Personal interview. 1996.

Colvin, Howard M. "The king's works before the Norman conquest." In *The History of the King's Works, the Middle Ages*, 1–17. Edited by Reginald Allen Brown and Howard M. Colvin. London, 1963.

Corson, Amédée Guillotin de. *Grandes Seigneuries de Haute-Bretagne*, vol. 2. Rennes, 1898.

Crick, Julia. "The Marshalling of Antiquity: Glastonbury's Historical Dossier." In *The Archaeology and History of Glastonbury Abbey*, 163–190. Edited by Leslie Abrams and James P. Carley. Woodbridge, 1991.

Cross, Tom Peete. *Lancelot and Guinevere: A Study on the Origins of Courtly Love*. New York, 1970.

Cross, Tom Peete, and William Albert Nitze. *Motif-Index of Early Irish Literature*. Chicago, 1952.

Cross, Tom Peete, and Clark Harris Slover. *Ancient Irish Tales*. Dublin, 1969.

Curle, Alexander Ormiston. "Report on the Excavation, in September 1913, of a Vitrified Fort at Rockcliffe, Dalbeattie, known as the Mote of Mark." *PSAS* 12: 125–69, 4th series. Edinburgh, 1914.

Dam, Jan van. *Zü Vorgeschichte des höfischen Epos: Lamprecht, Eilhart, Valdeke*. Bonn, 1923.

Dark, Kenneth Rainsbury. *From Civitas to Kingdom: British Political Continuity 300–800*. Leicester, 1994.

Davies, Wendy. "Property Rights and Property Claims in Welsh 'Vitae' of the Eleventh Century." In *Hagiographie, cultures, et sociétés iv*^{e}*-xii*^{e} *siécles*, 515–33. Edited by Pierre Riché. Paris, 1981.

Diune, Francoise. "La vie de S. Samson, à propos d'un ouvrage récent." In *Annales de Bretagne* 28, 332–56. Paris, 1912–13.

Diverres, Armel Hughes. "The Grail and the Third Crusade: Thoughts on *Le Conte du Graal* by Chrétien de Troyes." In *Arthurian Literature X*, 13–109. Cambridge, 1990.

Dumville, David N. "The Anglian Collection of Royal Genealogies and Regnal Lists." *ASE* 5: 23–50. Cambridge, 1976.

——. *Ireland in Early Mediaeval Europe Studies in Memory of Kathleen Hughes*. Cambridge, 1982.

——. "Early Welsh Poetry: Problems of Historicity." In *Early Welsh Poetry: Studies in the Book of Aneirin*, 1–16. Edited by Brynley F. Roberts. Aberystwyth, 1988.

——. *St. Patrick, A.D. 493–1993*. Cambridge, 1993.

Faral, Edmond. "Ovide et qualques autres Roman d'Éneas." *Romania* 40: 161–234. Paris, 1911.

Finberg, Herbert Patrick Reginald. "St. Patrick and Glastonbury." In *Irish Ecclesiastical Record*, 107. Dublin, 1967.

Foot, Sarah. "Glastonbury's Early Abbots." In *The Archaeology and History of Glastonbury Abbey*, 163–90. Edited by Leslie Abrams and James P. Carley. Woodbridge, 1991.

Frappier, Jean. "Chrétien de Troyes." In *Arthurian Literature in the Middle Ages*, 157–91. Edited by Roger S. Loomis. Chicago, 1959.

Gentil, Pierre le. "La légende de Tristan vue par Béroul et Thomas: Essai d'interprétation." *RP* 7: 111–129. Turnhout, 1953.

——. "The Work of Robert de Boron and the *Didot Perceval*." In *Arthurian Literature in the Middle Ages*, 251–262. Edited by Roger S. Loomis. Chicago, 1959.

George, Lloyd, ed. *Geirfa Barddoniaeth Gynnar Gymraeg*. Cardiff, 1931–1963.

Glendinning, Robert James. "Gottfried von Strassburg and the school tradition." *DVJ* 61: 617–638. Stuttgart, 1987.

Goetinck, Glenys. *Peredur: A Study of Welsh Tradition in the Grail Legends*. Cardiff, 1975.

Goodrich, Norma Lorre. *King Arthur*. London, 1986.

Gowans, Linda. *Cei and the Arthurian Legend*. Cambridge, 1988.

Graves, Robert. *The Greek Myths*. 2 vols. London, 1955.

Greene, David. "The Chariot as described in Irish Literature." In *The Iron Age in the Irish Sea Province*, 59–73. Edited by Charles Thomas. London, 1972.

Grimsby, John L. "The Continuations of Chrétien de Troyes." In *The New Arthurian Encyclopedia*, 99–101. Edited by Norris J. Lacy. London, 1991.

Grout, P. B., R. A. Lodge, C. E. Pickford, and E. K. C. Varty, eds. *The Legend of Arthur in the Middle Ages*. Cambridge, 1983.

Guyer, Foster E. *Dissertation: The Influence of Ovid on Chréstien de Troyes*. Chicago, 1921.

Hamel, Anton Gerardus van. "Tristan's Combat with the Dragon." *RC* 41: 331–349. Paris, 1924.

Hardy, James, and Will Hasty, eds. *Dictionary of Literary Biography*. Vol. 38, *German Writers and Works of the High Middle Ages: 1170–1280*, 185–206. London, 1994.

Haug, Walter. "Reinterpreting the Tristan Romances of Thomas and Gotfrid; Implications of a Recent Discovery." *Arthuriana: The Quarterly for the International Arthurian Society* 7: 45–59. West Lafayette, 1997.

Haycock, Marged. "'Preiddeu Annwn' and the figure of Taliesin." *SC* 14/15: 52–77. Cardiff, 1984.

Henderson, Jane Frances Anne. "A Critical Edition of Evrat's *Genesis: Creation to the Flood*." Unpublished Ph.D. diss. Toronto, 1977.

Hoffa, W. "Antike elemente bei Gottfried von Strassburg." *ZDA* 52 vol. 4: 339–350. Berlin, 1910.

Hucker, B. U. "Literatur im Umkreis Kaiser Ottos IV." In *Die Welfen und ihr Braunschweiger Hof im hohen Mittelalter*, 377–406. Edited by B. Schneidermüller, Weisbaden, 1995.

Hughes, Kathleen. *The Church in Early Irish Society*. Cambridge, 1966.

———. "The Welsh Latin Chronicles: *Annales Cambriae* and related texts." *PBA* 59: 233–259. London, 1975.

———. *Celtic Britain in the Early Middle Ages: Studies in Welsh and Scottish sources*. Cambridge, 1980.

———. *Church and society in Ireland, A.D. 400–1200*. Cambridge, 1987.

Hunt, Tony. "The Prologue to Chrestien's *Li contes del graal*." *Romania* 92: 359–79. Paris, 1971.

———. "The Significance of Thomas' *Tristan*." *RMS* 7: 41–61 (1981).

———. "Chrétien's Prologues Reconsidered." *Medieval Studies in Honor of Douglas Kelly*. Edited by Keith Busby and Norris Lacy. Amsterdam, 1994, 153–168.

Irby-Massie, Georgia L. *Military Religion in Roman Britain*. Boston, 1999.

Jackson, Kenneth Hurlstone. *Language and History in Early Britain: A Chronological Survey of the Brittonic Languages 1st to 12th C. A.D.* Edinburgh, 1953.

———. "The British Language during the English Settlement." In *Studies in Early British History*. Edited by Nora K. Chadwick. Cambridge, 1954, 61–82.

———. "The Britons in Southern Scotland." *A* 29: 77–88. Gloucester, 1955.

———. "The Sources for the Life of St. Kentigern." In *Studies in the Early British Church*, 273–358. Edited by Nora K. Chadwick. Cambridge, 1958.

———. "The Arthur of History." In *Arthurian Literature in the Middle Ages*. Edited by Roger S. Loomis. Oxford, 1959, 1–11.

———. *The International Popular Tale and Early Welsh Tradition*. Cardiff, 1961.

———. "On the Northern British Section in Nennius." In *Celt and Saxon: Studies in the Early British Border*. Edited by Nora K. Chadwick. Cambridge, 1963, 20–62.

Jackson, W. H., and Sylvia A. Ranawake, eds. *The Arthur of the French*. Cardiff, 2000.

Jackson, W. T. H. "Gottfried von Strassburg." In *Arthurian Literature in the Middle Ages*, 145–156. Edited by Roger S. Loomis. Chicago, 1959.

Jarman, Alfred O. H., and Gwillym R. Jones, eds. *A Guide to Early Welsh Literature*. 4 vols. Cardiff, 1976.

Johnston, James Brown. *Place-Names of Scotland*. London, 1934.

Jones, Gwynn T. "Some Arthurian Material in Keltic." *Aberyswyth Studies* 14: 37–93. Aberystwyth, 1936.

Jones, Thomas. "The Black Book of Carmarthen 'Stanzas of the Graves.'" *PBA* 53: 97–137. London, 1967.

Kelly, Anne. *Eleanore of Aquitaine and the Four Kings*. Cambridge, 1950.

Kelly, Douglas. "Chrétien de Troyes," *The Arthur of the French: The Arthurian Legend in Medieval French and Occitan Literature*, 135–185. Edited by Karen Pratt and Glyn Burgess. Cardiff, 2006.

Kelly, Fergus. *A Guide to Early Irish Law*. Vol. 3, *Early Irish Law Series*. Dublin, 1988.

Kelly, Thomas E., ed. *Le Haut du Graal: Perlesvaus, A Structural Study*. Geneva, 1974.

Kenyon, John R. *Medieval Fortifications*. Leicester, 1990.

Ker, William P. *Epic and Romance: Essays on Medieval Literature*. Dover, 1957.

Köhler, Erich. *Ideal und Wirklichkeit in*

der *Höfischen Epik: Studien zur form der Frühen Artus-und Graldichtung*. Tübingen, 1956.
Krey. "William of Tyre." *S* 16: 149–166. Cambridge, 1941.
Krueger, Roberta L. *Women Readers and the Ideology of Gender in Old French Romance*. Cambridge, 1993.
Lacy, Norris J., ed. *The New Arthurian Encyclopedia*. London, 1991.
Laing, Lloyd. "Timber Halls in Dark Age Britain-Some Problems." *TDGNAHS* 46: 110–27, 3rd series Dumfries, 1969.
———. "Archaeological Notes on Some Scottish Early Christian Stones." *PSAS* 114: 277–287. Darking, 1985.
Laurie, Helen C. R. *Two Studies in Chrétien de Troyes*. Geneva, 1972.
Lejeune, Rita. "The Troubadours." In *Arthurian Literature in the Middle Ages*, 393–399. Edited by Roger S. Loomis. Chicago, 1959.
Lewis, Ceri. "The Historical Background of Early Welsh Verse." In *A Guide to Early Welsh Literature*, Vol. 1, 11–50. Edited by Alfred O. H. Jarman and Gwillym R. Jones. Cardiff, 1976.
Lewis, Michael Jonathan Taunton. *Temples in Roman Britain*. Cambridge, 1966.
Lewis, Saunders. "Branwen." *LlC* 10: 230–3. Cardiff, 1968.
———. "Branwen." In *Y Traethodydd*, 137–142. Cardiff, 1969a.
———. "Branwen." In *Y Traethodydd*, 185–192. Cardiff, 1969b.
———. "Branwen." In *Ysgrifau Beirniadol* 5, 30–43. Cardiff, 1970.
Lloyd-Morgan, Ceridwen. "Narrative Structure in *Peredur*," *ZCP* 38: 187–231. Berlin, 1981.
———. "Breuddwyd Rhonabwy and Later Arthurian Literature." In *The Arthur of the Welsh*, 183–208. Edited by Rachel Bromwich, Brynley F. Roberts, and Alfred O. H. Jarman. Cardiff, 1991.
———. "Lancelot in Wales." In *Shifts and Transpositions in Medieval Literature*, 169–179. Edited by Karen Pratt. Cambridge, 1994.
Loomis, Laura Hibbard. "The Sword Bridge of Chrétien de Troyes and its Celtic Original," PMLA 4: 166–190. Columbia, 1913.
Loomis, Roger Sherman. "Tristram and the House of Anjou," *MLR* 17: 24–30. Cambridge, 1922.
———. "The Origin of Rivallon in the Tristan Legend," *MLN* 39: 319–328. Baltimore, 1924.
———. *Celtic Myth and Arthurian Romance*. New York, 1927a.
———, ed. *Medieval Studies in Memory of Gertrude Schoepperle Loomis*. New York, 1927b.
———. "Discussions: Cause or Coincidence, a Reply to Monsieur Ferdinand Lot," *R* 54: 515–526. Paris, 1928a.
———. "Calogrenanz and Crestien's Originality," *MLN* 43: 215–222. Baltimore, 1928b.
———. "By What Route did the Romantic Tradition of Arthur Reach the French," *MP* 33.3: 225–238. Chicago, 1936.
———. "'The Spoils of Annwfn': An Early Arthurian Poem," *PMLA* 56: 887–936. Menasha, 1941.
———. *Arthurian Tradition and Chrétien*. New York, 1949.
———. "Edward I, Arthurian Admirer," *S* 28: 114–127. Cambridge, 1953.
———. *Wales and the Arthurian Legend*. Cardiff, 1956.
———, ed. *Arthurian Literature in the Middle Ages*. Edited by Roger S. Loomis. Oxford, 1959b.
———. "The Origins of the Grail Legends." In *Arthurian Literature in the Middle Ages*, 274–94. Edited by Roger S. Loomis. Oxford, 1959b.
———. "A Survey of Tristan Scholarship after 1911." In *Tristan and Isolt: A Study of the Sources of the Romance*. Rev. ed. New York, 1960.
———. *The Grail: From Celtic Myth to Christian Symbol*. Cardiff, 1963.
Loth, Joseph. *Contributions à l'étude des romans de la Table ronde*. Paris, 1912.
Lovecy, Ian. "The Celtic Sovereignty Theme and the Structure of *Peredur*," *SC* 12/13: 133–146. Cardiff, 1978.
———. "Historia Peredur ab Efrawg." *The*

Arthur of the Welsh. Edited by Rachel Bromwich, Brynley F. Roberts, and Alfred O. H. Jarman, 171–182. Cardiff, 1991.

Mac Cana, Proinsias. "Aspects of the Theme of the King and Goddess," *EC* 6: 356–413. Paris, 1955.

———. *Celtic Mythology*. Hamlyn, 1970.

Mac Cana, Proinsias, Meic Stephens, and R. Brinley Jones, eds. *The Mabinogi*. Cardiff, 1992.

MacQueen, John. "Yvain, Ewen, and Owein ap Urien," *TDGNAHS*, 3rd series 33: 107–131. Dumfries, 1956.

———. "A Reply to Professor Jackson," *TDGNAHS* 3rd series 36: 175–83. Dumfries, 1959.

Mason, John Frederick Arthur. "The 'Honour of Richmond' in 1086," *EHR* 78: 703–704. London, 1963.

Mallory, James P., ed. *Aspects of the Táin*. Belfast, 1992.

———. "The World of Cú Chulainn: The Archaeology of *Táin Bo Cuailgne*." In *Aspects of the Táin*, 103–153. Edited by James P. Mallory. Belfast, 1992.

Matthews, John F. *Western Aristocracies and Imperial Court, AD 364–425*. Oxford, 1975.

Maynadier, Howard. *The Wife of Bath's Tale: Its Sources and Analogues*. London, 1901,

McCash, June Hall. "Marie de Champagne's 'Cuer d'ome et cors de Fame': Aspects of Feminism and Misogyny in the Twelfth Century." In *The Spirit of the Court*, 234–245. Edited by Glyn S. Burgess and Robert A. Taylor. Toronto, 1985.

Mertens, Volvert. "Eilhart, der Herzog und der Truchseß. Der *Tristant* am Welfenhof." *Tristant et Iseut, mythr européen*, 262–281. Edited by Danielle Buschinger. Göppingen, 1987.

Moore, Donald, ed. *The Irish Sea Province in Archaeology and History*. Cardiff, 1970.

Murray, James A. H., Henry Bradley, W. A. Craigie, C. T. Onions, and R. W. Burchfield, eds. *The Oxford English Dictionary*. Oxford, 1961.

Murray, Margaret Alice. *The God of the Witches*. London, 1931.

Nellmann, Eberhard. "Wolfram und Kyot als 'vindaere wilder maere,' *ZfdA* 117: 31–67. Wiesbaden, 1988.

Newell, William W. "Arthurian Notes," *MLN* 17: 277–8. Baltimore, 1902.

Newstead, Helen. "The Origin and Growth of the Tristan Legend." In *Arthurian Literature in the Middle Ages*, 122–133. Edited by Roger S. Loomis. Chicago, 1959.

———. *Brân the Blessed in Arthurian Romance*. New York, 1966.

Nitze, William Albert. "*Sens* and *Matière* dans les Oeuvres de Chrétien de Troyes," *Romania* 44: 14–36. Paris, 1915–1917.

———. "*Perlesvaus*." *Arthurian Literature in the Middle Ages*, 263–273. Edited by Roger S. Loomis. Chicago, 1959.

Nutt, Alfred. *Studies on the Legend of the Holy Grail*. London, 1888.

O' Rahilly, Cecile. *Ireland and Wales: Their Historical and Literary Traditions*. New York, 1924.

O' Rahilly, Thomas F. *Early Irish History and Mythology*. Dublin, 1946a.

———. "On the Origin of the Names *Érain* and *Ériu*, 7–28." In *Ériu* 35. Dublin, 1946b.

Owen, Douglas David Roy. *The Evolution of the Grail Legend*. Edinburgh, 1968.

———. "Chrétien and the *Roland*." In *An Arthurian Tapestry: Essays in Memory of Lewis Thorpe*, 139–149. Edited by Kenneth Varty. Glasgow, 1981.

Owen, Douglas David Roy, and Douglas Kelly. "Arthurian Romance in the twelfth and thirteenth centuries." In *The Arthur of the Germans*, 393–460. Edited by W. H. Jackson and Sylvia A. Ranawake. Cardiff, 2000.

Padel, Oliver J. "The Cornish Background of the Tristan Stories," *CMCS* 1: 53–82. Cambridge, 1981.

———. "Some South-Western Sites with Arthurian Associations." In *The Arthur of the Welsh*, 229–248. Edited by Rachel Bromwich, Brynley F. Roberts, and Alfred O. H. Jarman. Cardiff, 1991.

Warren, F. M. "On the Latin sources of *Thèbes* and *Énéas*," *PMLA* 16: 375–384. Menasha, 1901.

Watts, Dorothy. *Christians and Pagans in Roman Britain*. New York, 1991.

Webster, Graham. *The Pagan Celts and Their Gods under Rome*. London, 1986.

Webster, Kenneth Grant Tremayne. "Welsches Buoch." *Harvard Studies and Notes in Philology and Literature* 16: 203–228. Harvard, 1934.

Weinraub, Eugene J. *Chrétien's Jewish Grail*. Chapel Hill, 1976.

West, Geoffrey D. *An Index of Proper Names in French Arthurian Verse Romances 1150–1300*. Toronto, 1969.

———. *An Index of Proper Names in French Arthurian Prose Romances*. Toronto, 1978.

Weston, Jessie. *The Legend of Sir Gawain*. London, 1897.

———. *The Legend of Lancelot du Lac*. London, 1901.

———. *The Quest of the Holy Grail*. London, 1913.

———. *From Ritual to Romance*. London, 1920.

Whitehead, Frederick. "The Tristan Poems." In *Arthurian Literature in the Middle Ages*, , 134–45. Edited by Roger S. Loomis. Chicago, 1959.

Williams, Mary. *Essai sur la composition du roman gallois de Peredur*. Paris, 1909.

Williams, Sir Ifor. *Pedeir Keinc y Mabinogi*. Cardiff, 1930.

———. *Lectures on Old Welsh Poetry*. Dublin, 1944.

Wind, Bartina H., ed. *Les Fragments de roman de Tristan, poéme du XIIe siècle*. Paris, 1960.

Wolff, Ludwig, and Werner Schröder. "Eilhart von Oberg," *VL* 2: 410–418. New York, 1980.

Wynn, Marianne. "Wolfram von Eschenbach." In *Dictionary of Literary Biography*. Vol. 38, *German Writers and Works of the High Middle Ages: 1170–1280*, 185–206. Edited by James Hardy and Will Hasty. London, 1994.

Zimmer, Heinrich. "Keltische Beitrage. I. Germanen, germanische Lehnwdrter und germanische Sagenelemente in der altesten Überlieferung der irischen Heldensage," *ZDA* 32: 196–334. Berlin, 1888.

———. "Keltische Beitrage. III. Weitere nordgermanische Einflüsse in der Altesten Ueberlieferung der irischen Heldensage," *ZDA* 35: 1–176. Berlin, 1891.

Index

Numbers in **_bold italics_** indicate pages with illustrations.

Adamnan 66
Addanc 108
Alan Fergant 104
Andreas Capellanus 24–26, 28, 48, 64, 190
Andrew of Wyntoun 211
Aneirin 16, 19, 185
Angevin 21, 22, **_27_**, 156, 180
The Anglo-Saxon Chronicle 82, 174, 188
Annales Cambriae 6, 16, **_18_**, 20, 104, 129, 185, 206
Anonymous Vita Gildae 32, 33, 38, 42, 44, 197
Awdlau 148, 158

Bademagus 13, 42, 54–56, 188, 194
Bede 6
Belatacudros 12, 13, 76, 101–102, 105, 107, 129–130, 132, 134, 188
Beli 12, 93, 101–102, 130
Beowulf 47, 125, 193
Béroul 144, 147, 151, 152, 160, 161, 162, 183
Black Book of Carmarthen 34, 115, 158
Book of Llandaff 147
The Boyhood Deeds of Finn 56
Brân the Blessed 48, 93, 95, 100–102, 104, 115, 194, 199, 204
Branwen 150–151
Brengain 146, 150, 162, 177
Bretons 17, 21–22, 73, 93, 97
Breuddwyt Rhonabwy 109
Brittany 22, 37, 96, 115, 147, 153, 156, 178, 199
Brut 155, 161

Cadegr 12, 20
Caer Lloyw 113
Cagul 114
Canterbury 38
Caradoc of Llancarfan 38–40, 193; *Vita Gildae* 38–40
Carlisle 17, 82
Cei 32, 37, 39–40, 42–43, 60–61, 115, 132, 138, 185, 200, 202, 204
Cernunnos 101, 119
Le Chevalier de la Charrette 7, 9, 12–13, 22–24, 26, 28, 33, 35–36, 39–42, 48, 50, 57–58, 63–65, 67, 69–71, 75–76, 102, 104, 122–123, 129–130, 138, 144, 155, 162, 171, 172, 174, 192, 193, 196
Chevrefoil 147, 208
Chrétien de Troyes 5–8, 11–13, 14–15, 17, 20–26, 28–30, 33, 35–36, 38–39, 42–44, 46–47, 50–59, 61–70, 71–73, 75, 78, 79–82, 84, 86–88, 91, 93–96, 98, 101, 103–104, 107–114, 117–118, 122–131, 133, 134, 138, 143, 156, 179, 180–183, 188, 190, 192, 193, 197, 198, 199, 200, 201, 202, 204
Cligès 23–26, 36, 53, 54, 155, 181–182, 190, 195
Columba 66, 203
Le Conte du Graal 12, 14, 24, 51, 54, 73, 75–82, 87–90, 92–93, 96, 100, 110, 113, 114, 118, 122–123, 125, 128–132, 138, 144, 155, 162, 171, 172, 181, 183, 188, 196, 198, 200, 209

Corn 94
Cornwall 11, 17, 22, 139–140, 147–149, 152, 162, 177–178, 184, 205
Críth Gablach 49
Cú Chulainn 52–53, 58, 61, 65, 98, 150, 168, 194
Cu Roi 110
Culhwch ac Olwen
Cumbria 17, 32, 34, 49, 56, 58, 60, 61, 93, 103, 104, 110, 121, 148, 160, 177, 188, 191

David of Scotland 82, 129
De Excidio Britanniae 6, 134
Diarmid 149, 168, 170, 174, 176, 179, 205
Didot Perceval 96, 102, 103, 108–109, 117, 121, 133
Dínas de Lidan 146, 152, 160, 162–163, 167, 208
Diu Crône 31, 32, 42–44, 68, 96, 103, 112–113, 132, 195
Domesday Book 147
Drust 17, 146, 150, 153, 167–168, 170, 175, 178, 184, 205, 209
Dubricius 49
Dyfed 119, 149, 177, 201
Dysgyl 12, 76, 99, 101, 106, 107, 109, 116–117, 133–135, 200

Efrawg 103–104
Eilhart von Oberge 139, 141, 144, 152–153, 160–163
Eleanor of Aquitaine 26–27, 156–157, 160–162, 169, 176, 180–183

225

Eliffer 103
Enéas 155, 182
Erec 26, 54, 94
Erec et Enide 7, 14, 24–26, 36, 58, 67, 97, 101, 138, 182–183
Fionn MacCumhail 56, 61, 85, 88, 93, 128, 168, 172, 179
First Continuation 113, 121, 198
Fís Adamnan 57

Gahmuret 103–104, 110
Gauvain 13, 14, 17, 25, 31–32, 37, 46, 48, 50, 54, 56, 58–59, 65, 67, 75, 77–78, 81, 82, 93, 100, 102–103, 105, 107, 110, 113, 122, 123, 129, 133, 185, 186, 190, 195, 196, 198, 204
Gawain 97, 138, 174, 208
Geoffrey of Monmouth 5–6, 20–21, 25, 32–33, 35, 39–41, 44, 63, 133, 185, 191, 193, 201, 204, 207
Gereint 97, 104
Gildas 6, 32, 38–39, 97, 134
Ginover 190
Glastonbury 38–40, 85, 111–112
Gonemans 93, 100, 103, 105, 107, 188, 201
Gottfried von Strassburg 144, 147, 155, 162–163, 173, 183, 205
Grail Castle 77, 84, 89–90, 93–94, 96, 98, 101–102, 107, 111, 113, 115, 123–125, 127, 198
Gráinne 149, 168, 170, 174, 176, 179, 205
Gregory of Tours 57, 203
Guinevere 157, 170
Guvernal 152, 162
Gwalchmai 118, 121, 132, 138, 185, 204
Gwenhwyfar 32, 38–40, 44–45, 151, 176, 185, 191
Gwrgi 104
Gwrtheyrn 120
Gwynedd 19, 21, 119, 129, 149, 153, 160, 165, 177, 189

Hadrian's Wall 101
Hartmann von Aue 43–44, 58
Heinrich von dem Türlin 42–43, 113
Hengest 190, 193

Henry II 5, 23, 26, *27*, 73, 81, 156–157, 160–162, 169, 176, 181
Herodotus 48
Historia Brittonum 6, *18*, 19–20, 97, 129, 149, 177, 189
Historia Regum Britanniae 5, 29, 33, 41, 97, 191, 192
Honorius 119
Hrolf Kraki's Saga 47, 54, 124–125
Hundred Years' War 156, 181
Husdent 146, 151–154, 160, 167, 169
Hywel Dda 177

Iliad 52, 134, 187

Jandrèe 48, 51, 102, 188
Julius Caesar 65, 95

Kay 138
Keii 42–43
Kentigern 18, 49, 129, 203, 204
Keu 13, 14, 31–32, 39, 42, 60, 77, 93, 107, 113, 185, 190
Kingship stone 68–69
Kyôt 110–111

Lancelot 7, 13, 23–24, 26, 28, 31, 33–36, 46, 48, 50–52, 54–59, 64–69, 104, 113, 122–123, 174, 186, 191, 193, 195, 198, 204, 208
Lanzelet 31–33, 36, 41–42, 44, 52, 67, 96, 113, 193
Latimari 11, 22, 57, 95, 108
The Law of Hywel Dda 56, 177
Livy 48
Llyr 34, 102, 191
Louis VII 26, 156–157, 160, 181

Mabinogion 10, 33, 108, 143
Madness of Tristan 144, 164
Maiden Castle 103
Manassier 199
Marie de Champagne 8, 11, 14, 26–28, 33, *44*, 51–54, 57, 64, 66–67, 75, 82, 99, 123, 181–183, 190, 204
Marie de France 68–69, 71–72, 128, 143, 183, 208
Martin 120–121, 197
Medrawt 192
Meigle 66, 179, *180*
Meleagant 13, 24, 31, 39, 48, 51, 55–56, 62, 102, 133, 190, 195

Modred 17, 40–41, 138, 192, 208
Le Morte d'Arthur 103, 191, 195, 197, 198

Ninnius 19
Northern History 189
Northern Memoranda 16, *18*, 73, 196
Northumbria 18, 19, 175

Ovid 23–26, 64, 182
Owain 17, 138, 151
Owain 40, 109, 185
Owain son of Urien 192

"Pa Gur?" 32, 34, 43, 60, 110, 113–115, 128, *132*, 188
Paien de Maisières 182
Parzival 103–104, 109–111, 195, 197, 201
Patrick 49, 134, 203
Pelles 13, 93, 101, 130, 200
Pellinore 97, 101
Peredur 10, 48, 82, 96, *99*, 100, 102–104, 107, 109–110, 113–118, 120–121, 127, 130, *132*, 134, 199, 200
Peredur 17, 93, 102–107, 116, 118, 121, 130–132, 185, 201
Perlesvaus 38, 94, 96, 101–102, 111, 117, 121, 127, 132, 200
Perron 68–69, 126
Philip Augustus 28, 80
Philip of Flanders 8, 11, 75, 79–82, 85–86, 99, 107, 109, 114, 117, 122, 127, 130, 131, 134, 137, 181, 198
Picts 36, 65, 119, 174–175, 178
Pomponius Mela 114–115
Pope Gregory 57
Preiddeu Annwn 17, 33–34, 111, 114–*116*, 128
Prose Tristan 139, 144, 152, 163–164, 173, 205
Pryderi 93, 109, 159, 199

Red Book of Hergest 108, 115
Rheged 31, 53
Rhodri Mawr 20, 149
Rivalen 153
Robert de Boron 108, 164, 202

Samson 115–116, 132, 147, 203, 204
Sir Thomas Malory 113, 197, 198

Sovereignty 7, 96–97, 100, 123, 125–127, 180, 200
Strabo 48
Strathclyde 20, 129, 148, 175, 188, 189
Sword Bridge 13, 55–58, 62, 102, 179
Syre Gawen and the Grene Knight 51, 204

Tacitus 65
Táin Bó Cuailgne 52–53, 56
Taliesin 16, 19, 114, 134, 159, 188, 196
Tallwch 146, 153, 175, 205
Thomas of Britain 143–144, 150, 152–153, 155–158, 160–163, 166–167, 169–170, 172–174, 176, 180–184, 205, 208

Tochmarc Emire 49, 150, 172, 176, 184
Tri Thlws are Ddeg Ynys Brydain 95, 114–115
Trioedd Ynys Prydein 16, 33, 34, 158, 188, 191, 192, 204
Troubadour 5, 22–23, 57, 62, 95, 128
Trouvère 5, 22–23, 57, 62, 95
Twrch Trwyth 149, 159–160, 177, 207, 208

Ulrich von Zatzikhoven 41–**42**, 68, 192
Urien 17, 31–32, 48, 53, 73, 134, 152, 188, 191, 192, 196

Vita Cadoci 203
Vita Columbae 66
Vita Merlini 109

Vita Samsoni 114–115, 132–133
Vulgate 65, 103, 111, 113, 164, 188, 191, 198

Wace 25–26, 29, 81, 155, 182
Wauchier 109
Wigalois 68
Wolfram von Eschenbach 101, 109–110, 163

Y Gododdin 6, 53, 73, 129, 135, 159, 188, 196
Ymddiddan Gwenhwyfar ac Arthur 32–33, 39, 44, 60, 62, 195
Ymddiddanion 158
Yvain 22–23, 25, 53–54, 93
Yvain 7, 14, 17, 24–26, 40, 43, 58, 97, 138, 151, 185

www.ingramcontent.com/pod-product-compliance
Ingram Content Group UK Ltd.
Pitfield, Milton Keynes, MK11 3LW, UK
UKHW041949140426
5217IPUK00014B/708